Into the
North
Wind

Jill Homer

www.arcticglasspress.com

Distributed in the United States by Arctic Glass Press
Boulder, Colorado
www.arcticglasspress.com

Editor: Tonya Simpson
Cover Design: Jill Homer
Interior Design: Jill Homer
Chapter photos by Jill Homer and Seth Landon
Map of the Iditarod Trail from Iditarod Trail Committee

Cover: Jill Homer rides over the sea ice of the Norton Sound near Koyuk, Alaska.
Photo by Mike Beiergrohslein.

Back Cover: A view from Rainy Pass along the Iditarod Trail.
Photo by Jill Homer.

ISBN-13: 978-0692789865 (Arctic Glass Press)
ISBN-10: 0692789863

First Edition

This is a work of narrative nonfiction. Dialogue and events herein have been recounted to the best of the author's memory.

The Iditarod Trail

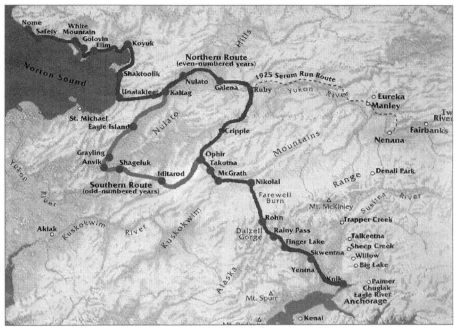

2016 Northern Route

	Distances between checkpoints in miles	Total distance from Knik
Knik to Yentna Station	57	57
Yentna Station to Skwentna	30	87
Skwentna to Finger Lake	40	127
Finger Lake to Rainy Pass	35	162
Rainy Pass to Rohn	40	202
Rohn to Nikolai	75	277
Nikolai to McGrath	52	329
McGrath to Takotna	18	347
Takotna to Ophir	23	370
Ophir to Cripple	73	443
Cripple to Ruby	70	513
Ruby to Galena	50	563
Galena to Nulato	37	600
Nulato to Kaltag	47	647
Kaltag to Unalakleet	85	732
Unalakleet to Shaktoolik	40	772
Shaktoolik to Koyuk	50	822
Koyuk to Elim	48	870
Elim to Golovin	28	898
Golovin to White Mountain	18	916
White Mountain to Safety	55	971
Safety to Nome	22	993

Contents

The Relentless Wind

When the wind sweeps in from the north, all that remains is white fury.

I raised a mittened hand to shield microscopic holes in my face mask from a flash-freezing blast of air. Ice shards pummeled my goggles and I squinted in spite of them, unable to see anything through the whiteout. The view was featureless either way — a moonscape of black ice and snowdrifts along Alaska's western coast. The treeless Shaktoolik Peninsula wasn't distinguishable from the frozen sea, which started two miles beyond and stretched an unbridgeable distance to the next point of civilization. I might as well have been standing on the moon, alone, buried to my knees in snow and shivering in my warmest coat as I leaned against a useless bicycle, exhausted.

I pressed both mittens against an ice-rimmed hat, increasingly desperate to shut out a high-pitched roar that echoed as unfocused terror. I was frightened with nowhere to run. I was battered with nowhere to hide. I was vaguely disgusted with myself for purposefully wandering into such a dire situation, yet again. A raging ground blizzard at the edge of the sea ice had been the backdrop of my worst nightmares — but in reality, I was on vacation.

The itinerary of this "vacation" was a solo bicycle tour of a 250-mile section of the Iditarod Trail, following the ice-bound coast along the Bering Sea. At the time, my partner, Beat, was attempting his third thousand-mile crossing of Alaska as part of an organized event, the Iditarod Trail Invitational. A dedicated runner, Beat traveled on foot. My plan was to start ahead of him in the village of Unalakleet, pedal and push a heavily loaded fat bike to Nome, and greet him at the finish.

Beat and I are a well-matched if somewhat unlikely couple. He's a Swiss software engineer with a doctorate in physics, a swimmer's lithe body and a runner's bold heart. I hail from Utah — sturdy Mormon pioneer stock — and stare at words for a living. We met during the summer of 2010 at an ultramarathon in Montana, where I was living at the time. Beat was completing a hundred-mile race through the rugged Swan Mountains, and I was a sleep-deprived volunteer at the finish line. He had the most captivating smile I'd ever seen, even after thirty-four hours of difficult running through the wilderness. I was a cyclist, not a runner, but Beat said I should take it up. I countered that I'd need some guidance if I were to venture into such a punishing sport. There's a longer story of course, but six months later, I finished my first hundred-mile race and then moved to California to live with him. We've been prodding each other into bigger and bolder adventures ever since.

When I set out from Unalakleet in March 2015, Beat was farther behind than I'd anticipated. Two weeks earlier, as he and three other Iditarod Trail Invitational racers approached the most remote, least-traveled segment of the route through Interior Alaska, a storm buried the trail in two feet of fresh snow. Breaking trail through knee-deep powder, they struggled to travel ten miles over each exhausting day, and then temperatures dropped to forty-five below. By the time they emerged in the Yukon River village of Ruby, having not seen another human in nine days, all four had narrowly escaped the brink of survivability. A woman on foot, Loreen, had a badly frostbitten hand, and her cycling husband, Tim, decided to evacuate as well. Beat and his good friend from San Francisco, Steve, entered a race against the calendar. Already deeply fatigued from their trail-breaking odyssey, they walked upwards of fifty miles a day on the Yukon River to make up time. In addition to a thirty-day race cutoff, the volatile weather of spring was fast approaching. Even if Beat and Steve ignored the race constraints, they might have to contend with the slushy trails and dangerously thin ice of the season that Alaskans call "Break-up." Of course, the idea that spring would ever arrive was difficult to conceptualize while gasping into windchill so low that the back of my throat froze.

It was three days before the spring equinox, and wind gusts only gained ferocity as relatively warm air over the Pacific Ocean siphoned frigid air from the

Arctic. This narrow but exposed passage across the frozen Norton Sound was a veritable wind tunnel from which there was no escape and nowhere to hide. Years earlier, the local Malemuit tribe funded the construction of an emergency shelter cabin on a peninsula that juts into the sound like a broken finger. They painted the cabin bright orange so it could be spotted in a whiteout. When I squinted through shards of ice swirling around my face, I could see a speck of color, even though the cabin was still six miles away.

I'd been moving so slowly throughout the day that I'd made plenty of calculations, only to determine that six miles was an impossible distance. This was day four of my trip. Battling these winds, I'd managed to achieve only about fifty miles of forward progress in that time. As it was, I was only eight miles beyond Shaktoolik, a village I'd made my third attempt to leave seven hours earlier.

The first attempt happened before dawn the previous day. I stepped out of the school — the only public building in town and thus where travelers stay — to gales raging at fifty miles per hour. Truck-sized snowdrifts had piled up in the village's single street overnight. Even after I found a way around them, I couldn't locate the trail as blowing snow and darkness created television static-like confusion.

I tried again after first light, as a cheerful man operating a front-end loader cleared the piles of snow blocking the road. He waved at me — a mostly unidentifiable human riding a bicycle while wearing a veritable moon suit. I waved back. The Iditarod Sled Dog Race was in full swing, and more than twenty mushers were holed up at the village's checkpoint, waiting out the storm. A volunteer pointed me to the trail, which also was buried in drifts. From there, I wrestled with my bike for three hours, making less than three miles of progress before I opted to return to Shaktoolik. The school librarian told me she wasn't surprised to see me back in town, as even the caribou hunters were staying home that day.

"If the caribou hunters don't go, you don't go," she said with an ominous tone.

For the rest of the day, I sat in the teacher's lounge with wind-blocking tape still stretched across my face, checking musher standings and weather forecasts online. The weather station at the airport recorded a temperature of three above zero and north winds of thirty-eight miles per hour, gusting to sixty. Overnight lows were forecast at ten below zero, and the librarian speculated that the caribou hunters were going to sit out the following day as well. But as the frigid night fell, mushers became impatient and trickled out of their checkpoint in groups. I vowed to make one more attempt at first light. As it was, I had only a day and a half of food left in my bicycle bags. Mushers had almost entirely cleared out the village store of dry goods, so resupply was impossible. I really only had one more chance to salvage my trip.

The following morning, nothing had changed. The wind still roared from the north, and the front-end loader operator was clearing drifts that had again buried the street. The caribou hunters had again opted to stay home. But I could see new evidence of dog teams — fresh feces and dog booties filled to the brim with drifted snow and scattered along the trail like colorful rocks — so I knew a number of mushers were attempting the sea ice crossing. By afternoon, I was questioning the wisdom of following mushers. Those guys are crazy, and they had an actual race to finish. What the hell was I doing?

The North Wind answered only with a deafening roar, like an approaching freight train that would never arrive. To secure both my bike and my body, I wedged the front wheel into a drift and propped my leg against a pedal as I turned my back to the wind and hunched down. After seven strenuous hours, I was terribly hungry and thirsty. But the windchill only allowed for infrequent breaks — just long enough to reach into my coat and pull out my hydration tube, or grab some trail mix wedged into a bag on the top tube of my bike. There was never time to do both before an unnerving sensation of ice entered my blood. I pulled my face mask down and felt the wind flash-freezing the skin around my cheekbones. At the moment I was more desperately thirsty, so I frantically unzipped multiple layers to reach the hose more quickly. This was a poor choice, as cold air poured into my breached defenses, and I began to shiver violently.

I yanked up the zippers and whirled around, now desperate to start moving again. Motion was my only means of generating heat — without motion, I would freeze to death. This was a daunting reality to face once I conceptualized what that actually meant — that something as simple as a twisted ankle or a seized bicycle wheel could kill me. On my bike I carried a sleeping bag rated to fifty below, along with a waterproof bivy sack and thin sleeping pad. In an emergency these items would probably keep me alive, but I could only guess how long I could remain pinned down while exposed to this wind. When I was already shivering from the cold in my warmest clothing, it was difficult to put faith in any of my gear. I was deeply afraid.

Just then the wind's roar amplified to jet engine decibels, and I knew a major gust was charging south. I knelt onto the snow and placed my head against the frame of my bike — as though this pile of lightweight metal and rubber could shield me from an ice hurricane. The force of the gust rattled my whole body, and for several seconds I was utterly helpless. When I stood again, I felt blind. A thick ground blizzard obscured the horizon, and any semblance of a trail had long since been erased by blowing snow. When I glanced over my shoulder, my own footprints were already wiped clean, leaving no evidence that I had passed through moments earlier. I was little more than a ghost moving through a great white expanse — except that ghosts have no mass and cannot feel the wind.

Because the trail no longer differed from the rest of the landscape, I'd depended on a line of wooden stakes to find my way. A good number of these stakes had blown over, and the swirling ground blizzard had intensified to the point that I could no longer find them in the distance. Initially I didn't panic about this, since I had both a compass and GPS to keep me moving in the right direction. But as I waded into deeper drifts, I understood the perils of venturing away from the established path. Even though the trail was buried beneath drifted snow, there was still a packed base underneath. Off trail, I punched through unconsolidated snow that swallowed my hips. I must have looked like a wounded caribou as I thrashed through thigh-deep snow, yanking my overturned bike beside me. I could only hope an opportunistic wolf wouldn't mistake me for one.

Wrestling my eighty-pound bike through knee-deep drifts had been maddeningly difficult. But as I stepped onto a pristine white surface and felt my legs sink to the waist, frustration flushed away in a cold rush of terror. The bike punched in below the wheels, and with my heavily fatigued shoulders and back, I couldn't summon the strength to lift it. Leveraging my bike, I tried to pull myself out of the drift, but I might as well have been sinking in wet cement. When I looked down, I could see wind-blown snow gathering around my torso — slowly burying me deeper.

"They're going to find me here," I moaned out loud, as though trying to motivate my own muscles to work harder. "They're going to find my frozen body buried to the waist in this drift. This is how I die."

But who would find me? I looked over my shoulder, desperate to see evidence of humans, but even my own tracks had already blown away. It was as though I'd never taken those steps at all.

Fatigue forces a strange kind of detachment between intellect and emotion, and my primitive self resented the ambitious woman who dropped her out of the sky into this cold, featureless hell. Still, she realized that this hell was "our" choice. Every step I'd ever taken led me to this place. The same could be said for anyone at any moment, and none of us really know where our paths will lead. But we all must choose a path.

Most would say I picked a strange one. The merciless environment of the Alaska backcountry is a rare choice for people like me — a white, middle-class woman raised in a sheltered religious culture where I was taught that my role in life was chosen before I was born. I spent a happy childhood clinging fervently to this notion. But somewhere along the way, I lost faith in the American Dream. To get married, secure a career, have children, buy a home, buy more possessions, and strive only for a comfortable life shielded from the chaos of the world — it all felt inauthentic, deceitful even. The particles of the universe explode all around us whether we acknowledge them or not. People and emotions evolve and change whether we want them to or not. Homes and possessions can disappear with the strike of a match, or not — but the truth remains that everything is ultimately temporary.

The American Dream was just that — a fantasy that progress is infinite, people are static, and happiness is as simple as checking off a to-do list. Even as a religious and routine-driven child, I observed comfortable lives rotting under their own stagnation, people clinging to shadows of love, people whose souls were charred by smoldering hurt and anger, whole families imprisoned by debt and fruitless obligations. Even then, it was difficult for me to believe that God wanted this for His children — this fearful inertia. The winds shift, the seasons change, water flows from mountain to sea to sky, and particles expand and collide and decay because the entire universe is simply energy. How are we different?

As I grew into an adult, I became more convinced that motion was the virtue I sought. Motion expands perspectives, encourages knowledge, and cultivates understanding and empathy. If we're moving through a place, we inevitably become a part of it, dependent on the terrain, infrastructure and inhabitants. Staying in one place allows a person to become intimately familiar with it, but as with all things familiar, curiosity eventually fades and quiescence sets in. Comfort breeds discontent, discontent breeds anxiety, and soon we're locked in lives of quiet desperation that Thoreau described, our hearts beating with a longing that we've mistaken for fear. I've fallen into this trap before, clinging to the familiar as discontent encompassed me like a lukewarm pool. Each time I emerged, damp and shivering in the breeze, were the moments I felt most free.

Out on Alaska's icy expanse, thousands of miles from home and hundreds of miles from the nearest accessible road, I was as free from familiar routine as I'd ever been. I was as dependent on motion as I could possibly be — and I was trapped in a snow dune. Yes, somewhere in this messy journey, I'd lost my way. A surge of adrenaline rushed against the deepening chill. I dropped the bike and punched my arms frantically into the wind. This full-body flailing finally created the momentum I needed to extract myself from the drift, tumbling out of the snow onto a patch of hard ice. Gasping for breath, I turned to grab the overturned bike and pull it forward.

It was an exhaustive effort. My heart raced, and every nerve in my body fired jolts of relief and terror. Where would I find the strength for six more miles of deep snowdrifts? And that was just to reach a shelter cabin. From there, thirty-five more miles of sea ice still stood between me and the next village. Thirty-five miles at less than one mile per hour, no opportunities for rest, locked in a strenuous effort that was surely burning at least six hundred calories an hour, with only enough water-carrying capacity to last ten hours, and only four thousand calories of food. My primitive mind ruled, but you don't have to be good at math to see the imbalance. When all but the mileage subtracted to zero, could I survive?

My primitive mind recognized this pointless fretting and put the rest of my intellect in lockdown. It had come to this: survival mode. Survival mode is an instinct-driven state that records very little in long-term memory, so the next six miles have been lost in a cerebral blur. But shortly after my frightening battle with the snow dunes, I spotted a wooden stake and made my way back to the trail. Then continued, exhausted, for five more hours, until I reached the orange cabin at the neck of a broad bluff — Little Mountain.

I slumped toward the cabin, dizzy and disoriented. I couldn't remember eating or drinking anything since the snow dune incident. As soon as I stepped through the door, a startling sensation pierced my body. It felt as though an enormous weight lifted from my shoulders, and warmth surrounded me. It was the sensation of being out of the wind. The sensation of peace.

My frozen breath swirled in the still air inside the cabin, where a thermometer confirmed it was three degrees. It felt practically tropical without windchill. The plywood interior included a wooden bunk and standing-height table, as well as a tiny wood stove with a broken pipe and door, stuffed to the brim with partially burnt trash. Clumps of paper and charred coffee cans littered the floor. Ash and cigarettes coated the bunks. But this cabin had four walls and a roof, and I couldn't have been more grateful if it were the Emirates Palace.

I sat down on the bunk and nibbled on trail mix, but my stomach churned and I continued to feel out of sorts. I needed to cook dinner and melt snow for drinking water soon, while I still had any fumes of energy left. But these tasks were too daunting. They both required stepping outside. Instead, I fished my satellite phone out of a bicycle pannier and turned it on, pointing the antenna toward the tiny window. More than anything, I just wanted to hear Beat's voice.

The phone beeped to life and alerted me to a new text message. The message said only, "Zane died. Phone's on. Call at 6."

"Wait, what?" It was a shocking piece of information to receive out here. Zane was Steve's wife. I visualized Steve emerging from the hell he and Beat had been through, and hearing this news. Out here in the jaws of the merciless wind, I couldn't imagine experiencing the same: Fighting the battles Steve had fought, enduring the grueling efforts and brutal cold, surviving it all only to discover his entire life had fallen apart. And now he was so far away from home, so far away from anything.

The phone's service cut out, so I charged outside to boost the satellite connection, momentarily forgetting my intense fear of the wind. It was after six, but Beat's satellite phone was still on, and he picked up my call. I could scarcely hear his voice over the screaming gales. Zane was found in bed at her and Steve's apartment in San Francisco, Beat told me. No foul play suspected, but nobody knew what had happened. Beat said he and Steve were currently waiting in a tiny village on the Yukon River, Koyukuk. They would leave that evening on a flight to Galena and then Anchorage. Beat would accompany Steve because he wanted to be there for his friend, and because after all they'd been through together, he didn't have the heart to continue toward Nome without him. This was the end of the race for both of them.

All of the blood retreated from my fingers and toes, and my face felt flush. I told Beat that I would turn around as well, return to Unalakleet by bike, and buy a plane ticket to Anchorage. It might take me a few days to make it back, but I'd get there as soon as possible.

Although I entertained plenty of thoughts about quitting, as soon as I said the words, relief washed over me. Relief was followed by shame. Shame melted into disappointment, and then bewilderment. Death elicits a pendulum of emotions, and as I sprinted back to the cabin with my bare fingers still wrapped around the satellite phone, I became overwhelmed by the weight of them. I didn't know Zane well, but I did know her. My memory conjured the image of a petite woman with blonde hair and kind eyes, wrapping her arms around adult sons who were twice her size. She wasn't much older than me. She didn't share these risky hobbies — her own husband's penchant to wander deep into the Alaska wilderness with only the supplies he could drag in a sled. Steve had survived a situation that not many people in the first world could, but he was alive and his wife was gone.

I collapsed on the ash-covered bunk and curled up in a fetal position, burying my face in half-frozen hands. Wind gusts knocked against the cabin's thin walls like a Big Bad Wolf, so I moved my hands over my ears to quiet the roar. Grief rippled through my chest, and I shivered as I continued to imagine what Steve and Beat must have been experiencing in that moment. It was so bleak. I needed to break away somehow. After pulling myself off the bunk, I fumbled with stiff fingers to put on my down parka and pants, then returned to the wind.

Little Mountain rises only about three hundred feet above the sea, with a broad slope encircling the east face and sheer cliffs on the west. Although my limbs were numb and I didn't have an ounce of glycogen left in my muscles, I was determined to stand on the peak. These would be my last steps north, and I needed them to count. My boots punched through flaky layers of crusted snow as I ascended. Sweat trickled down my back in spite of the cold. The final fifteen feet were nearly vertical, and I drove both arms into a dense cornice to pull myself up the wall.

"So futile," my intellect said to the primitive self that strove to complete this climb.

All of it was futile.

This tour along Alaska's western coast had been a test run for my own long-standing dream of traveling the full thousand miles to Nome. It was a dream nearly ten years in the making, since I first moved to Alaska and discovered endurance winter sports. As I pushed myself through ever-longer and tougher challenges, Nome always seemed like a step too far. It took meeting Beat to begin to believe anything was possible, but even then, I never felt ready to tackle the full Iditarod Trail. Finally, in late 2014, I set a plan in motion to make my first attempt during the 2016 Iditarod Trail Invitational. To gain the experience I thought necessary, I reserved 2015 for preparations — everything I did that year was fixed with an eye on reaching Nome from Anchorage under my own power.

Simmering beneath a gut-wrenching mixture of sadness and relief was disappointment that my test run had failed, and failed badly. In four days I'd managed to travel only sixty miles, which is six percent of the distance to Nome, and those sixty miles had unraveled every ounce of experience and strength I'd mustered in ten years of endurance racing. I'd ridden a mountain bike 2,700 miles along the Continental Divide and walked 350 miles on the Iditarod Trail, and I'd never felt so beaten or tired. I knew even if this tragedy hadn't happened, I didn't have the energy or strength to attempt the rest of the sea ice crossing. I was done either way.

The top of Little Mountain was a broad plateau, windswept and brown with clusters of blueberry branches sticking out of intermittent patches of concrete-hard snow. It was so flat I couldn't discern the high point, so I marched to a pile of rocks near the northern edge. On the largest rock, I stood up straight and pulled my face mask down, facing the full brunt of the gale, forever raging southward — the North Wind. Tears had soaked the piece of tape I'd stuck to my face as wind protection, and I could feel ice forming around the edges. All around me, the rippled surface of the sea ice stretched toward distant mountains. The sun hovered low over the southwestern horizon, casting a pink glow. Only the orange shelter cabin punctured the illusion of standing on another planet. Even though Shaktoolik was only fourteen miles away, it had taken me nearly eleven hours of exhaustive effort to reach this point, and in this moment it was another planet. Little Mountain surely was a lonely place — the loneliest I'd ever been.

"Why?" I called out to the wind. "Why?" It was the only word I could think to say. There were no others.

The North Wind answered only in the same deafening roar, racing effortlessly past my shambling body. How does the North Wind generate all this energy? Where did it begin? Where does it finally stop? Many questions filled my mind, but the same unanswerable one was all I asked aloud. "Why?"

With a numb face to match my fingers, I turned my back to the wind and hiked back to the headwall, bounding down the slope I'd crawled up. The North Wind ushered me forward as though that were its answer: "Leave this place. Go home."

I strongly doubted I'd ever return to Little Mountain.

Growing Old Along
The Great Divide

Why?

Anyone who participates in endurance sports will frequently encounter this question — both from others, and from within. Why would any person choose to engage in long and intense blocks of physical labor, suffer discomfort and illness, risk injury, spend large amounts of money on gear and invest hours in training, all for no reward?

Those who don't participate in endurance sports assume those who do are either deranged, self-flagellating, or need to stroke their misguided egos by asserting that they are strong or tough. When confronted, endurance racers generally furrow their brows and mumble equivocal platitudes: "I do this as a challenge to myself," "To see if I can," or "Because it's there."

But really, why?

I've been attempting to answer this question for more than ten years, ever since I happened across a brochure for a hundred-mile winter bike race in Alaska and decided on a whim to sign up. I come from a decidedly nonathletic background — I was terrible at sports as a child, bookish and nonconformist as a young adult, and possess a physical disposition better suited to working in windowless offices than climbing mountains. For these reasons, I felt better equipped to offer some sort of understanding to nonparticipants. Despite a decade of trying — publishing thousands of photos and writing millions of words in blogs, newspaper articles, magazines, and books — the answers only became more ethereal, and the question more opaque.

Most of the answers we find in endurance sports are contradictions. We suffer to feel alive. We exhaust our bodies to fill our souls. We compete against others to bond with them. Beat will rant about the insignificance of sport amid all the issues facing the world, but much of his free time is dedicated to participation, as is mine. I have raced many thousands of miles, both as a mountain biker and a trail runner, and feel no more satisfied or accomplished than I did at the starting line of my very first race. I fear I'll never be satisfied. But no, fear isn't the correct word at all. I'm glad I'll never be satisfied. Sport is an enduringly beautiful way to stay in motion, experiencing life.

The failed bike trip on the Iditarod Trail rightly crushed my own self-assurances about the "why." After Beat and I reconnected in Anchorage, we went for slow hikes in the foothills of the Chugach Mountains and talked about our experiences on the Iditarod Trail. We discussed how Steve was coping, and reconfirmed how much we valued our relationship. It was during these talks that we openly committed to the second part of the Nome dream I'd fostered, which was to coax Beat to sign up for the Iditarod Trail Invitational in the bike division, and ride together. The roar of the North Wind swiftly faded into the whispers of memory, and I became excited about the prospect of traveling across Alaska with Beat.

One week later, I lined up to run White Mountains 100, a hundred-mile race on remote snowmobile trails in the mountains north of Fairbanks, Alaska. I'd finished this race four times on a bicycle, and this was my first year in the foot division. Exhausted but upbeat, Beat "paced" me for the first sixty miles as an unofficial participant. Eventually he needed a break to take care of his own issues, and I surged forward, hoping to finish before the thirty-hour mark. My own legs were wind-battered and sore, but they carried me to my best hundred-mile finish yet. Sometimes these snowy miles are not so hard. Nome, I decided, was a great idea.

There was still an entire summer ahead of us, and the prospect of preparing for an effort as daunting as the Iditarod brought me to an equally outlandish training idea: the 2,740-mile Tour Divide. The mountain bike race traverses the Continental Divide from Canada to Mexico, and I'd completed it once, six years earlier. My twenty-four-day finish stood as a women's record for three more years, and if I had to rank my athletic accomplishments, the 2009 Tour

Divide remains at the top of the list. It was ridiculous to consider this nearly three-thousand-mile race through the rugged Rocky Mountains — often touted as "The Hardest Mountain Bike Race in the World" — as training for a thousand-mile race across frozen Alaska. But in my mind, it made sense. Alaska requires complete self-sufficiency, and the self-supported nature of the Tour Divide would help me refresh these skills, as well as work on strategies to maximize efficiency. Skills and strategy are more valuable than simple fitness. Multi-day endurance races are largely about the long game: Slow and steady actually can win the race.

I trained through the spring in California, and felt strong and fit when I arrived in Banff, Alberta, for the June 12 start. It was odd to return to this place with six years of experiences separating me from an event that had such a monumental impact on my life. I felt like a wholly different person, but this was still the same quirky mountain town, with the same types of wide-eyed rookies, the same pre-race chatter about mud and snow, and the same 2,740-mile journey. Only now it was in front of me, not behind.

As I lined up at the Spray River trailhead with 150 other cyclists, I was filled with a strange dread. A voice in my head whispered, "You shouldn't have come back here." I dismissed this thought as silly, but the fear wouldn't leave. As the field took off, I rushed up to my Banff friends, Leslie and Keith, for one last goodbye.

"I just need one more hug," I said as tears poured down my cheeks. I had no idea why I was crying; there was no reason to be so upset. I was heading out for a grand adventure — one that had more knowns than unknowns. There were dangers along the Tour Divide route, but they were nominal compared to the relentless menace of winter in Alaska. Leslie and Keith wrapped their arms around me and said I'd be fine.

"I'm so scared; I don't know why," I said through happy-sad sobs. "Thank you."

As I pedaled south through narrow valleys crowned with snowy peaks, dark clouds gathered overhead. It started raining, and then the rain turned to hail, then to chunky flakes of snow. This was normal for June in the Rockies, and I'd gotten caught up in the thrill of chasing folks who left me in the dust after my starting line meltdown. I didn't stop to put on my raincoat, reasoning that my numb fingers and toes would warm up soon enough. To generate heat, I pressed harder into the pedals. Hard breathing in the cold air tore at my throat.

The rest of the first day was filled with miles of thick mud, crashes, more rain, rainbows, then a clearing just as night descended. I pedaled hard until I'd covered 155 miles, and found a nice spot next to a river to lay out my bivy sack. In Alaska, common wisdom dictates that you avoid camping near waterways, because the coldest air sinks into the lowest spots. But I was in a different place — the Canadian Rockies in mid-June — and the riverbank offered a forested canopy and drinking water for morning. I congratulated myself on this efficiency.

The alarm went off at 5 a.m., and I awoke from a stupor so deep that it took me several seconds to realize where I was. My arms and legs were numb, and my core temperature was low. Shivering commenced before I even peeked out of my sleeping bag, seven years old and likely no longer insulated to its thirty-two-degree rating. The mossy ground was coated in thick frost. I'd fallen asleep in my wet clothing and soaked the interior of my bag. The zipper was frozen shut. It took several minutes of thrashing to free it, and by then I was very cold. I darted around camp and did jumping jacks to ignite blood circulation. As soon as I could move my fingers, I checked the temperature on my bike computer. It was minus four Celsius — twenty-five degrees.

I fumbled to pack up as quickly as possible. After I generated enough heat, I made a poor decision to drag my bike into a frigid creek and wash away some of the mud. As I pedaled away from camp, my limbs were utterly numb again. Still, it was summer and skies were clear. I knew warmth was not far away.

By midday, mucous was streaming out of my nose and a pounding headache rattled my skull. A sore throat was the final signal that I'd caught a potent cold virus. By the time I crossed the United States border in the early evening, I could hardly breathe through the snot, which only aggravated my muscle soreness, coughing, and fatigue. By then, I'd ridden 270 rugged miles and climbed four mountain passes in the span of thirty-six hours. I went to sleep hopeful I'd feel better in the morning.

Montana heated up, with daytime temperatures climbing into the high eighties. Windstorms swept brown clouds of dust through the canyons. The cold virus moved into my lungs, pushing mucous deeper into overtaxed airways as I ground the pedals up mountain after mountain. I stopped to cough up green gobs of phlegm. The hacking tore at my lungs and left my throat raw, but briefly cleared my airways and opened short bouts of vitality. These energy bursts only proved how lousy I felt most of the time, even for an endurance race. I'd grown accustomed to maintaining forward motion by staying warm and fed, but out here, all energy came from oxygen. My airways were too clogged to filter the dusty, high-altitude air, and I was becoming startlingly weak from limited oxygen.

My routine was simple but strenuous. Each day, I set an alarm for 5 a.m., rising with first light into frosty mornings. I'd put on the damp clothing that hung from the frame of my bike, pack up my bivy sack, sleeping bag, and pad, and stuff a few handfuls of trail mix in my mouth before continuing down whatever dirt path I'd collapsed beside the previous night. I'd cough and sputter as my legs warmed up with the sun. Usually I enjoyed a couple of good hours of pedaling between morning coughing fits and afternoon dust storms. Each day there was usually a small town in which I could stop and refuel. I'd purchase a meal, more trail mix, cheese and dried meat; I was trying to stay away from simple sugars as part of my nutrition strategy, but this was proving more and more difficult. Sugar seemed to be the only fuel source that produced any energy anymore. Candy gave me wings, and although this energy was short-lived, I began to depend on guilty fistfuls of gummy bears and M&Ms to propel me through afternoon slumps. The slumps deepened. By nightfall my mind was foggy and my body was a shell. I'd forced myself into survival mode, until I could scarcely remember crawling under a cluster of pines or a clearing near a cattle fence to fall asleep.

When I was awake, the hours ticked by with muted urgency, like the pulse of a ventilator in an otherwise quiet hospital room. This is what my breathing sounded like — a rhythmic whoosh and hiss, harmonized by high-pitched chirps. The night coughs were becoming worse, and occasionally I'd wake up in a panic because I'd stopped breathing. I'd claw at the zipper of my bivy sack and push my face into the cold mountain air, hacking until the obstruction landed on the dirt. One night I stared at the gob in fascination while it glistened in the silver moonlight. I imagined that ball of mucous was the last stronghold of the virus. Tomorrow, surely, I'd feel better.

Mornings always were better, marginally, and only because I'd spent six hours drifting in and out of consciousness, resting my legs and clearing my lungs. But if I looked for a pattern, I could easily track how my health was deteriorating with each passing day of the Tour Divide. I was wheezing sooner on each hill, taking more stops to catch my breath, and shutting down earlier each night. Decreasing stamina is a given in endurance racing, and a big part of the challenge is figuring out the best way forward. My condition was never so bad that I couldn't manage, and so I viewed quitting the Tour Divide as exactly that — quitting a race I could manage. I did not want to quit. The Tour Divide was my race, my greatest accomplishment to date. By 2015, I'd practically become one of the old guard in this burgeoning sport. People looked up to me. In a way, I couldn't bear to let them down.

Although I wasn't willing to admit this to myself, the Tour Divide had become a piece of my identity, and quitting the race was the same as quitting myself. What my mind also wasn't willing to accept was the reality that pushing my body so hard while I was clearly sick with bronchitis also was a way of quitting myself. I was doing something so prevalent in endurance sports that I should have been able to recognize it instantly — sacrificing my body in favor of my ego. There's a fine but important line between mental toughness and reckless stubbornness, and I had long since crossed it.

Still, at the time, this was difficult to conceptualize because my head was so addled by oxygen deficits and fatigue. My primitive mind spent more time in the driver's seat. And primitive mind, which can still remember what it was like to be stalked by tigers, understands only that forward motion takes priority over all. When I was facing the North Wind in Alaska, this was true. I needed motion to survive. But the Rocky Mountains are a more subdued wilderness, and my route was a long series of dirt and gravel roads. There was shelter, water, and food at regular intervals, and the summer sun allowed long, rejuvenating breaks. Forward motion was physically unnecessary. What I needed was to stop. Eventually my body forced this when I experienced my first asthma attack while climbing steep pavement in Grand Teton National Park. Hyperventilating for several minutes was a scary experience, but as soon as it was over, I chalked it up to pushing too hard.

"Take it easy," I said aloud. "Don't rush." I took a fifteen-minute nap on a picnic table as a precaution, only to wake up with seventeen new mosquito bites and still-ragged breaths.

That night, again, I scarcely made it to somewhere safe before I collapsed. It was at the top of a pass, in a frigid picnic area near ten thousand feet. I stashed my bike in an outhouse to deter curious grizzlies while subconsciously hoping the bear would come and eat me instead. The strain, the wheezing and the battle for oxygen was making me miserable. But in the strange coping mechanisms of the mind, I didn't fully recognize this. The crimson sunsets and snowcapped mountains reminded me of happy memories. As I pedaled along the dusty roads of the present, I spent more time drifting through the past, stubbornly refusing to acknowledge my afflictions. The deeper I retreated, the faster time passed — many miles disappeared entirely into feverish dreams. But I always had to emerge — sunburned, mosquito-bitten, gasping through a DEET-saturated face mask as relentless summer winds pushed mucous and dust deeper into my lungs.

While crossing the high desert of Western Wyoming, I became too tired to formulate the elaborate daydreams that had been sustaining me. The sagebrush plain spread out toward the horizon, capped with the distant peaks of the Wind River Mountains. I just stared forward, thinking about nothing, feeling pain but only in the most visceral way, as though I was suffering in a dream. Only when my stomach growled did I snap to alertness, and re-focused on the horizon as I reached into a bag of trail mix. Every muscle in my body sagged. My heart beat in shallow murmurs. The sun was again moving low on the horizon, saturating the desert in orange light.

"Where had I been, all this time?" I wondered. "Where did I go?"

As sugar filled my bloodstream and a semblance of lucidity returned, I thought, "This is what it must feel like, to be very old. To be worn out by life."

When my grandfather was dying in a nursing home, my mother and I went to visit him on a Sunday afternoon. We walked past the rooms of others who were dying in the nursing home, sitting alone in beds and on chairs, staring at televisions. This is what my grandfather did as well, as the sun rose and set beyond the shades that darkened his only window. We talked, but only of banal things, and I couldn't understand how he could have so little to say at the end of his life. If I believed I was nearing the end of my life, I would use every last breath to wring joy out of existence. I would not wither away in a nursing home if I could help it. I would limp into the mountains, as high as I could go, even if I was never seen again.

Now, on the sagebrush plains of Wyoming, I understood. I understood what it must be like to gaze into a horizon without seeing, to think only in banalities, to crave only sleep and oblivion. The incandescent beauty of the wilderness meant little to me. I too could go into a dark room and stare at a television and it wouldn't make much difference, because my body was all used up. Where the body goes, the mind follows.

No. I refused to believe I was done. What was that poem about refusing to go gently into that good night? To rage, rage against the dying of the light?

I wanted to believe this illness was something I could control, part of the mind-over-matter challenge I'd been seeking in my dozens of endurance races, as though bronchitis was nothing more than a devil in my heart. Through the grapevine of social media networks, I'd learned that several other racers ahead and behind me were coping with respiratory issues and bronchitis. Perhaps a virus had been shared amid close quarters in Banff, and the air was particularly bad with consistent strong wind, high pollen counts, and dust. A handful of sick racers had quit; just as many were still on the trail. One woman went to the hospital in Helena, Montana, and was still out in front of the field, on pace to shatter the women's record.

I unapologetically race for my own reasons — most of them cerebral — but I'd be lying if I claimed I was unaffected by peer pressure. Other racers managed to either out-think or out-muscle their illnesses. So I knew it was possible.

While cycling through my memory archives, I often drew on the experience of completing a seven-day foot race in Nepal while battling food poisoning so severe that I couldn't eat or drink for most of the week. My body was seriously depleted and weak, but I knew it was a rare chance to experience the Himalayas, so I pushed through the discomfort and had an incredible — if exhausting — experience. I imagined I'd reach an even higher plane of satisfaction if I could banish the devil bronchitis and finish my second Tour Divide.

So I ground on, coughing and sputtering my way along the rolling foothills of the Wind River Mountains and into the Great Divide Basin. As I approached the sandy plain that lacked so much as a trickle of flowing water, the wind picked up and heat bore down. Brown clouds of dust streamed across the desert, and I felt a visceral fear not unlike the terror of watching ground blizzards obscure the sea ice in Alaska. Even with fabric wrapped over my nose and mouth, the high-velocity dust found its way into my throat and pushed deeper into my airways, intensifying the cough. A paste of sweat and dirt coated most of my exposed skin, and dizziness clamped down before the top of every hill. I needed to take increasingly longer breaks, slumped over the handlebars and yanking the buff away from my face as I gasped away from the wind. There were more than a hundred shadeless, dry miles between there and the next town of Wamsutter, Wyoming. I realized, too late, that I had every reason to feel this gnawing fear.

"They're going to find my body out here, pinned underneath this bike, skin blackened by the sun and lungs filled with dust. This is how I die."

Conditions on the dirt road continued to deteriorate until it was only two faint tire tracks worn into the clay surface, scarcely visible amid the yellow grass and sage. I wouldn't have believed it to be a route used by anyone since Mormon pioneers pulled handcarts along the Oregon Trail, but the GPS pointed me in that direction. After meandering through the rusty remnants of an abandoned oil-drilling site, the trail shot upward, cutting a direct line along the rolling crest of a shallow ridge.

Each short but steep hill took ages to climb, as I walked beside my bike and stopped every three or four steps to gasp for air. Even though I'd only gained a few hundred feet of elevation, I could see for a hundred miles in every direction — the distant snow-capped peaks to the north, the sagebrush plains to the east, the pink horizon to the west. I was moving south, where the late evening sunlight cast shadows over the fluted cliffs of this ridge. The geography of the Great Divide Basin was startlingly complex, and between gasps I found myself grappling with frustrating calculations — "I'm sixty miles from Wamsutter. I have three liters of water. I'm moving at two miles per hour uphill, about ten downhill. Fifteen more hours? Twenty?"

Failure to reach a conclusion was followed by more disturbing observations about how "they" would find my body if I collapsed. Each coughing fit left me feeling dizzy. I needed to lie down, but I was frightened and fear drove me forward. I was in survival mode, low on energy, using each breath-catching stop to cram string cheese and chocolate in my mouth, fearful that any lull in momentum might cause me to drift to sleep while standing. I needed to reach Wamsutter before morning — I was convinced my life depended on this. If I camped in the desert and drank most of my water during the night, the heat and wind of another day out here would surely kill me.

Minutes trickled past as darkness settled, and the furnace blast of wind calmed to a breeze. The track dropped off the ridge to a more manageable grade along a dry stream bed, and the surface of the road gradually improved. The night was starry and cold as heat dissipated into the clear sky. I was an old woman again, alone in a dark room, staring unseeingly at television static. Suddenly, an abrupt jolt broke the reverie. I was lying in the dirt. I'd fallen off my bike. Disoriented and confused, I sat up and looked around.

"Where did I go?"

Behind me, wheel tracks meandered drunkenly along the edge of the road before veering abruptly into the ditch. I concluded I'd either fainted or fallen asleep on my bike, and this realization brought a new wave of frustration and anger. I was losing control. I could no longer trust myself to even reach Wamsutter, let alone Mexico. It was hopeless. Everything had been exhausted. GPS told me Wamsutter was twenty-eight miles away. I decided I could sleep for a few hours and still make it there before the heat of the day.

I pushed my bike fifty yards off the road and spread out my bivy sack in a narrow strip of sand between clumps of sage. As I pulled off my shoes and climbed inside, I noticed streaks of white light shooting across the sky — faint spotlights across a wash of stars. Although exhausted, I was mesmerized by these lights, and watched them for several minutes before a green wave emerged, rippling along the black edge of the northern horizon.

"Northern Lights?" I found their presence confusing, and glanced around to make sure I hadn't experienced another lapse in my awareness of time. The sage desert was rendered in nighttime's cinematic silvers and grays, but it was undoubtedly the desert. I was still in southern Wyoming, at a latitude far south of those typically exposed to the aurora borealis. It wasn't impossible ... but was it real? Was I hallucinating? I scooted my bag sideways so I could lie down and watch the green light as it danced over the desert. It was so beautiful. It was so comforting, like a signal from the heavens that the world was good and the North beckoned, always, even as I suffered through this long journey south.

"It's going to be okay," I said aloud. My voice chirped as I talked, which startled me, so I cleared my throat and said in a more soothing tone. "Everything will be okay."

I didn't want to stop watching the light show, but within a minute the decision was made for me, and oblivion returned.

Hard-Fought Failures

Two weeks later, on a withering 102-degree afternoon in Salt Lake City, I decided to roll out of bed and attempt a walk.

I'd effectively been in bed since my parents rescued me in Frisco, Colorado, after I dropped out of the Tour Divide. I managed to cover several hundred miles after I rolled into Wamsutter, where I learned that there'd been an intense solar flare, and the Northern Lights I witnessed were not a hallucination. Rejuvenated by this sign from the universe — and a half gallon of cold Pepsi — I continued pedaling south.

The dust and heat factor only worsened as I entered the oil fields of southern Wyoming. I caught a third wind in northern Colorado, with the high Rockies beckoning and the kindness of a trail angel to spur me onward. I visited a medical clinic in Steamboat Springs, where a doctor diagnosed me with bronchitis and prescribed antibiotics and an inhaler. The prospect of medication renewed my optimism, but the following day everything fell apart in spectacular fashion. Beyond Steamboat Springs, I grappled with frequent asthma attacks that the inhaler only tempered. More often these attacks forced me to curl up in culverts under the thin shade of aspen trees for a half hour or more, until I felt well enough to pedal. Finally, a fever and intense nausea left me too weak to climb stairs, let alone ride my bike up mountains.

There was finally a moment when I accepted that I had to quit, and the realization settled over me like smog as I limped into Kremmling, Colorado. But pride wouldn't let me quit there. Kremmling is the home of old wounds — it's the town where my ex-boyfriend quit this race during his only attempt in 2008. The following year, I promised myself that never, no matter what, would Kremmling be the end of my road. So in 2015, I pedaled fifty more miles to Silverthorne, taking frequent breaks while lying in ditches or on the hot gravel of road shoulders. I spent the day wheezing and coughing despite incessant inhaler hits, and drinking sun-heated fruit juice because it was the only calorie source I could keep from throwing up — barely.

While I was slumped over the handlebars, gradually descending on a paved road at only six or seven miles per hour, the stupidity of the lengths I'd taken this ride became uncomfortably clear. There was usually such thrill and satisfaction in facing fears and overcoming great challenges, but this was just sad. I'd traveled seventeen hundred miles for what, exactly? This wasn't fun or triumphant. At times I was so delirious that I could scarcely keep my decades straight. The only force I'd overcome was common sense. Shame washed over me, and I realized it wasn't because I was planning to quit this race, but because I hadn't quit earlier.

Despite this prevailing shame, it still took me another day to make the final call. I wallowed in a hotel room in Silverthorne, sleeping in fitful spurts and waking drenched in sweat. I was too weak to carry my bike down the hotel stairs, so I hiked one mile to a pharmacy to pick up a new antibiotic prescription. This one mile took nearly an hour to walk as I sat down on curbs and slumped against trees next to the sidewalk, gasping for breath. While standing in line at the pharmacy, my prevailing fear was whether I'd find the strength to walk back. Outside the building, I called my parents in Salt Lake City, who said they could drive out to Colorado the following day. With that I felt the familiar rush of guilt, and just enough relief to crawl back to the hotel.

Most of the next week passed while languishing in bed at my childhood home, battling pneumonia. My mother drove me to Target to purchase a second set of clothing to replace the outfit I'd worn for seventeen hundred miles, and I nearly fainted while walking across the parking lot. The July sun was intense, and I understood why weather forecasters issue heat warnings for the elderly and the sick.

My first real venture back into the living world, three days later, did not yield encouraging results. I made it three blocks before the wheezing returned, and turned around after six. Some form of active recovery had always yielded positive results in the past, but I was a brittle shell of my athletic self, full of holes. Good health is life's most valuable gift, and I never appreciated it the way I should have. The devil bronchitis drained all of my vitality and zeal for life, leaving plenty of room for loathing and regret.

Eventually I felt strong enough to board an airplane, and flew home to California. Beat was also just returning from a similarly arduous 1,400-mile mountain bike race in South Africa, and would soon be gearing up for his annual duo of two-hundred-mile mountain runs in Europe. Beat's endurance seems to have no boundaries, and flexibility in his work as a software engineer at Google allows him to push limits where few have ventured. All the while, he refuses to take himself seriously and only engages in training when it's convenient and fun. I admire his attitude, but when I aspire to it, I find myself failing spectacularly.

I now had two of what I considered egregious failures in just half a year, and my illness — which was later diagnosed as pneumonia — proved resilient. Short ventures on the mountain bike brought on asthma attacks, and I could only run at a moderate pace before I began hyperventilating. Friends who had experience with chronic asthma urged me to dial back my efforts, but I was simply engaging in a minimum of activity to keep my mental health intact. The Tour Divide had ravaged my mood. When I abruptly stopped riding my mountain bike fourteen hours a day and spent the next two weeks in bed, my thoughts went to dark places I rarely encounter. Post-adventure blues are usually present, but when they're wired into personal failure and a steep decline in health, the results can be devastating. I feared depression, and didn't want to slip into a downward spiral. So I fought back in the best way I knew how.

As Beat geared up for his Alps adventures, I reconsidered a race I had signed up for earlier in the year, and subsequently backed out of (but didn't remove my name from the roster) when I decided to race the Tour Divide. The Ultra Trail du Mont Blanc is a 104-mile foot race around Mont Blanc, the largest mountain in western Europe. The route crosses through France, Italy, and Switzerland over a multitude of mountain passes that add up to more than thirty-thousand feet of cumulative elevation gain: equal to climbing from sea level to Mount Everest. The race organization gives runners forty-six hours to complete the race, which sounds like an amble, but most certainly is not when steep grades and technical trails reduce an all-out effort to two miles per hour. In mountain racing, thirty-minute-miles are absolutely a respectable running pace.

Of course, my body was desperately overworked and under-trained. Most of my spring training had been on a bike. Seventeen hundred miles of the Tour Divide is an exhaustive effort even without pneumonia, and lung recovery was slow. My fitness remained poor in early August, just three weeks before the start of UTMB. I told everyone who asked that I would not be racing in Europe. Even Beat heard a noncommittal, "Let's see how I feel before the start." But in my daydreams, UTMB had redemption scrawled across its daunting elevation profile. The Ultra Trail du Mont Blanc is another one of those races frequently touted as "the toughest in the world." I wanted to run it untrained, eight weeks after quitting the Tour Divide and still recovering from pneumonia. What could go wrong?

At this point, many readers of this book are no doubt rolling their eyes at my hubris. On the surface I may appear as another endurance masochist taking misguided moon-shots to defy my own decline. If I must be truthful, this was part of the draw, but only a small part. Even if the race itself was a disaster, there was so much beauty to witness, interesting people to meet, joy to savor, and pain to endure. There was so much life to experience. Languishing in a French hotel room when this opportunity was right in front of me — this, I convinced myself, was the poor choice. So a few days after Beat set out for his two-hundred-mile odyssey, I lined up with twenty-five hundred fiercely fit international runners in the central square of Chamonix, France.

And yes, there were disasters. The disasters were small, but they started early, just three miles after the gun went off at six in the evening. All of Chamonix erupted in cheers as thousands of runners surged into the streets of this upscale mountain town. The temperature was eighty-six degrees: unseasonably warm for late August. The crowd was thick, and most runners seemed to sprint off the starting line. Although I intended to pace myself, even ten-minute-miles — my typical pace for short trail runs — siphoned me into the back of the pack. I groaned and took longer strides to boost my speed, but I was so focused on monitoring my breathing that I failed to recognize the early signs of stomach distress. By mile three, my gut was gurgling, and nausea moved through my body in unwelcome waves.

Slowing my stride was necessary but futile; the damage had been done. I hiked up the first twenty-five-hundred-foot climb while fighting off dizziness. The long descent loosened my bowels to the point that I was trotting awkwardly with my cheeks clenched for nearly an hour. My eyes darted everywhere in search of a private nook, to no avail. With hundreds of other runners surrounding me, I was too proud to squat next to the trail, and too rushed to bushwhack into the woods. By the time I reached a bathroom at the first checkpoint, there were smears of blood across my backside. In my desperation to prevent a messy accident, I failed to notice the considerable chaffing that rubbed my skin raw.

Even though I still had control of my breathing, nausea and open wounds just thirteen miles into a hundred-mile race do not bode well. I cleaned myself thoroughly with antibacterial wet wipes, which evoked a searing pain so intense I can only compare it to pouring acid into a third-degree burn. Once I finally stopped seeing stars, I limped into the darkened cattle fields, holding my breath to block a nauseating aroma. After becoming so dizzy I nearly passed out, I hunched over to vomit a small amount of clear liquid — I'd only ingested water since starting the race — and then coughed until I could walk again. I was barely holding myself together.

At the second checkpoint in the French resort town of Les Contamines, I staggered toward a bench and laid on my back. I still hadn't eaten anything, and hoped fifteen minutes of rest, some broth, and maybe some plain bread would help me get my stomach back. Just as I laid down, a woman approached me and pointed sternly at her watch. A voice over the intercom spoke in several languages before translating the message to English: "We remind you that you must leave by twelve o'clock." I glanced at my phone. It was 11:55.

Disheartenment sliced through my raw gut. I was only twenty-two miles into UTMB, and already running against cutoffs. If I failed to meet one, I'd be pulled from the race. If I wanted to not fail, I was going to have to chase these cutoffs with my sour stomach, questionable lung capacity, and searingly painful butt wounds for every one of the next forty hours. There would be no time to rest.

But oh, what redemption I'd achieve if I overcame the odds! As I shuffled away from more cow pastures with a John Wayne-like gait, I made frustrating calculations that only served to flood my system with stress hormones. Overcoming every issue without accumulating more seemed highly unlikely, and yet I cringed at how devastated I'd feel if I quit. But if I didn't quit, there were so many worse ways to fail.

Still, humans are strange animals, and the chemicals that respond to sickness and stress also fill our bodies with elation and awe. The rocky trail rose above tree line, offering the route's first unobstructed views of towering mountains surrounding a cirque. The full moon cast limestone cliffs in luminescent shades of silver, with contours so deep they hinted at a fourth dimension. In front of me, a steep pass rose like a fortress wall, rendered black in the moon's shadow. At the apex of the pass, a star-filled sky appeared to drain into a single stream of white light. It was the headlamp-lit procession of a thousand runners marching up Croix du Bonhomme, nearly three-thousand feet higher. They appeared to be floating, like fallen angels ascending toward a heaven they would never reach. The scene was dystopically beautiful, and for long minutes I marched in awe, free of frustration and fear.

By the bottom of the pass, I was again grinding my teeth in agony as I mopped up fresh blood with wet wipes. The open sores between my butt cheeks rubbed together with every footfall, and were becoming deeper and more painful as the miles ground away at my skin. My stomach had settled enough that I could take in a few handfuls of candy, but this new energy only serve to highlight the searing pain that was not going away — not as long as I kept moving.

It was mile thirty-three. I was avoiding failure math at this point. The check-point already looked like a disaster-area refugee camp, with most of the other runners slumped on benches, bandaging bloody feet, lying face-down on the grass, or hunched over bushes, vomiting. We were the back of the pack — the sickly animals struggling and stumbling just to stay with the herd. There were twenty minutes before the cutoff, and I could almost feel the hot breath of imaginary wolves bearing down on this sad place. Those still sprawled on the ground were next in line to be picked off by the wolves. I gulped down chicken broth and waddled out of the aid station, refueled mainly by fear.

The sun rose over the next pass as the back-of-packers crossed into Italy. The pass after that was an expanse of table-sized boulders that required crawling. In my rush down the other side, I caught my foot and tumbled headlong into a minefield of sharp boulders. Usually when I trip, my anxious brain interferes, causing me to tense up and slap the ground like a dead fish. Here I was so resigned to fatigue and pain that even that terrifying pull of gravity didn't prompt an emotional reaction. Instinct directed me to tuck and roll over the rocks, and I more or less landed on my feet without hitting anything sharp. For several seconds I froze in this crouched position, overcome with disbelief that I just unintentionally cartwheeled over a boulder field and somehow emerged unscathed. My shoulder throbbed and I was frightened to start moving again, convinced that after the shock subsided I'd find a broken bone. Finally, a British runner who witnessed the fall from two switchbacks higher passed me.

"Are you hurt?" he asked.

"No," I wheezed, then cleared my throat. "Actually, I think I'm fine."

Renewed adrenaline propelled me over the next few passes as the day heated up. The cutoff wolves fell a few paces behind. I had more than an hour on them when I reached the halfway point in the Italian village of Courmayeur, so I took advantage of the extra time to tend to my feet and eat a plate of pasta. I should have continued moving, as the temperature topped ninety-seven degrees by the time I returned to the trail. I was back at the cusp of the time limit and facing not only a massive climb, but also the slow-moving procession of the back-of-pack.

A narrow trail funneled runners upward through the pine forest. Trees provided thin shade while keeping the crowd condensed into a hunched, sweat-soaked assembly line. The fixed pace felt unconscionably slow, but every time I tried to pass people, I became so winded that I had to stop and catch my breath. Beige clouds of dust swirled from a sun-baked trail that two-thousand runners had trampled into fine powder. I pulled a buff over my mouth to prevent dust from entering my lungs, but I couldn't contain the wheezing.

This was a familiar spiral. While I had suspected it from the beginning, I remained incredulous that my airways were still so reactive two months after contracting pneumonia.

"This is a mistake."

The forest ended abruptly at a sharp point on the ridge. Above that elevation, the trail contoured a grassy slope with views of the granite spires and glaciers of the Mont Blanc massif, still ten-thousand feet higher. This is the postcard view of UTMB, so majestic that it's distracting to all but the most self-absorbed runners — which most of us are by hour twenty-one. Only when I stopped for "oxygen breaks" could I remove myself from my own distress for long enough to experience what it was I came for. I lay on my back in the tall grass and watched the mountain's dark clouds dissipate into the blue sky overhead.

I made the next checkpoint's cutoff, barely, just as a volunteer was urging a seventy-year-old Swiss man to put down his plate and leave before the clock ran out. The caliber of athletes at the back of the pack continued to impress me — a lot of them were young, strong-looking men with no visible injuries, and their presence among those who were struggling bolstered my conviction that this race was in fact very hard. But the older runner impressed me most of all, because he put down his plate of food and marched out of the tent with a fierce look on his face. I later learned that he arrived in Chamonix minutes before the final cut-off, becoming the oldest UTMB finisher ever.

I was more resigned. My face was not fierce. In all likelihood, it betrayed the fear I felt as I hiked toward Grand Col Ferret with my back to the setting sun. Was my breathing going to become progressively worse? Would I spiral back to pneumonia, with days of gasping in bed? The early discomforts of the race — bloody chaffing, raw gut and a bruised shoulder — still gnawed at me, but I'd become wholly preoccupied with concerns about my overall health. Continuing to hike up yet another pass after an entire night and day of hard breathing couldn't be doing my lungs any favors, and yet something inside my brain balked at the notion of turning around and quitting. The effort was futile, and I knew that, but I was going to see it through to the bitter end. At least, I was going to see Switzerland.

But I didn't see Switzerland, not really. The pass that marked Italy's border with Switzerland was still beyond my line of sight when awareness began to fade — again slipping into survival mode as my brain shut down unnecessary emotions to conserve oxygen and energy. I remember the nearly full moon rising into a purple sky, and then darkness clamped down as I shuffled downhill. This was still "running" — it was all I had left from my deflated fight-or-flight instinct. But I didn't make it all that far before two race volunteers who were sweeping this section of trail caught up with me. And this was it. I'd reached the back of the race. The cutoff wolves culled everyone behind me. I was next.

Eventually I caught up to another wounded deer of a runner, and the sweeps circled around him while I shuffled ahead. The trail contoured a steep hillside, with a rocky surface barely wide enough to fit two shoes. The woods below were thick and quiet, as black as a bottomless hole. I fantasized about walking off the ledge and disappearing into the darkness — not a legitimately suicidal thought, but more a method of imagining away the discomfort and discouragement. I still had to get myself to the next point of civilization, whether I met the time cutoff or not. The sweeps had said my chances were not good.

"You'll need to really run," were the words he used in an abrupt French accent.

"I'm doing the best I can," I replied, which is a phrase I often say to myself when I'm about to fail.

But I couldn't honestly say I was doing the best I could. My legs were still strong, and I hadn't been out of breath since I started descending. Still, there were worse scenarios than failure, and I needed the cutoff wolves to take me out before my ego caused any more damage. There was relief in this again — shame and relief — as I shuffled toward the shuttered village of La Fouly, where I missed the cutoff by fifteen minutes.

In that amount of time, the aid station had been cleared and most of the tables removed. A volunteer directed me in broken English to join the other culled runners on a bus. I misunderstood his instructions and limped to the village bus station, where there was no bus scheduled to arrive for ten more hours. The Swiss village was too small for taxis, and hotels were closed for the night. Beat was participating in another race and my parents, who were also visiting Europe for the week and touring Zermatt that day, had no reliable means of communication. For twenty minutes I sat in the abandoned bus station as my leg muscles stiffened and my core became chilled in the cool evening air. Finally it dawned on me that no one was coming, and the runners' bus already left. Eventually my parents would find me and drive me back to Chamonix, but at the time I believed I would have to remain there until morning.

It's these ridiculous scenarios — shivering in sweat-soaked Lycra on a bench in rural Switzerland, having not slept the previous evening, after running and hiking seventy-one miles with more than twenty-two-thousand feet of climbing, and wheezing while I pondered how to keep myself warm — that bring out the most critical introspection.

"This has all gotten out of hand," I thought as I removed a pair of gloves and the last bits of food from my pack. "I need to take a step back from all of this and figure out what I'm actually trying to accomplish."

The goal of endurance sports always seems to be bigger, tougher, and scarier. The numbers don't matter as much as the escalation. The more we participate in endurance challenges, the farther we need to push ourselves to reach the threshold of the unknown, wherein we find the optimal experiences we seek. The fear, the joy, the pain, the passion, the love — we feel it all so much more intensely on the edge of livability. It's this intensity that brings us back, seeking ever-greater challenges.

Modern life is steeped in the mundane, built around the assumption that the edge of livability is a dangerous and uncomfortable place we would all do well to avoid. If this is true, how did the most comfortable and safe society in the history of human civilization become so anxious, hateful, and fear-driven? I know I tend to succumb to anxiety when I've become too comfortable. Sedentary routine brings out my worst characteristics, which have nothing to do with becoming fat or unfit, and everything to do with a dulling of experience. A gray hue washes over my days and I slowly become more complacent, less imaginative, more fearful and less content.

When these negative emotions take over, I wonder if this is how others experience life — the strangers who rage at me from their cars, obsess about products, panic over trivial setbacks, or seem fixated on their outward appearance. Why do we get so worked up over trivial details? How much perspective have we lost in our focus on comfort?

Comfort, I'm convinced, is the enemy. Adversity keeps us sharp, which is why we seek salient experiences, even when our own safety-driven consciences deem these activities unnecessary or insane. We go to the edge because that is where we feel the most alive. Still, it makes sense that our pursuit of this edge of livability would eventually go too far, and we'd fall into an unlivable condition of long-term injury, illness, or death.

The poet T.S. Eliot coined a phrase popular with endurance athletes: "Only those who risk going too far can possibly find out how far one can go." This remains true — but how often do we genuinely assess the costs of that risk, and contemplate what will happen if we truly go too far?

Maybe too far is having permanently shredded lungs. Or maybe it's simply being cold, exhausted, and alone on a bench in Switzerland, loathing myself in ways that comfort always managed to dull.

Pursuit of Experience

B
eyond this mire of self-loathing, illness, and failure was my Alaska dream, inexplicably intact.

After Beat and I returned from Europe in late September, I made an appointment with an asthma specialist and tentatively ventured back into training. My Iditarod fitness plan was conservative but time-consuming: Moderate-intensity efforts increasing in duration until I re-established a firm base of endurance. The March bike trip proved I wasn't strong enough to manage a fully loaded fat bike in difficult conditions, so I also joined a gym and incorporated twice-weekly weight lifting. The doctor confirmed that my lung function was abnormally low and prescribed treatments for exercise-induced asthma.

These were all positive developments, and yet uncertainty was like quicksand, sucking me deeper the more I struggled against it. I was thirty-six years old, and it seemed logical that my health and vitality had already passed its pinnacle. This was the downward arc of life. My body was aging and breaking down. Before 2015, the inevitability of my own decline had been a distant notion. Now it had a tangible presence in my lungs, and there was no denying that I was less fit than I once was, despite my best efforts. Declining fitness was just the first step on that rapidly steepening slope toward death. Like many people do when they ponder their own mortality, I kept my more outlandish dreams closer to my heart. There was still great adventure in me. There was Alaska.

The Alaska dream deserves a backstory, because it's not a particularly common dream, even for an endurance athlete's mid-life crisis. The endeavor lies on the far fringes of what is already a fringe sport. "Winter ultra-distance cycling" doesn't end up on many athletic resumes. The combination of long distance, absolute self-sufficiency, difficult trail conditions, remoteness, cold temperatures, and intense storms tend to be a strong deterrent. The Iditarod Trail Invitational is more of an expedition than a race. The average cyclist takes more than twenty days to reach Nome. Challengers need not only a strong desire to succeed and a willingness to suffer, but also the time, funds, and gear it takes to finish. Since the inaugural year of the thousand-mile race in 2000, sixty individuals have completed the route at least once. Thirty-nine rode a bicycle, fifteen were on foot, and four skied. Only seven were women.

Although only a small number of athletes participate in the human-powered Iditarod, its roots run deeper than many modern sports. People first rode bikes long distances across the frozen North during the late nineteenth century, when prospective miners sought inexpensive modes of travel to gold fields during the Klondike Gold Rush. Northern gold fever coincided with an era when bicycles were the hottest new technology, not unlike television in the 1950s or personal computers in the 1980s. Bicycles were so trendy that newspapers in Seattle advertised Klondike-ready bikes, specifically designed to be ridden in extreme conditions. These models — dubiously upgraded "safety" bicycles with heavy steel frames, solid rubber tires and a fixed-gear drivetrain — sold by the hundreds, and several miners actually rode them across Alaska on tundra and ice.

One of these men was Max Hirschberg, who rode from Dawson City to Nome in 1900. Hirschberg followed the "two-inch trail" set by the slim runners of dog sleds, pedaling the distance in two and a half months. Along the way he suffered from snow blindness, exhaustion, and exposure. He nearly drowned crossing the Shaktoolik River, struggling in frigid chest-deep water for two hours and losing all of his money — fifteen hundred dollars in gold dust — in the process. The bicycle's chain broke while he was crossing the sea ice of the Norton Sound, so he rigged his coat as a sail and coasted with the wind on top of glare ice the rest of the way to Nome.

The Gold Rush ended and most miners left Alaska, but the pathogens they brought with them remained. Alaska Natives had no natural defenses to these germs, so outbreaks of flu and diphtheria were rampant in villages. Nome was hit with a diphtheria epidemic in 1925, prompting the "Great Race of Mercy" as a relay of dog teams shuttled antitoxin serum to the village on Alaska's remote western coast. Dozens of lives were saved thanks to the teams' persistent progress in horrific weather and trail conditions. Mushers were hailed as heroes and their lead dogs were memorialized in bronze statues. Fifty years later, the serum run became an inspiration for the Iditarod Sled Dog Race.

Flu and diphtheria outbreaks abated, but not before killing thousands of people. By the 1930s, populations in most rural Alaska towns were a fraction of what they were in previous decades, and land-based mail routes saw less traffic as planes became more widely used. The largest of these mail routes was the Iditarod Trail, which connected the port town of Seward to villages in the Alaska Range, the Interior, the Norton Sound, and Nome. The Iditarod Trail had all but disappeared when the snowmobile was invented in the 1960s, and the use of sled dogs began to decline rapidly. A homesteader named Joe Redington Sr. fretted that Alaska was losing touch with its cultural heritage. Redington was a sled dog advocate, and believed the tradition of mushing could be preserved through sport. He was a quixotic figure with big dreams, and went straight to the most outlandish: A thousand-mile race across Alaska on the historic Iditarod Trail. Redington overcame a fantastic number of obstacles to see his dream through to reality. The Iditarod Trail was restored and the first Iditarod Sled Dog Race was held in 1973.

As sled dog racing gained popularity in Alaska during the 1980s, Redington challenged a local group of cyclists to organize their own race on the Iditarod Trail, competing in what was then still a fledging sport: mountain biking. The first Iditabike race was held in 1987, with twenty men and six women taking on the 210-mile challenge. Two riders from outside Alaska set a blistering pace for the first forty miles of packed trail on what these days would be regarded as terribly skinny tires for snow riding. Farther out, trail conditions worsened, and the cyclists spent the next fifteen hours pushing their bicycles sixty miles to the halfway checkpoint. Thirteen of the twenty-six starters went on to finish the race — the winner in thirty-three hours and the first woman in forty-two.

Iditabike changed to Iditasport and continued to draw respectable fields through the late eighties and nineties. The organizer added multiple disciplines — foot and ski — and longer distances — a 350-mile race to McGrath in 1997, and the thousand-mile race to Nome in 2000. The race's organization fell apart in 2002, but one racer who had finished the 350-mile distance four times was committed to keeping the event alive. With the help of several other racers, Bill Merchant formed the Iditarod Trail Invitational — a no-frills event with no required gear, no set course, limited support, and no prizes. Merchant's wife, Kathi, now manages most of the logistics of this event, while Bill is happier with the title of "trail crew," working behind the scenes.

I stumbled onto this scene, largely by accident, shortly after I moved to Homer, Alaska, in 2005. While shopping at an outdoor retailer in Anchorage, I came across a brochure for a hundred-mile bike race on the Iditarod Trail, the Susitna 100. I had no experience with endurance sports and no idea that riding bikes on snow was even a thing, but I was captivated. I signed up for the event, trained through my first dark winter in Alaska, and finished the grueling slog in twenty-five hours — soaking wet, dehydrated, depleted, and exhausted. Everything about the experience should have been a deterrent. Winter endurance cycling is one of those activities that looks fun from a distance, but in practice, actually is not — similar to heavy drinking. And yet, similar to heavy drinking, it continues to draw people back, almost against their will. Is winter endurance cycling an addiction? I'm inclined to say no, and yet I can't deny that I was hooked.

Since 2005, every year has involved some form of racing a snow bike or racing on the Iditarod Trail. I completed my first 350-mile race to McGrath in 2008, and dropped out of the race with a severe case of frostbite in 2009. I completed the Susitna 100 on foot in 2011 and 2012, and went on to challenge the 350-mile distance on foot in 2014. By 2015, I'd raced more than a thousand miles on the Iditarod Trail alone, and six hundred more on other Alaska routes. Through all of this, the full thousand-mile distance was always a pipe dream — a step too far. It was too remote, too dangerous, too much time in the cold, and too difficult. I told myself I didn't want this. And yet, I can't deny that I did.

Finally voicing this desire and signing up for the full distance was a major investment of everything I'd committed to the sport over the past decade. That alone may be why it was so difficult to let go. My training progressed nicely as fall settled into winter. Pulmonary function tests continued to show slow improvements. Beat and I spent Christmas in Fairbanks on a gear-testing trip that inspired confidence. In early January 2016, we'd both signed up for a two-hundred-dred mile snow bike race in Idaho. Organized by an Iditarod cyclist and southern route record-holder named Jay Petervary, the Fat Pursuit followed groomed snowmobile trails through the Greater Yellowstone area.

Beat was already feeling uncertain about riding a bicycle on the Iditarod Trail. Although our Fairbanks trip went well, he had some issues with cold feet and hands. The forty-five below cold snap of the previous year was still fresh in his memory, and he expressed concern about managing a bicycle in temperatures that low. The lowest temperature I'd experienced on a bicycle was thirty-five below, and I conceded that my own experience was limited. But I'd managed to keep myself warm then, and figured I could survive.

We traveled to Idaho in hopes of better testing conditions, but temperatures were perplexingly mild — overnight lows of fifteen above, with highs in the thirties. The Fat Pursuit had a required gear list, so our bikes were loaded with sleeping bags, stoves, and extra food. I hadn't taken the time to cull my gear, reasoning that I needed the training, and the load was nearly as heavy as my full Iditarod set-up. The race started in a hotel parking lot at 5:30 p.m., just in time to catch the pink rays of sunset before darkness cloaked snow-frosted pine forests and the granite spires of the Tetons. Beat surged ahead with the rest of the pack, and I fell off the back almost immediately.

"It's okay," I assured myself out loud as I pedaled atop soft snow along a wide power line corridor. "Steady pace, deep breaths." But inside, I agonized over my position. It was far too soon to be in last place.

The route veered away from the power line easement onto a narrow cross-country ski trail, then wove around streams to cross a valley. I could see cyclists' red taillights blinking in the distance, and became more dismayed at how far ahead the closest one appeared. I was clearly crawling. This was embarrassing. I stood out of the saddle to add more power to my pedal stroke, and chased the taillights into low-lying hills. I was winded even on the flatter terrain, and then the trail began to climb and descend a series of steep drainages. My option was to either max out my effort to pedal to the top, or get off and push my bike. Anxiety steered me to the first option. After three hills, no matter how hard I gasped, all of the air seemed to disappear before it reached my lungs. My vision flickered briefly and I panicked, throwing my bike down and kneeling on the trail until I caught my breath.

This just wasn't right. I was three months into Iditarod training that had been going well, and six months into recovery from the Tour Divide and pneumonia. My allergy season had long since passed — even if the weather was somewhat mild for Idaho, it was still the middle of winter. I'd only been racing, slowly, for three hours. Many of my training rides were far longer than this. There was no reason to have such pronounced issues with my breathing so early in the race — unless I had a more serious problem than I'd anticipated.

I was concerned about my overall health and the implications of pushing my lungs too hard. But I also knew the Fat Pursuit was my last chance to prove myself. I had too many failures. If I couldn't pull this one off, then I had no chance of completing the ride to Nome. The Iditarod Trail Invitational was less than seven weeks away, five times as long, and probably ten times as difficult, if not more.

"Breathe, just breathe," I chanted. It would become my mantra.

Just as it hadn't for any of my prior last-ditch efforts, my breathing did not improve. I no longer cared that I was so far behind the field, but I still couldn't ride slowly enough to soothe the huffing or slow the hyperventilation. The course veered steeply downhill to a waterfall on an out-and-back journey of more than three miles. On my way out, I didn't see anyone returning. I was at least an hour behind the next rider, and likely falling farther behind. The worst part was that I still needed to reach the first checkpoint at mile ninety of the course, which was still sixty miles away. I leaned against a metal railing — part of a scenic overlook that was closed for the winter — and gazed toward the quiet roar of a waterfall that I could not see through the darkness.

"Well, that's just great," I muttered, speaking aloud as though I were scolding an indignant child who never learned. "You do these things to yourself."

The night passed as these breathless hours do, in tedious desperation. I overheated despite the fifteen-degree temperature, so I removed my hat, gloves, and outer coat, leaving only a base layer and light jacket to shield my body from the icy breeze. When a chill set in I felt grateful — because it was invigorating, because it distracted from my breathing difficulties, and because warm blood rushed from my extremities to my core, which almost felt like strength.

The route crossed the Warm River — which was mostly frozen — and climbed into the foothills toward a ridge that would top out above seven thousand feet. I stepped off the bike and pushed for miles. In doing so, I actually managed to catch a handful of riders. One was sleeping, two were hunched over their stoves and melting snow for drinking water, and one woman was weaving all over the wide trail. She was pedaling slower than I was walking. I thought my condition was improving, but when she asked how far it was to the first checkpoint, I could barely speak the words between gasps.

"Bout ... thirty ... miles. I think."

It began to snow, and then the flakes started to fall hard and fast. The hat went back on even though my body was overheating again. A thickening layer of fresh snow made progress even slower. The trail had been soft to begin with, and several inches of new snow buried the lower rims of the bike. The effort is similar to plowing through mud or sand — any time surface resistance deepens, energy expenditure increases at what feels like an exponential rate.

My mind slipped backward, drifting to the past in re-imagined memories that nearly tricked me into believing they were real. I was back on the Tour Divide, in 2009, riding the sandy ATV trail where it drops into the Warm River Valley just a few miles away. Aspen trees towered overhead, with green leaves fluttering in the breeze. The sandy moguls had reminded me of the Iditarod Trail, and I rode them like a BMX rider positioning herself to catch big air. I was strong then, and remembering this invincibility caused me to sigh. But then it was 2015, just after sunset when I left Island Park and resolved to ride until I dropped from fatigue or oxygen deprivation or both. A drought year had dried the sand. It was churned up and deep, like a bottomless bowl of sugar, slower than even the slowest snow. I cried that night. Actually, during the 2015 Tour Divide, I cried nearly every night. But that night I continued to cry as I drifted to sleep in my bivy sack, hip throbbing from a recent crash on the sand, and lungs filled with dust and phlegm.

I snapped back to the present as snowflakes brushed against my eyebrows and nose. The route launched into a long descent, and the new snow was slippery and uneven. The bike was all over the trail. I could scarcely hold on, but the adrenaline did offer a fresh hit of badly needed energy. This didn't translate to oxygen, though, and as soon as the trail veered upward again, I had to step off the bike so I could breathe.

Some fifteen hours after the race started, the sky was still dark — because it was January — but strips of violet light were beginning to appear through the trees. Snowfall had ceased, but low clouds remained. Dawn came in a barely perceptible lightening of grays. I kept looking at my watch and attempting to calculate arrival times. The first hard cutoff wasn't technically until West Yellowstone at mile 120, but I had to gain some certainty that I could make it. I wasn't going to force my ragged lungs into thirty more miles over the Continental Divide if all was doomed.

The failure math checked out; even my slow pace would suffice, but I wasn't going to be able to rest. Similar to UTMB, it meant two nights without sleep, and no guarantees that my condition wouldn't worsen over that length of time. It was daunting. My ego, common sense, and the guilt-ridden inner comfort-seeker were locked in a fierce battle to either drive my body forward or convince it to quit. Despite being outnumbered, ego was winning.

"Just go to West Yellowstone," I said aloud. "It will take all day, but at least you can make it that far."

First I had to reach checkpoint one, which was a tent camp in the woods, ten miles from the nearest road. The trail returned to a power line easement, where I could see ahead for miles. All was gray sky, black woods, and white ground, with only hints of mountains through the fog. The horizon seemed to prove that I was not making any progress, even though my legs continued to turn the pedals and my throat was raw from hard breathing. I pedaled harder, but nothing happened. The next five miles could have taken one hour or seventeen. I lost track. I lost heart.

Beat was standing next to a small propane heater when I arrived at the tent camp. He had been there for almost three hours, and continued to wait for me because he was worried.

"You ... need to go," I wheezed. "I ... am crawling. You'll ... never ... make the ... cutoff ... if ... you stay ... with me."

"How are you doing?" he asked. "What's going on?"

"Breathing. ... Having ... trouble. Again."

"I knew it," he said. I could see he was shivering in his down coat and tights.

Morning temperatures were in the twenties, and he'd been standing outside in his damp clothing.

"You … shouldn't have waited," I breathed out. The wind was returning to my lungs, slowly, only because I'd stopped.

"What are you going to do?" he asked.

"I'm going to head for West … Yellowstone," I said. "Need to at least try. I can't … stay here long. But I need more water. Maybe … some soup."

I'd been pedaling about as hard as my air intake would allow for fifteen hours, more than ninety miles. I needed a lot more than soup. But soup was all they had. I looked toward the two volunteers behind the table. They were none other than Bill Merchant — the founder of the Iditarod Trail Invitational — and Tracy Petervary, Jay's wife. Tracy was an accomplished Iditarod cyclist herself, with finishes on both the northern and southern routes, including the women's record on the southern route. Both were people of whom I thought highly and admittedly felt intimidated around. People who both knew I intended to make a bid for Nome the following month. They were the last people I wanted to face in this situation.

Beat escorted me to the heater and instructed me to sit down.

"Thanks," I said. "I won't be here long. I don't need to sit."

"Jill, you don't look okay," he said. "Is this really what you want to do? You don't want to get sick all over again."

"No."

Tracy brought me an open can of lukewarm chowder. Beat, ever the pragmatist, continued to press for the smart decision and not compromise my lungs any further. I started crying, so I held my breath and buried my face in my jacket, because I was deeply ashamed. Of all places, it had to be here, at mile ninety of a relatively easy training ride — at least easy compared to the Iditarod — having my meltdown in front of two people who I least wanted to witness me having a meltdown. Beat, my partner in many adventures as well as in life, has witnessed plenty of my meltdowns, and wrapped an arm around me.

"I don't know … why I'm having problems now," I blubbered. "I feel like there's something wrong with me."

"It's okay," he said. "You're having a bad day. It happens."

"They've all been bad days, lately," I sniffed, and held my breath again to suppress the sob I could feel building in my gut.

"Look, we don't have to do this," Beat said. "Let's call it here. I'll ride back to the start with you. We'll go home and figure it out."

I was still holding my breath and biting my lip. I nodded weakly.

Tracy smelled trouble and stepped in. People quit races for lots of reasons and usually regret it later, so she tried to be helpful when she urged me to continue.

"You came here to ride, didn't you?"

I shrugged. I did come here to ride — but not to force myself through two-plus days of hypoxic despondency. Tracy meant well, but her urging only heightened my shame. It was just biking. Why couldn't I do it without gasping?

Beat interjected. "She had pneumonia last summer and it's been a long recovery. The last thing she needs now is a relapse." He turned to me. "I'll ride with you. We should go back."

I conceded, but the worst shame was yet to come. As we wheeled our bikes away, I turned to face Bill, who nodded at me sympathetically. Bill had witnessed some of my worst Iditarod missteps. He and Kathi were riding to Nome in 2008 when they passed me in a deadly cold swamp called the Farewell Burn. I'd become desperately sleepy and rolled out my bivy sack in a low-lying hollow where the temperature was thirty-five below zero. The winds were picking up, and it was still early in the night. It was a terrible place to bed down, and any veteran would have continued moving if they had any sense. Bill called out to ask if I was okay.

"Yes," I replied. "Just tired." Bill said nothing more. He respects people enough to let them make their own mistakes.

He again didn't offer up advice or criticism after I dropped out with frostbite early in the 2009 race. But in 2010, I received a cryptic message from him about "needing to have a talk" before I could enter the ITI again. This e-mail was prompted by my online advocacy of satellite-based trackers, which Bill despised. His views were understandable — at the time, the technology was relatively new and devices were prone to malfunctioning and miscommunication that could prompt unnecessary search-and-rescue efforts. Bill wanted to explain why my insistence on trackers would not be tolerated in the ITI. It was a simple disagreement, but I was going through a difficult time in my life, and took this message personally. I felt as though a respected mentor was breaking up with me.

I vowed to never return to the ITI. But later that year, I met Beat. Much of our courtship was propelled by outlandish endurance challenges, and I was the one who urged him to try winter racing in Alaska. He wanted me to take up ultrarunning, so we raced the 2011 Susitna 100 together, on foot. Beat was hooked. He walked to McGrath in 2012 — a year of heavy snowfall, low temperatures and high drop-out rates. He went to Nome on the southern route in 2013, the northern route in 2014, and then there was the intense expedition through the snowbound Interior in 2015. In just four years, Beat took this strange hobby further than I had dreamed in a decade. By then, I was just trying to keep up. Bill respected Beat, and I believe this helped me re-enter the fold when I signed up to walk to McGrath in 2014. My return to the race that year had been so triumphant. But here, looking into Bill's eyes, which were kind but sad, I felt hopeless.

"I guess that's it for Nome," I said to Beat as soon as we were out of earshot. We'd only been pedaling for three minutes before I was winded again and needed a break.

"We'll talk about it later," Beat said. "First we need to get back to the road."

Giving Up,
Then Giving In

Despite my silent boycott in 2010, the Iditarod Trail Invitational always felt like a family. It's an event that draws people in without fanfare and inexplicably lures them to return, year after year. Even if they haven't raced in a decade, no one ever leaves the ITI, not really. The annual reunions are filled with a unique cast of characters that society would never bring together were it not for a unifying interest in suffering in the cold.

The 2016 gathering was full of familiar faces. There was Bill, of course — the old-fashioned, grizzled sourdough whose autobiography would invite chills, but who had a kind and empathetic side as well. His wife, Kathi, hailed from Germany and had a steely matter-of-factness about the most daunting aspects of Alaska.

There were the folks who had been around since almost the beginning: Tim Hewitt, the sixty-year-old lawyer from Pennsylvania who had walked to Nome an astonishing eight times since 2001. His wife, Loreen, had joined him for at least the short race nearly every year since 2008, and walked to Nome herself, setting the women's foot record in 2014. Jeff Oatley of Fairbanks held the overall bike record to Nome after an astonishing ten-day ride in 2014, and had more finishes on the short course than anyone else. His wife, Heather Best, held the women's bike record to McGrath and continued to lower it every year.

Then there was the second generation — a group I counted myself among. These were people who first signed on in the mid-2000s, before most of the information surrounding the race was widely available, and there were still a lot of unknowns. Jay and Tracy Petervary lived in Idaho and had raced nearly every year since 2007. Both had ridden bikes to Nome twice, and Jay returned for a third finish in 2015, making it through the abandoned Interior just before the storm hit. Shawn McTaggart, a shy and unassuming woman from Anchorage, was the only woman to walk both the northern and southern routes of the Iditarod Trail. Eric Johnson, a doctor from Utah, had finished the route to Mc-Grath six times, but even after several attempts, had never reached Nome.

The third generation was people who joined the fray after 2010, when the popularity of the Iditarod Trail Invitational started to explode. (And by explode, I mean that more than a handful of people had heard of it.) This group included Beat as well as most of the fastest individuals — cyclists such as Kevin Breitenbach, John Lackey, and Tim Bernston, who have blitzed the 350-mile course in less than two days. There was Dave Johnston, an Alaska-based ultrarunner with a laid-back, surfer dude personality and an ability to run farther than all but a few others in the world. He holds a McGrath foot record that most believe will never be broken.

Then there were the rookies — wide-eyed individuals who had read everything they could find about the race, and who still didn't have a true understanding of the adventure in front of them. They had meticulous race plans that were going to fall apart in ways they never anticipated. They had top-of-the-line gear that was going to rip, bike parts that were going to break, food that was going to become inedible, and water containers that were going to freeze shut. In short, they had all of the potential for all of the mistakes that all of us made when we were rookies. I envied them most of all.

In this family, the last Saturday in February was like Christmas Eve. This was the day when we converged from our disparate corners of the world to gather around the tables of a pre-race meeting at a hotel in downtown Anchorage. Jittery nervousness hung in the room like static electricity, and we distracted ourselves with small talk about the weather (Very warm. Too warm. It was forty degrees outside and the streets were bare, scoured of all of their usual mid-winter snow.)

Inevitably, the conversation would turn to whether I was racing this year. For the past several years, I'd attended the pre-race meeting with Beat even though I wasn't racing, so it was a natural question.

"Well," I'd say in a drawn-out breath. "I'm signed up to ride to Nome …"

After dropping out of the Fat Pursuit in January, I came down with a stomach flu and then a cold that put a deeper notch in my fitness. Beat also contracted his second respiratory infection of the season — although we never seemed to share these bouts of pneumonia or bronchitis, at least one of us had been sick for most of the past six months. January trickled into February. I told Beat that I was going to downgrade my participation to the 350-mile division, if I raced at all. Since our training season had been less than ideal, Beat decided to ditch the plan to ride a bike to Nome and stick to what he knew — traveling on foot. He reasoned that because he wasn't in great shape, he didn't have the stamina or experience to risk a cycling effort. However, a thousand-mile hike with a heavy sled was okay.

"You know how crazy that sounds, right?" I replied. But I didn't argue. Our plan had always been to ride to Nome together. In early February, it appeared that neither of us would.

Because Beat no longer planned to ride, he insisted I borrow his fat bike. The lightweight titanium frame had been built by a company called Eriksen, and it was custom-designed by another elder of the sport, Mike Curiak. Mike is a wheel-builder in Grand Junction, Colorado, who began racing the Iditarod Trail in the mid-1990s. He raced the first Iditasport Impossible in 2000 and set a record that wasn't broken for fourteen more years. By the mid-2000s, he'd branched out to unsupported expeditions. A meticulous engineer, Curiak refined his equipment every year, designing and building a new bike before testing it out in the field. The old bikes were sold, and Beat had acquired three of them at this point — an art collector of sorts. Arguably no one had more experience cycling the Iditarod Trail, or a better understanding of exactly what equipment was best for the job, than Mike Curiak. When the Eriksen became available, the prospect of piloting the perfect bike helped soften the disappointment that Beat and I wouldn't travel together.

Most cyclists love to geek out on new gear, but I am not one of those cyclists. I'm content to take suggestions from others, tend to become comfortable with what I have, and refuse to give up my well-used bikes until they've been ridden into the ground. I'd probably still be riding my first fat bike, a 2007 Surly Pugsley with outmoded geometry and rusting parts, were it not for Beat, who is without a doubt the most dedicated gear geek I have ever known. As an athlete, Beat prefers the typically minimal sport of running. But as an engineer, he gravitates toward the latest and greatest technology, and his gear collection reflects this. Although he is six inches taller and forty pounds heavier than me, we have the same inseam measurements, so we can comfortably share bicycles. And because I'm the more avid cyclist in the relationship, I tend to be the prime benefactor of Beat's gear enthusiasm.

After I'd recovered sufficiently from the Fat Pursuit and resumed training, Beat set me up on his Eriksen. With only five weeks until the race, it was rushed introduction, but Eriksen and I got along well. The bike was light and nimble, as well as robust and comfortable. I took Eriksen out on steep hill repeats and mountain bike trails, aiming for at least fifteen hours of training per week. In the friendly climate of coastal California, I began to feel strong again. Still, I couldn't garner much optimism. After all, well-groomed dirt singletrack and seventy-degree sunny days bear zero resemblance to conditions I'd encounter in Alaska. Even after racking up more than thirty-thousand feet of climbing per week and increasing my weight limits at the gym, I knew this training was a shallow mimicry of the strength I'd need to battle deep snow and high winds. If I lost control of my breathing in such conditions, it wouldn't take much for the situation to change from difficult to deadly.

Pessimism is a powerful force, but even repeated blows to my confidence weren't quite enough to kill my long-suffering Nome dream. Although I'd slacked on all of the preparations necessary for the thousand-mile race, I never removed my name from the roster. Two weeks before the start of the race, it became necessary to declare my intent. The Iditarod Trail Invitational provides only limited support, and almost none beyond the 350-mile finish line of the short race. As such, athletes who intend to continue toward Nome must mail supplies to remote villages through the United States Postal Service. Because services in the villages are extremely limited, boxes must contain all the food necessary for each segment of trail. Some athletes also mail themselves replacement items, such as bicycle tubes, medical supplies, and batteries. It's difficult if not impossible to proceed in the race without these supplies in place, and slow mail service necessitates sending boxes at least two weeks early. If I sent out my boxes, there was still a chance I could aim for Nome. If I didn't, my decision to stop in McGrath would be final.

Beat refused to advise me one way or the other. "It's your decision," he insisted, but added, "They're only groceries. If you don't go on, you're out a couple hundred dollars. But, if everything goes well and you get to McGrath feeling good, and you didn't send the boxes ..."

"I'd always wonder what if," I interjected, and sighed. "I hate what ifs."

Beat had already procured a few hundred dollars' worth of high-calorie-density food for his boxes. In an effort to waste as little as possible when I inevitably stopped in McGrath or sooner, I gleaned my supplies from his rejected items: Ziplock bags of peanut butter, trail mixes made of peanuts, almonds, M&Ms, and dried cranberries, crunchy granola bars, Snickers bars, chocolate, bags of crackers crushed and vacuum-sealed, a few bags of beef jerky, mashed potato powder, two freeze-dried meals for each box, and gummy bears.

Since the calories didn't quite add up, I went out and bought a few of my own treats: peanut butter cups, fruit snacks, shelled pistachios, and dried cherries. It was a lot of sugar — it was almost entirely sugar — and I recognized that. But a decade of endurance racing history has shown me that when I have a sour stomach, there's not a lot I'm willing to stuff down my gullet besides sugar. Also, when I'm cold, ingesting sugary food helps my body fire up the internal furnace. Sugar fuels quick energy and heat, and if you keep the calories coming in, you can avoid energy crashes. I compare it to feeding a wood stove with kindling. Sure, logs are better, but logs won't do you much good if you can't keep the fire lit. Sugar was easy and it was effective. Of course, this food didn't provide many nutrients for an endeavor that could take nearly a month, so I added multi-vitamins and salt tablets. When thrown together it looked terribly unappetizing, but I reasoned that I wasn't going to actually eat much of this food, anyway.

Beat and I packed everything into fifteen flat-rate boxes, and I carted them to the post office on an unseasonably hot February day in Los Altos, California. The boxes looked ridiculous stuffed in the back of our Subaru Outback, and even sillier when stacked on the counter of the tiny neighborhood post office. One customer who watched me hoist the heavy boxes over five separate trips finally asked what I was mailing to Alaska. It's one of those social interactions where you consider whether you're going to tell a long, confusing story, or just lie. I usually pick the latter.

"They're supplies for schools," I mumbled, then rushed away before he could ask more questions, hoping the post office workers didn't overhear this and decide to check. The boxes were all marked "Please Deliver to School" — the only public buildings in these villages — so it made my lie plausible, but also inexplicable. Who sends boxes of candy to schoolchildren?

One week before the race, I finally loaded Eriksen with all of the supplies I planned to carry on the Iditarod Trail. The rear rack contained a small bag with my down parka, booties and down pants, for quick access. There were two narrow panniers with spare clothing — extra hat, mittens, balaclava, wind-resistant pants and shell, primaloft shorts with attached knee warmers, extra underwear and socks — as well as a stove, pot, fuel bottles, repair kit, freeze-dried meals, nylon waders (used for open water crossings), two trash bags (to protect gear or clothing in the event of rain), and a toiletries kit. In the triangle of the bike was a fitted frame bag that contained the rest of my food — up to four days' worth — a waterproof bag with electronics, headlamp and spare light, bicycle pump, anti-chafing lube, blister tape, and wet wipes for hygienic purposes. I planned to carry three liters of drinking water in a hydration pack on my back, where I also stored my camera, inhalers, pills, and wind-blocking skin ointment. The sleeping bag, waterproof bivy sack, and pad were rolled into a bundle on a front rack, which Beat had modified so we could attach it to the bike's fiberglass suspension fork with soft straps. An hour before sunset on Sunday afternoon, I took the load out for a final test ride on trails near my neighborhood.

The sleeping gear filled a big red bundle that blocked the view of the front end of the bike, and I didn't notice as the front rack slipped a few millimeters downward with each bump on the trail. As I launched into the final descent at eighteen miles per hour, the rack's metal platform came down onto the front tire, stopping the wheel and flipping me over the handlebars. My body hit the ground with such force that all I could see for several seconds were white sparkles on black. When my eyes finally refocused, I sat up and hoisted the overturned bike off my legs. The sudden movement sent a shock of pain through my right shoulder. Sensations were returning; my shoulder throbbed fiercely, my right hand and knee burned with trail rash, and my ears were ringing. I spent another minute clutching my shoulder and moaning before I finally decided it would be prudent to stand up and figure out what was broken.

All of my limbs appeared to be intact. The bike was also fine — after the front wheel stopped moving, the bike cartwheeled and landed more or less on top of me. Moving stiffly through a fog of pain, I shifted the bivy bundle to the rear rack, then raised the front rack and re-tightened the straps. After a little more moaning, I was able to continue riding home.

The following day, my entire body felt as though I'd been hit by a truck. It was painful to get out of bed and walk to the bathroom.

"At least you have six more days," Beat assured me as I lamented my battered limbs. "Plenty of time to recover."

Beat boxed up the bike and we packed our bags for the flight to Anchorage. I didn't know if fortune could be any more discouraging of my Nome ambitions, or whether I wanted to find out. I limped into the pre-race meeting with bruised hips and a battered ego, but unbroken intent. Still, most people at the meeting were friends and acquaintances who knew about my recent health setbacks and athletic failures, so I wasn't about to broadcast more unearned hubris. When I said that I was "signed up" to ride to Nome, my emphasis was on the gamble, like "signing up" to win the lottery.

My skepticism was not well received. In any intensive endeavor, fate is not kind to those who don't maintain unflagging commitment. Trekking across Alaska isn't easy in the best of circumstances. There are endless reasons to quit and only one to continue: Because you want it, badly, despite anything that stands in your way. Others who had made this commitment gave me looks ranging from half smiles to full side-eyes when I shrugged and said, "Maybe." Another Nome sign-up, a man named Joe Stiller, shared my slightly battered status with a pre-race injury to his knee. He'd driven a large van all the way from South Dakota to spectate the race. After the pre-race meeting, he took up a vigil in the hotel lobby to show off his fat bike, fully decked out with ultralight gear and a half dozen electronic gadgets. Unlike me, Joe had no intent of starting this year's race with an injury; he was here because he already had the time off work, and wanted to observe and learn in preparation for the following year's event.

"I don't DNF," he said forcefully, referring to the "did not finish" status designated to race failures such as myself. "When I start the ITI next year, I'm going to be a hundred and ten percent all in."

"I admire that attitude," I replied, but silently responded to his veiled criticism with my own. So many things can go wrong in the Alaska wilderness — frostbite, broken bones, debilitating illness, a thousand things you never prepared for. You can't know what will happen, so you can never claim that failure isn't an option. I'd clung to a dogged determination not to fail for far too long, and now I was grappling with the long-term effects of possible lung damage. Sometimes you need to quit when you're ahead, sometimes you need to quit when you're still alive, and sometimes — but only sometimes — you should shoot for the moon.

"I agree it's something that takes a hundred percent, which I can't claim to have," I continued. "But Nome is a difficult dream to let go."

✳ ✳ ✳ ✳ ✳

The following morning, sixty-five participants gathered with bikes, sleds, and one set of skis in front of the hotel. We prepared to board a bus that would take us from Anchorage to the official start of the Iditarod Trail on Knik Lake. I barely succeeded in hoisting my loaded bike over my shoulders and onto a moving van, but considered this a success all the same. The interior of the bus was sizzling with solar heat, tense silence and nervous chatter. Beat and I squeezed into a narrow bench seat and quietly discussed what we would do if one of us ended up back in Anchorage much earlier than the other. He felt severely under-trained after his month-long bout with pneumonia, so neither of us assumed it would automatically be me, although that was implied.

"If asthma is going to be a problem, I'm going to know early, maybe by tonight," I said. The first and second checkpoints at miles fifty-seven and ninety were the easiest places to quit the race — involving an air taxi flight that costs two to three hundred dollars. After that, the Iditarod Trail becomes remote and the airstrips more difficult to access. Evacuations can take up to a week if the weather is bad. I glanced out the window toward the snow-capped peaks of the

Chugach Mountains and pondered what it would be like to quit in time to sleep in a bed that same night. Ending up back in Anchorage on the first day was the most logical scenario, but the thought filled my gut with such dread that I had to shut it out. Instead, I fretted about pushing my bike through slushy water.

Anchorage and the surrounding regions were experiencing unprecedented warmth that winter. The global weather pattern El Nino pumped a steady stream of warm air into the Far North, resulting in temperatures above freezing and frequent rain. Snowfall had been minimal, and after two weeks with daytime temperatures regularly reaching forty degrees, the landscape was a patchwork of bare ground and wet ice. Much of the chatter in the bus centered on crossing open water and whether there would be a trail at all, as the Iditarod only exists in winter as a ribbon of snow packed down by snowmobile traffic. In the summer, it's all swamps, alder-choked hillsides, spongy tundra, and rivers — utterly impassable unless frozen. The forecast called for rain showers, and we expected to spend the first day wading through swamps and slush while wearing soaked clothing. When temperatures are in the thirties, wet clothing and feet create a high risk for hypothermia. This was my most immediate concern.

The bus pulled over at the Knik Bar. I stepped out into the moist, too-warm air, feeling faint. The Knik Bar had been the starting point of human-powered Iditarod racing since the 1990s, but this year it was closed for the season. Still, the proprietor opened the doors to a darkened interior and fired up the grill to cook cheeseburgers for racers' nervous stomachs. I sat in a corner and picked at the grease-soaked bun, worried that I might vomit at any moment.

All of my big endeavors scare me, but this was by far the worst I had ever felt before a race. My fear didn't necessarily center on failure, which I had spent a year embracing. It wasn't about dying — a risk that is always lurking whether we acknowledge it or not. It wasn't about missing Beat. I regretted that we wouldn't be traveling together, but took comfort in the fact that we were both carrying satellite phones, which would allow us to remain connected. No, this unsettled fear had more to do with facing the loss of something I loved. Choking out on the Iditarod Trail, both literally and figuratively, felt like a final straw. This was my last chance. If I didn't succeed, there was nothing else to face but the reality of my declining health and the necessity of walking away from endurance racing. But I would not go gentle into that good night.

I spent so long stewing over the burger that I nearly missed the line-up under a banner at the shoreline of Knik Lake. I rushed out and grabbed my bike, which I hadn't even test-ridden since I put it together in the Anchorage hotel room. The lake looked partly thawed; puddles on top of the gray ice were so deep that water rippled in the breeze. A male runner turned to me and asked, "Think the ice will hold?" I laughed nervously.

Beat pulled up beside me with his massive sled, built with a sturdy fabric cover that doubled as a bivouac-style shelter. Other runners occasionally teased Beat about the size of his haul, but he maintained that security matters more than speed in the scheme of a long expedition. No one could argue with his track record. I shared his views on preparedness. I harbored deep insecurity about my own abilities, and needed to feel prepared for all of the worst-case scenarios I could imagine, of which there were many. Heading out into the frozen wilderness with a head full of fears and no safety nets would only ensure a decision to quit. Still, whether I could actually manage eighty pounds of bike, food, and supplies remained unproved.

"So are we all going to go plunging into Knik Lake now?" I asked Beat. "The ice looks a little anemic."

"Nah, it's solid," he replied. "I checked."

Somebody fired a gun into the air and the field took off across the lake, splashing through puddles and sliding on the wet ice. All of the runners and one skier veered right, where the Iditarod Trail begins. The cyclists went left toward a series of gas-line easement trails and roads on a route that's longer but tends to be faster for bikes. Both converge at Flathorn Lake, around mile twenty-five. From there all racers follow the Iditarod Trail, although most veterans have their own secret shortcuts. Even the most creative side routes are sanctioned in race rules, which stipulate only that racers must reach every checkpoint under their own power. How they get there is their own problem.

I rolled beside Beat for a few seconds as we said our final goodbyes. When I pushed the power button on my GPS, it wouldn't start. The blank screen incited a quiet panic. Why didn't I test it earlier? What if it didn't work the entire trip? I depended on it for navigation and had only rudimentary paper maps as a backup. Beat helped me re-start the unit as I shivered in the cold wind, inadvertently planting one of my water-resistant (I hoped) boots in a puddle. Finally the device fired up. Beat and I shared one last hurried kiss, and with that veered our separate ways toward the unknown.

Whisked Into
The Wilderness

The field of forty-eight cyclists streamed across the waterlogged surface of Knik Lake, churning up wake that splashed against the shoreline. I caught the pack where a trail climbed up a steep embankment. A traffic jam formed as wheels spun and bikes tipped over on the icy surface. Nearly all of us, myself included, had fat bikes equipped with tires that were embedded with carbide studs to grip into ice. I'd lived in coastal California for the past five years, and my ice-riding skills were rusty at best. I shimmied the handlebars and pedaled furiously in an attempt to generate the friction needed to propel my bike up a surface that had as much traction as an oil slick.

Wet ice coated the trail through the low hills of the Susitna River Valley. Birch trees crowded the narrow corridor. Beneath the trees, the forest floor was bare. The only reason there was still frozen matter on the trail was because snowmobile traffic had compressed snow into hard ice. Patches of mud intervened, and deep puddles ensured that everyone had wet legs and mud-splattered backsides within the first few miles. Clouds darkened into sleet squalls. I put on the rain jacket that I didn't intend to bring, but decided at the last minute that I couldn't afford to rely on non-waterproof coats. After all, it was winter in Alaska.

Rain pelted my jacket, my insulated handlebar mitts, my bivy bundle containing the down sleeping bag I hoped would keep me dry and warm in temperatures down to fifty below, and my panniers full of things that would be useless to me if they were wet. Anxiety roiled in my gut. The feeling was even worse than the nervousness I felt before the race, which was a new experience.

Generally, the doom I feel before a big endeavor melts away when I finally start. At that point, I've done everything I can do to get ready, and usually relax when I realize that the only task ahead amounts to putting one foot in front of the other. Situational problems such as poor weather always bother me, of course, but this was different. Even after I reminded myself of the water-resistant reinforcements I'd made — including putting the sleeping bag inside the bivy sack, and stuffing all of my spare layers into Zip-lock bags — I continued to battle an urge to panic. Why was I so frightened? What certain doom was my intuition detecting this time?

A few dozen race fans spread out along the first twenty-five miles of the course. I was a knot of stress, but tried to smile and wave as I passed groups of cheering strangers parked next to road crossings, and friends riding their own bikes along the trail. The trail petered out and the route became little more than snowmobile scratches across barely frozen swamps. Spindly spruce trees stuck out of the brown ice. Wispy fog lifted to reveal Mount Susitna, a lone mountain towering over the river valley. Contrasted beneath dark rain clouds, Mount Susitna was an almost blinding shade of white, cutting a sharp profile of a reclining woman that inspired the mountain's nickname — "The Sleeping Lady."

Nearly every year since 2006, I've returned to the Susitna Valley for an Iditarod-based race or adventure, and every year I've looked to The Sleeping Lady for comfort. This year, I could scarcely look up for fear of hitting any small bump at the wrong angle and crashing down on the ice. I fell in line with five other riders. We passed the last group of fans on the shoreline of Flathorn Lake and rolled onto a smooth surface that perfectly mirrored the stormy sky.

There was no snow on the lake, revealing ice fractured with pressure cracks. Just a few weeks earlier, southcentral Alaska experienced a magnitude-7 earthquake that left deep, rippling imprints in the region's frozen waterways. The cracked ice had refrozen, but it appeared fragile from the vantage of a bicycle seat. A dizzying vortex encompassed my thoughts, and I gripped the handlebars tighter in an effort to stay upright.

Back in 2009, I put my foot through a patch of weak ice while walking my bike across Flathorn Lake, dunking my right leg to the thigh. A series of poor decisions immediately afterward resulted in dropping out of the Iditarod Trail Invitational with frostbite on my right foot, followed by two months of recovery and nerve damage that persists to this day. Also persisting is a phobia of ice, and lake ice specifically. Even though logic reminds me that lake ice is generally more stable than river ice, my anxiety hits a fever pitch whenever I need to cross a frozen lake. For seven years, Flathorn Lake has been waiting to pull me into its icy depths. Of this I was convinced.

"This is how I die," I thought as the ice groaned ominously. The group had pulled away, and I could scarcely muster the wherewithal to continue turning pedals.

A panic attack seemed imminent when I passed Joe Stiller, who was standing in the middle of the frozen lake with his space-age bicycle lying sideways on the ice, and one hand clasped around a video camera. I wanted nothing more than to get off this lake, and couldn't believe he was willing to just stand there as though the world wasn't going to collapse underneath him.

"Say something," he called out to me.

"Ice, eek," I squeaked. Saying this out loud made me aware of my own ridiculousness. Of course there was ice. After all, it was winter in Alaska.

Relief washed over me as I reached the other side of the lake, where there was finally some real snow cover. Its consistency was similar to a wafer-thin crust over granulated sugar, and there were blades of yellow grass sticking out of the surface, but it was snow. Since my group had surged ahead, I assumed I was near the back of the race. But another cyclist caught up as I was trying to locate the unmarked point where the trail veered into the woods. He was a tall man with broad shoulders and chest, wearing a bicycle cap, a wool shirt, and bib shorts — clothing better suited for a midsummer spin on trails rather than a winter wilderness race. His bare knees were sticking out of a pair of gaiters, and he was grinning through a short, salt-and-pepper beard. He looked vaguely familiar but I couldn't place his name. He must have known me or at least who I was, because the first thing he asked was, "Where is Beat?"

"Oh, he's back a ways … walking. He decided to drag a sled again this year."

"Why?"

"Long story, but I've been sick and assumed I wouldn't be able to start the race, so he decided to stick with what he knows. Because walking is more fun."

"Ha!" the man laughed. He thought I was being sarcastic. Fat-bike racers frequently refer to runners as "fun haters" because they could be riding bikes, but inexplicably chose the more difficult and tedious method of travel. Even when trail conditions deteriorate and cyclists are reduced to pushing their heavy bikes through deep snow, they still feel their method is superior because at some point, they'll be rolling again. And it's true — even during years that saw the worst trail conditions, when runners led the race for more than two hundred miles, bikes always prevailed to reach the finish line first.

Still, foot travel has its advantages. For starters, runners and walkers don't have to constantly scout for the path of least resistance through highly variable snow conditions, so they have more opportunities to gaze up at the scenery. They move at a more consistent speed, so progress is more predictable. They have fewer mechanical concerns to address. And there's something inherently satisfying about traveling such a long distance, through such difficult terrain, under what is truly your own power — without mechanical or gravitational assistance.

My walk to McGrath with Beat in 2014 remains one of my most cherished life experiences. It was meditative and rewarding, and bolstered our relationship in ways that I hadn't anticipated. It also was intensely physical, and after seven days I was wracked with deep exhaustion, muscle soreness, and shin splints. I will continue to defend the reasons why I think hiking the Iditarod Trail has potential to be more "fun" than cycling, but concede that it's significantly more painful.

"Biking is fun as long as it's fun. But when it's not fun ..." I trailed off.

"Skiing would be fun. But walking?"

The man stopped to fiddle with something on his bike before I learned his name, but caught back up to me hours later, shortly after the trail veered onto the Yentna River. A briefly intense snow squall dissipated to flurries, and the gray sky was darkening with dusk. After all this time, I expected to be more settled into the journey, but stress was still twisting knots into my muscles. The unexpected pain caused me to wince as I looked over my shoulder.

Since I last saw him, the man had put on a jacket and removed his sunglasses, but his knees were still bare.

"How's it going?" I asked.

"Well, I fell into some overflow back there," he answered. "Yeah, I was trying to take a picture while going through those puddles. I dropped my camera. Fell all the way in. Shouldn't have done that."

His tone was upbeat for somebody who was no doubt soaked as the frigid nighttime hours approached. I probably would have become unhinged if I'd fallen into open water, given how stressed I felt over nothing at all. But this guy was still grinning. For the next hour we rode side by side on the hard, bumpy river ice. I learned his name was Mike Beiergrohslein. He was a pharmacist and father of two teenagers in Eagle River, Alaska. He'd signed up to ride to McGrath, but just two weeks earlier he managed to secure enough approval from his family and employer to join the Nome roster. This entailed sending the organizers an extra two hundred dollars for one more drop bag, and then he had to quickly cobble together supply packages to send to village post offices. Like me, Mike felt under-prepared and was going to "see how it goes."

A brisk wind displaced the clouds, and temperatures plunged with the clearing sky. Mike and I reached the first checkpoint, a river lodge called Yentna Station, around 7:30 p.m. The lodge was crowded with a dozen others whose faces showed signs of strain after fifty-seven miles. A few ordered food, but I was feeling jittery and didn't want to spend too much time getting comfortable. The day's relative heat had left me terribly thirsty, and I continuously refilled a paper cup with two liters of lukewarm water and fruit punch from jugs on the counter. I chatted with Troy, a muscled Australian who had a deer-in-the-headlights demeanor, and a woman who seemed incredulous that the lodge's bathroom was a bucket in a storage closet.

I made my escape just a few minutes before Mike, who was outside and still rearranging stuff in his bike bags. I expected he'd catch me again, but didn't see anyone else for the next thirty miles. My clothing was damp with sweat, and the night felt menacingly cold. It was too hazy for stars, and a stiff breeze whistled along the river bank. When I turned to face the wind, the chill seemed to drain all of the air from my lungs. While my breathing was labored, it wasn't constrained enough to cause concern. I took a few hits from my inhaler as a precaution, but discovered it had frozen in my chest pocket and emitted squirts of cold liquid rather than air.

Nighttime in the Alaska backcountry invites awareness of both the immediate and the infinite. My headlamp illuminated an island of light in seemingly endless darkness, highlighting the smallest details. Patches of overflow that would have looked like puddles in daylight became open holes to the bottom of the Yentna River. Blue ice gave way to packed snow, and scratches in the trail told elaborate stories about those who came before. The breeze licked at my lower back. I attempted to follow perfectly straight tracks in the snow and imagined the fast racers sprinting up this river at unconscionable speeds. The overcast sky reflected no light, and I was still a long way from anywhere, here at the beginning of a thousand miles.

Three miles from the second checkpoint, the trail veered onto the Skwentna River, which was more wind-swept than the Yentna. The surface was riddled with strips of gray ice that were indistinguishable from the surrounding snow. A gust of wind caught me off guard and washed out the rear wheel, toppling the bike on hard ice. I landed on my outstretched right hand, and then my bike and body continued skidding along the ice for several more feet before stopping. My wrist was throbbing, but I was relieved that I had avoided hitting my head. It made me angry that after ninety miles of being overly tense and careful on the ice, I managed to crash here.

I swung a sore leg over the saddle and resumed pedaling, but the front wheel refused to move in a straight line. The shimmy was enough to force me off the bike. I tried several times to wrangle the handlebars into submission, only to tip off the saddle again and again.

"Crap, I've forgotten how to ride a bike," I thought, squinting into the darkness in disbelief.

I glanced down at the handlebars and realized they weren't aligned with the wheel — the crash had knocked the stem loose, and the front end of the bike was skewed at a sharp angle. Laughing, I fished a bike tool out of my frame bag and readjusted the stem. As I tightened the bolts, I felt a sharp, tingling pain in my right hand.

"That's strange," I thought, slapping the fingers with my other hand to reboot circulation. I brushed it off as a symptom of the cold. Temperatures had plunged to single digits, and the wind carried a harsh bite.

Anger and confusion about the mishap dissipated quickly as I wove through the woods toward my favorite stop en route to McGrath. Skwentna Roadhouse is a commercial watering hole for snowmobilers, pilots, summertime boaters, and the quirky locals who carve a rough living off this land in the foothills of the Alaska Range. Similar to the original roadhouses sprinkled across Alaska during the Gold Rush, Skwentna offers beds and hearty meals to worn-out travelers. It has the last indoor plumbing available to racers for two hundred miles, and if you're really feeling indulgent, you can even take a shower. During the Iditarod Trail Invitational, the friendly proprietors keep vigil at all hours of the night, and will cook a full breakfast for anyone who orders one, even if it's two in the morning.

I was thrilled to arrive at Skwentna at the still-early hour of 11:30. Quick math revealed I'd averaged more than nine miles per hour, which is blazing fast for ninety miles of wilderness trail on a heavily loaded fat bike. My breathing remained under control, and I was pleasantly surprised by how fresh I felt.

Most of the cyclists ahead had moved on to the next checkpoint, eager to put in miles while conditions were good. I pondered whether I had another forty miles in my legs that night, but decided I needed to be conservative if I wanted to keep Nome on the radar. Fatigue seemed to be the main trigger for my breathing difficulties, and there was little to gain by pushing hard so early in the race. I sat down at the table with Andrea and Julie, two women who were racing to McGrath. They also were pondering whether to stay or go.

"Skwentna is a nice place to sleep," I said, with a raspy voice that startled me.

Julie and Andrea congratulated me on making such good time with my Nome-loaded bike, which probably weighed at least twenty pounds more than the bikes of most of the McGrath racers.

"That tailwind helped," I rasped. "I'll probably slow way down tomorrow."

✳ ✳ ✳ ✳ ✳

I tossed and turned for most of the night, sprawled on a bottom bunk in a hot upstairs room shared with Julie, Andrea, and another woman, Kimberly. Many endurance racers experience sleeplessness after a day of hard effort — our bodies are filled with adrenaline and stress hormones, heart rates remain high, and muscles stiffen. Personally, I retain a lot of water during endurance efforts. My extremities swell, and once I stop moving, I often need to get up to pee every hour. Sleep is badly needed to boost recovery, but the discomfort involved with flushing out lactic acid and rebuilding torn muscle fibers keeps me awake. After a few days, my system seems to normalize, and exhaustion becomes deep enough to trump most pains.

Normalization of extreme effort is a subject I find incredibly interesting. Scientists have yet to do much research into the adaptations of humans, but one scientist found incredible abilities in Iditarod sled dogs. A professor named Mike Davis spent years tracking Alaskan huskies as they raced across the ice and tundra, and discovered these dogs rapidly adapt to sustained strenuous exercise. During their first hard day of running, sled dogs display most of the metabolic changes that human endurance athletes experience: depletion of muscle energy reserves, increased stress hormones, evidence of cellular breakdown in proteins, lipids and DNA, and oxidative stress. In subsequent consecutive days of exercise at the same intensity, these breakdowns reversed. Within four days, the metabolic profile of the dogs returns to where it was before the race began. Instead of breaking their bodies down to a point of no return, sled dogs gain fitness as they run.

Sled dogs are arguably the world's greatest endurance athletes, with an aerobic capacity that is four times greater than an elite human athlete, cells that are crammed with energy-producing mitochondria, and an efficient digestive system that allows them to burn enormous amounts of fat and calories during high-intensity efforts. Most humans require the quick-burning energy of carbohydrates, and experience a system shutdown in the form of nausea and vomiting if they try to ingest more than three hundred calories an hour, even if they're burning far more. Still, the biology of dogs and humans isn't all that different. People likely possess more endurance adaptations than most of us even realize.

Is it possible we can become stronger as we go? The key, I have always believed, lies in management of the mind — adjusting our own expectations about what we can and cannot achieve, and focusing on the positive attributes of every experience. We — all of us — are more capable than we believe. However, the past year's failures showed me the ways I succumb to weakness, even when I'm resolved to find strength. If I push my body too hard, real and long-term damage can follow. So how do we find balance? The ancestors of huskies tapped into the secret eons ago, but humans have been more content to avoid physical discomforts that are no longer necessary for survival. The sample size of humans with both the opportunity and willingness to seek the limits of endurance has been small. I realized that I was hardly an ideal specimen for experimentation.

Still, despite a difficult day of pedaling, a crash, and a night of almost no sleep, I felt fantastic as I pedaled away from Skwentna Roadhouse in pre-dawn darkness. I was doing it! After all of the doubt and anxiety, I'd made it through the first day, and this was the litmus test I needed. One small concern was pain and numbness in my right hand. The previous night, I assumed cold temperatures had caused the issue. But after six hours in a warm building, my hand continued to tingle and occasionally release electric shocks of pain. It hurt mildly to grasp the handlebars, so I balled up a mitten to hold between my palm and the rubber grip.

Darkness hung over the snow-blanketed swamps outside Skwentna and followed me into the cavernous woods of the Shell Hills.

"Is it ever daytime in Alaska?" I wondered. In late February, southcentral Alaska receives about nine hours of daylight — which seems like plenty until you contend with fifteen hours of night. I hit mile one hundred just after six a.m. Monday morning, when I'd seen all of four hours of sunlight and twelve hours of darkness.

As dawn crept over the southern horizon, thick fog enveloped the Shell Hills. The air became murkier as I descended out of the woods and pedaled into a gray, featureless pall that I assumed was Shell Lake. A headlight surged through the fog and pulled up beside me. The snowmobile belonged to the husband of a friend and frequent Iditarod foot racer, Anne Ver Hoef. Michael Schroeder had a cabin on Shell Lake, and ventured out first thing in the morning to greet Iditarod cyclists as they passed through. He offered a handful of chocolate-covered acai berries and warned of several miles of overflow on the swamps beyond the lake. This news was hardly a surprise given the warm conditions of the previous day. But could I distinguish wet, bad ice from solid ground? When I looked down, I could hardly see my own boots through the murky air. I missed the clarity of night.

Gray light gave way to shades of violet, then turquoise. But the world remained eerily two-dimensional as I pedaled across snow-covered swamps. Brown puddles added jarring detail to the featureless landscape, and I dismounted my bike to creep around each one, whether it was frozen or not. As I did this, another cyclist, Jim Ishman, passed. He was the first racer I'd seen since Skwentna, and chirped a loud hello as his rear wheel shattered the thin layer of the ice I was creeping around. Jim clearly had a much higher tolerance for risk than me, and it was interesting to watch him navigate this terrain. The temperature was about fifteen degrees — moderate by Alaska standards, but still hazardous if one were to break through a deeper puddle and tip over in slushy water. It wasn't a chance I was willing to take, but I envied Jim's technical prowess.

Jim put a boot down at the edge of the water so he could stop and chat. This made me cringe — my boots were supposed to be waterproof as well, but this knowledge didn't inspire the trust I'd anticipated. Most Iditarod cyclists purchase an expensive, bulky boot manufactured specifically for winter cycling by the company 45North. The boots are outfitted with cleats for clipless pedals, which I think is the main appeal, but they also boast several pounds of heavy-duty insulating materials.

For years I used rigid mountaineering boots for cold-weather cycling. But after competing in winter races on foot, I'd come to the conclusion that flexible, lighter footwear has more versatility. When feet aren't encased in a hard structure, they can more efficiently generate their own heat through movement. My system consisted of waterproof hiking boots, gaiters, and for colder temperatures, a water-resistant overboot insulated with primaloft material. I was confident my footwear would take me farther in comfort, and would probably still promote heat retention if I soaked a boot, but I remained terrified of this prospect. I'd probably feel this way even if I had my own pair of 45North boots — which to me looked like heavy clodhoppers. Wet feet are one of my fears, and as much as I'd like to believe that gear can help alleviate fears, this is rarely the case.

"Did you come from Skwentna this morning?" I asked.

"No, I bivied on the trail just before Shell," Jim said. "Two hours sleep and breakfast at Shell Lake Lodge. Now I feel like a million bucks."

I didn't believe him — the part about feeling like a million bucks — but didn't voice this skepticism. Although I felt relatively good when I set out in the early morning, my own sleepless night was catching up to me. My head was as bleary as the fog-shrouded swamp.

Jim motored ahead and I continued to pick my way around overflow. Morning haze lifted as though it were a curtain, slowly revealing mountains bathed in pink light. This was the beginning of the Alaska Range, and the mountains' proximity startled me. Had we really come so far so soon? This valley seemed far displaced from the muddy, ice-crusted swamps of the Susitna Valley. The ground was blanketed in several feet of snow, and the trail cut through it like a curled ribbon, rippling over each pillowy mound. It resembled a pump track, which is a mountain biking term for a bermed course of dips and rises, specifically designed to give the rider an exhilarating roller-coaster sensation. The riding was sheer fun, which helped dissolve anxieties and boost energy.

By the time I arrived at Winter Lake Lodge, mile 130, all bad feelings were forgotten. I felt like a million bucks. The high-end lodge hosts an Iditarod Trail Invitational checkpoint in the kitchen of the main building, away from view of paying customers who fly in from Anchorage on chartered planes. A small dining room table was crammed with racers who had finished the 130-mile race, as well as racers in the longer distances who were preparing to head out. It was noon, so I ordered a lunch dish of rice, tortillas, beans, and chicken, prepared by a young man who worked at the lodge. A Midwestern cyclist who had decided to drop out of the 350-mile race with back pain, Charly, had been tracking the race all morning via a Wi-Fi connection on his phone. Charly informed us that the leaders had slowed to a crawl over the next segment, where the route begins to climb into the mountains.

"It's all the new snow," I speculated. "The Iron Dog had to break trail through three feet of powder, and there's probably not much of a trail base beyond here."

The Iron Dog is a two-thousand-mile snowmobile race that took place two weeks earlier. With the Iditarod Dog Sled Race not starting until the following week, the Iron Dog had been the only traffic on the more remote sections of the Iditarod Trail up to that point, which effectively made them our trail-breakers. There had been a major snowstorm during the Iron Dog, and the physics of more than a hundred snowmobiles driving as fast as possible over fresh powder had created a deep rippling effect on the trail, commonly referred to as "whoop-de-dos" or "moguls." The bumpy conditions were a bane for everybody who followed.

Julie and Andrea were just getting ready to leave, and seemed especially nervous about the possibility of pushing their bikes for the next thirty miles.

"This section is always slow," I shrugged, which they knew because they were both veterans. I remembered crawling up hills so steep that I had to punch my fists into the snow to keep from sliding backward when I walked the trail in 2014. The weight of the sled was almost more than I could manage, and that only weighed forty-five pounds. After restocking my bike with food and supplies from the Winter Lake drop bag, it was back up to seventy-five or eighty. Would I even be able to drag it up those hills? Of this I had no certainty, but I knew that if I kept crawling forward, eventually I'd get somewhere.

"Maybe it takes twelve hours and maybe we decide to bivy before Puntilla," I said to Andrea. "It's not really a big deal."

How Did This Become My Life?

H ow did this become my life?

It's a question everyone must ask themselves from time to time. My own inquiries resonate the most when I am wrestling a bicycle through somewhere uncomfortable and far from home.

This foray into the Alaska Range was no exception. The morning fog lifted into an overcast afternoon, and I had been walking uphill for most of the four hours that passed since leaving Winter Lake Lodge. Despite an exhaustive effort, I hadn't yet reached the next milestone — the Happy River Steps — twelve miles beyond Finger Lake.

The questioning of life choices usually begins when some random childhood memory crosses my mind, such as building snow pumpkins in the backyard, when I was nine years old and it snowed a foot before Halloween. That memory cycled back to nights when I couldn't sleep as an anxiety-ridden pre-teen, staring at the dim light reflected in a neighbor's basement window and hoping that somebody — anybody — was also awake, so I didn't have to feel like the only person in the world.

I was a timid and fearful child, and not much more confident as a young adult. So how did I grow into this? How was I the kind of person who purpose-fully seeks out situations where I'm forced to be utterly self-reliant, in places so cold and remote that if I stopped moving for too long, I'd simply die, and there's a chance no one would ever find my body? Was this rebellion against all those aspects of my personality of which I'd always been ashamed? Was I confronting real danger as a way of battling a growing number of irrational fears? Endurance adventures seemed to be not just an instigator, but also a healer of physical and psychological decay.

As an example, there was the day I lost my fear of flying. Before this day, I was one of those reluctant air travelers who winced at every jolt of the aircraft, clutching the armrests in quiet terror as the plane went in for a landing. Then in 2008, I completed my first Iditarod Trail Invitational on a bike. As the plane lifted off the ice-coated tarmac in McGrath, I felt a startling lack of anxiety. I was as calm as I'd ever been, watching the shadow of this metal tube float thousands of feet over the Kuskokwim River Valley — the place where I'd been locked in a real battle for survival the previous day.

"That didn't kill me. This isn't going to kill me," I thought. I've felt comfort-able on planes ever since.

Surviving my first Iditarod certainly did not cure all of my fears. After years of similar confrontations, I was still afraid of death, of solitude, of pain, of failure. Failure was a particularly insidious fear, because it was the only one over which I had control. I'd chosen this dangerous and difficult pursuit, and I alone was responsible if I failed. Despite all the stories I told myself — about the victory of overcoming all the obstacles it took just to reach this point, or the unavoidable mishaps that made previous failures not my fault, or insisting that the beauty of these experiences mattered more than the outcome —deep down, I knew the onus was on me. So fear persisted. It was a heavy burden to bear.

The Happy River Steps arrived abruptly at a point where the rolling forest drops into a gorge hundreds of feet deep. Nearly all of the elevation that we'd been valiantly gaining since Skwentna is lost here, as the cliffs end at the con-fluence of the Happy and Skwentna rivers. The trail descends in a series of steep drop-offs. In 2014, I opted to slide down these "steps" on my butt, holding my sled in front of me and digging heels into the snow to steer and brake. This year the steps were coated with a smooth crust of glare ice. With limited traction on foot, the safest way down was to ride. It was an exhilarating and terrifying exercise in releasing all control, because there was no slowing down until the bottom.

The final step was almost vertical, with an overhanging lip where the fearless Iron Dog drivers launched off a twenty-foot riverbank. As their snowmobiles plunged from the cliff, the spinning tracks dug a deep trench down the center of the trail. I hit the brakes and scanned the hillside for the footprints of other riders who perhaps found a way around. But no, everyone had ridden it. I paused only a few seconds and lied to myself — "there's no other choice" — then slid as far back as I could against my rear rack, let go of the brakes, and launched into the void. The front wheel didn't touch the snow until the bike had plummeted twenty feet, but I managed to put the rear wheel down and steer to a stop. It is amazing what one can do even when every strand of logic tells us we can't.

The trail continued across the Happy River and along the Skwentna, skirting open leads into the river before veering up an equally vertical, twenty-foot embankment. This was the Happy River Steps in reverse, climbing back out of the gorge just as steeply as it descended. Some riders would be less intimidated by the downhill steps than me. But no matter what, in this direction, gravity is not on your side.

I pedaled my seventy-five-pound bike to the base, where I found two others, Leah Gruhn and Lars Danner, who teamed up to drag their bikes up the wall. Lars scrambled up first, anchored both feet in the deeper snow off the side of the trail, and reached down as Leah shoved her overturned bike from below. As he clasped the handlebars to prevent it from sliding back down the hill, she scrambled above him to grab it. They repeated the process until they'd leveraged her bike to the top of the wall, then returned for his.

As I watched them struggle from several hundred meters away, I understood that I was never going to lift my bike up this embankment on my own. I'd have to break it down first, removing the bags and carrying it up in shifts. Clearly that was going to require at least a half hour if not more, for twenty feet of progress.

Leah and Lars were just completing their task when I arrived, and I expected them to continue up the hill. Instead, without asking whether I needed help, Lars boot-skied back down to the river. Leah positioned herself from above as Lars and I worked together to shove my obese bicycle toward her. I grunted a breathless "thank you" as Leah clasped the bike and lunged backward. She was a much stronger woman than I, and managed to dead-lift the bike several feet before laying it down on top of the cliff. My contribution was relatively little, and I felt embarrassed. This was still a competition, and Leah and Lars were under no obligation to help me.

"I thought I was going to have to break down my bike. You just saved me at least a half hour," I said.

"No problem," Leah shrugged, and hoisted her own bike. I followed behind her but soon lost ground, and then I began to lose my breath. Although no longer vertical, the remaining climb out of the gorge was still incredibly steep. It took all of my strength just to take a few steps before pausing to get my breathing under control. Leah and Lars were climbing out of sight. I grasped at the pocket beneath my coat to find my inhaler, but I couldn't clasp the zipper with my still-numb right hand, and couldn't let go of the bike without losing it down the gorge. I continued in halting steps, desperately gasping against a sensation that my airways were closing.

Near the top of the climb, I finally hit a grade shallow enough to lean my bike against a tree, and took several hits of the inhaler. Having failed to warm it in my hands first, it continued to spit half-frozen squirts of liquid rather than airway-opening spray. Still, the idea of medicine was psychologically calming. I was just getting my breathing under control when Jim Ishman passed me again. He looked strong, with his shoulders lowered and face fixed in a steely gaze as he nodded at me. Even though I understood that all of us were positioned together in the mid-pack, I felt awe for my competitors' strength through this daunting gorge, and their unwavering approach toward the mountains still in front of us.

From what little I knew of Jim, he was a family man from Colorado with a stout build and a beard — not really the type most would envision when picturing endurance cyclists. Leah was a geologist from Minnesota, tall and blond and exactly my age — the kind of sporty woman I looked up to in high school. Lars was a lawyer in Anchorage, the kind of suited professional who was probably far more successful than his hobbies would let on. We were, on the outside, fairly typical, middle-aged suburban white people. How did this become our life?

As short as the first day had seemed, the second day of the Iditarod was interminably long, with gray skies casting dull light over the slow-moving miles. The trail rumbled over moose-stomped holes in a series of long, narrow lakes. Each lake ended in another impossibly steep climb. The route continued to parallel the Happy River across forested slopes high above the gorge, and the constant rolling in and out of creek drainages meant that for every ten feet of elevation gained, at least eight would be lost again. It's a hard way to climb to a modest elevation of 1,800 feet — the altitude of Puntilla Lake — but the effort and the sharp rise of pyramid-shaped mountains on both sides makes the place feel much higher.

For most of the next eighteen miles I walked with my bike, coasting descents but quickly forced off of the saddle after a few hard cranks at every steep rise. As we neared Puntilla, trail conditions continued to deteriorate, with a stiff wind dusting the already soft trail with fresh powder. We crossed an open swamp, where I could see Lars a half mile ahead, but his shin-deep footprints were already half-buried in drifted snow. At one point I caught up to Lars, and he mentioned looking forward to riding his bike again once we traversed the swamp. I didn't have the heart to speculate that these soft, wind-drifted trail conditions weren't likely to improve before Rainy Pass, some thirty miles beyond.

Daylight faded the way it does on an overcast evening, almost imperceptibly through shades of gray. I arrived at Puntilla Lake Lodge just before ten, which meant it took me nine hours to cover the preceding thirty miles. Still, I wasn't unhappy with the progress so far, given I was still fewer than thirty-six hours into the race.

Puntilla is another luxury wilderness lodge accessible only by plane, snow-mobile, dog team, and the occasional human-powered nut. I've read enviable reviews about gourmet meals and soft bedding, but I've only experienced the log shack where the lodge offers an unmanned Iditarod checkpoint. The shack holds a few bunks, several cots, a generator for light bulbs, a plug-in hot water thermos, and a wood stove. Drinking water is collected from a nearby spring and stored in large buckets, smelling strongly of sulphur. The tarpaper-covered window seals leak profusely with melted ice, the mattresses are pocked with mold, and the few scratchy wool blankets appear to have not been washed in at least a decade. The accommodations are Spartan, but not unappreciated. We realize how difficult it is to provide amenities out here.

Arriving at the far end of the mid-pack, I entered the building to find it stuffed to the brim with reclining bodies. All of the bunks and cots were full. Two people were curled up on a couch, and the floors were covered with yet more bodies and dozens of boots. I tiptoed around to find a place large enough to fit me, but was bewildered to find none. The wind was howling outside, and the temperature had dropped to four degrees. While I considered continuing up the trail to camp, any indoor space on the Iditarod Trail — even the most un-comfortable ones — remain far too enticing. When I decided to hunker down next to the table, Lars pointed out that I was blocking access to the drinking water. He wasn't wrong, but I felt annoyed because he'd used the fifteen minutes before I arrived to set up a relatively spacious nest on the remaining floor space.

"People can step on me," I grumbled. "I'm tired and there's nowhere else to sleep."

With that, I stuffed in earplugs, curled up in my billowing down sleeping bag, and passed out entirely. This was surprising, as I'd slept so poorly in a nice bed in Skwentna, but eventually fatigue overcomes discomfort. Lars would later tell me that the wood stove went out and the temperature on the floor dropped to thirty-eight degrees, but this was still balmy compared to the outdoors. Peo-ple tromped in and out, grazing from the ramen noodles and hot chocolate on the table and collecting water from the thermos that was directly above my face. None of this woke me up until somebody grabbed one of my shoulders and shook me heartily.

"We're leaving now," he yelled. "Do you want one of the beds?"

I jolted up and blinked in confusion. A half dozen bikers were milling about, putting on boots and packing up small bags. Where was I? Who were these people? Before I could even nod in agreement, the man yelled, "Good luck to Nome!"

The group was already out the door before I gained enough coherence to hoist my sleeping bag to one of the now-empty beds. Half of the mattress was soaked with melted ice from the ceiling. Rather than reject the bed, I simply spun my sleeping bag around so the wet part was at my feet. Squinting at the clock, I noted it was two in the morning, which I thought was far too early to leave. Not only because I wanted more sleep (I badly wanted more sleep), but because the thirty-five miles over Rainy Pass were known to be the most beautiful miles on the Iditarod Trail. Leaving now meant seven hours of darkness before the sun rose again.

Rainy Pass is one of the most scenic sections, but it is also one of the most volatile. Violent storms move in with little warning, and it's not uncommon to see fifty-mile-an-hour winds and temperatures dipping to forty below. Reaching the pass before noon was my goal, so I set an alarm for 4:30. I woke up promptly, but by the time I mowed through two ramen squares and a bowl of instant oatmeal, it was close to 5:30. Oh, well. The temperature outside was a relatively comfortable eight degrees, the wind had abated slightly, and skies had cleared to reveal the stunning contrast of snow-covered peaks bathed in moonlight.

The trail rose sharply out of Puntilla Lake, where the black spruce forest thinned to a few hearty stragglers, and the and the glacier-carved Ptarmigan Valley opened up beneath a violet dawn. With my headlamp beam fixed on bike tracks and footprints over the otherwise untrammeled trail, I could see where the leaders of the race had walked through several inches of new snow, but several who followed were able to ride on top of their tire tracks. I tried riding and was surprised to find good traction, but it was difficult to steer the bike straight enough to stay inside a trail that was only as wide as my own tires. As soon as the front wheel jumped out of the track, it was buried to the hub in crusted snow.

"Better to walk."

Pushing my bike, I had the freedom to gaze at my surroundings rather than endlessly scanning for rideable lines. Frequently I stopped to look back as strips of pink light pushed through low clouds still hovering over the peaks. Daylight revealed a glistening white valley broken only by sharp bands of rock and the occasional alder branch, wooden tripod, or lone tree. The rising mountains were bald under a thick layer of snow, and the monotone appearance of the landscape gave it a singular power. I was awestruck, pulled into a reverie that had no concept of time or miles.

Twelve miles past Puntilla Lake, the Iditarod Trail turns away from the Ptarmigan Valley and enters a narrow gully toward Rainy Pass. Traversing the valley requires a final crossing of the Happy River. At this altitude, the river is more of a robust creek, and is usually frozen and covered in snow. This year, for the first time in anyone's recent memory, the river was fully open with knee-deep water gushing through its widest channels. Hiking up and down the bank where others had already scouted, I found no ice bridges or channels narrow enough to jump.

Thanks to my inherent fear of open water and frozen feet, I was well prepared to wade difficult water crossings. I pulled on a pair of nylon hip waders, cinched them up tight, and attached the drawstring to cords in my pack that I'd added to ensure the waders wouldn't slip down. With that, I was able to hoist the saddle of my bike onto my shoulder, and spent several minutes taking careful steps to maintain my balance.

Pleased with the problem-free crossing, I observed another rider preparing to cross as I packed up my waders. He pulled on trash bags and secured them only with rubber ice cleats over his boots. His system was much more precarious, but he crossed without issue as well. Later I heard stories from riders who shared waders by throwing them across the river. Others removed all of their footwear and crossed the frigid stream barefoot. Mike had the best story of all. He carried waders, but encountered another Nome racer, Robert Ostrom, who had nothing waterproof to pull over his boots. Mike carried his own bike across, then ferried Robert's bike, then returned a third time to collect Robert. The smaller but still full-sized man climbed onto Mike's shoulders, and held on tight as Mike waded across. Any slip would have sent both of them plunging into the river, where the water temperature was barely above freezing and the current was strong enough to potentially push them downstream along rough gravel. I viewed this as an astonishing display of confidence on Mike's part and trust on Robert's, but for Mike it was all in good fun.

The day grew warm as I neared the pass. The last wispy clouds had retreated to the south, and bright sunlight reflected off the snow. I'd removed my hat, gloves, and jacket, and could feel the still-cool breeze between wet strands of hair. I'd hiked for more than seven hours that morning, and could feel the skin on my feet stewing in hot juices beneath a pair of vapor barrier socks. A half mile below the pass, I laid out my coat in the snow and plopped down to remove my boots and socks so my feet could dry out in the sun. Exposing wet skin to the breeze revealed that the ambient temperature was indeed still freezing, but it felt wonderful to sit with my legs extended, wiggling my naked toes at foreboding peaks in the Alaska Range. Handfuls of cheese crackers and jerky completed the pleasant mountain picnic.

I reached the pass around two in the afternoon, meaning it took me nine hours to travel eighteen miles. On the Iditarod Trail, on Rainy Pass, I considered this fantastic progress. I celebrated by remounting the bike and attempting to surf the soft-powder descent by locking out the brakes and steering with my hips. It was difficult to avoid the thigh-deep holes punched by other riders who'd attempted the same and crashed, and I soon found myself tumbling end over end, laughing through a mouth full of snow when I finally came to a stop.

The trail dipped below timber line and continued to contour Pass Creek, descending steeply into a narrowing canyon choked with alder branches. At times the route wound through the bed of the creek itself, which was deceptively slick with patches of white ice. Rounding a rock outcropping at full speed, I hit one of these ice patches and slipped sideways, crashing hard on my right side. My hand, which was already numb from the first day's crash, and my forearm, which was still cut and bruised from the California crash a week earlier, throbbed with intense pain. I laid on the ice, clutching my arm and fretting that I'd broken a bone. That would be a difficult problem to have in a narrow canyon where planes couldn't land, still two dozen bumpy trail miles from the nearest building. For all of the hazards I expected to encounter in Alaska, I never gave bicycle crashes their proper consideration.

After letting the pain course through my body, I was sufficiently satisfied that nothing was broken. Still, my arm was sore and throbbed painfully whenever I gripped the handlebar. I attempted to steer one-handed through the thickening maze of alder branches and stream ice, but fear of crashing again coaxed me to endure the pain.

A few more miles of tender steering brought me to the top of the Dalzell Gorge, an infamous segment where Pass Creek empties into Dalzell Creek and cascades down a narrow gorge with sheer rock walls on both sides. The "trail" is a series of ice bridges over the creek, prone to collapsing into the rushing water. When I walked through this gorge in 2014, there was no snow cover at all, and I had to anchor sharp cleats and trekking poles into wet, sloping ice as my sled yanked toward open leads. I was terrified of taking a bike through the Dalzell Gorge, even more so now that my arm was compromised.

Just as I braced for the icy descent, I saw another cyclist pushing his bike toward me. Bartosz was a Polish man, bald and barrel-chested with a beak-like nose. He was a rookie in the 350-mile race.

"What are you doing?" I asked, since he was walking in the wrong direction. "What's wrong?"

"I am looking for hotel," he said in a particularly garbled Polish accent.

"Oh, ha ha," I laughed, presuming he was making a joke. We were on the western side of the Alaska Range, deep in a frozen gorge, still a hundred miles from the nearest village. Even Alaska doesn't get much more remote than this spot.

Bartosz responded with a confused look that led me to believe he was genuinely looking for a hotel. "I just saw it," he said. "It was right over here some-where." As I scrunched my face into a concerned frown, he moaned, "I am sooooo sleepy."

I realized that it was Bartosz I saw late the previous evening in Puntilla, as I briefly awoke while snoozing in the wet bed. He was sitting in a chair, holding his boot next to the extinguished wood stove. He told another rider that he'd soaked his foot in a river, and was only going to stay long enough to dry his boot. I doubted that he succeeded in drying his boot, and probably hadn't slept at all, possibly since the start of the race two days earlier.

"Hey, I think you're hallucinating," I said. "There's no hotel."

Bartosz continued to look confused. "I just saw it."

"Well, we're only eight miles from Rohn," I said, referring to the next check-point — a tent camp next to an uninhabited shelter cabin that was used once a year during the Iditarod Sled Dog Race. "Why don't you stick with me and we'll ride there right now? Easier than finding a hotel?"

Bartosz beamed and nodded vigorously. We continued down the trail, with him hugging my rear wheel but saying nothing as we swooped into the gorge. There were a few rollers with steep climbs. I felt compelled to crank up them to save face, and still Bartosz had no problem keeping up with me. Clearly this guy was a strong rider, even if a bit bonkers.

We hit the creek bottom, where I expected to encounter deadly glare ice. Instead we found smooth snow and robust ice bridges supported by tree trunks. A week earlier, the Iditarod Dog Sled Race had sent a half dozen volunteers to Rohn to work on the trail, in response to complaints from mushers about dangerous conditions during previous years. The trail they built was profes-sional grade, with banked turns that seemed custom-built for mountain biking. The volunteers even cut notches through ice walls — at some point earlier in the winter, an ice dam blocked the gorge, forming a temporary lake that later washed out and left behind shelves up to six feet thick. Frozen waterfalls draped from the cliffs, and the route continued to wind through narrow passages in a dense canyon forest. Even a sore arm couldn't diminish the thrill of this descent.

Bartosz and I popped out of the forest at the Tatina River, where the nar-row Dalzell Gorge empties into a much wider canyon. We pedaled over a be-nign-looking ice bridge onto the main river channel. I even stopped to capture photos of Bartosz in front of the canyon's towering peaks. Just two days later, warm temperatures created open leads in this same spot, forcing a few cyclists and foot racers to bash through the woods along the river bank. One foot rac-er, Peter Ripmaster, attempted a crossing and crashed through a precariously refrozen ice bridge, plunging over his head in frigid water. Before the current could push him under the ice, he managed to spread his arms onto a solid shelf and pull himself out of the river, flopping like a seal as ice shattered around him. Everything from his clothing to his sled was soaked and quickly freezing. All he could do was sprint the remaining four miles to Rohn, where he was able to dry his gear overnight. If it had been any colder than the thirty degrees it was at the time, he might have succumbed to hypothermia before he reached the tent camp. What happened to Peter was my worst nightmare — the scenario to which I gave the most headspace during nighttime fretting sessions — and I admired him for continuing toward McGrath after that incident. If I had nearly drowned in the Tatina, I no doubt would have quit the race immediately and called in a thousand-dollar air taxi flight out of Rohn.

Two days before Peter's plunge into the Tatina, skies were blue and the river was a tranquil plain of snow-covered ice. Sunset was still more than an hour away when I arrived at the tent camp, situated at the confluence of the South Fork of the Kuskokwim River. The checkpoint was designated "Rob's Roadhouse" in honor of a longtime volunteer who died during an Alaska wilderness race in 2014. Rob drowned after his packraft capsized in the Tana River. His death was a reminder that we may view the world as a beautiful playground, but it remains indifferent to our presence. Life hangs by a delicate thread everywhere.

At Rohn I stayed only long enough to enjoy a bratwurst cooked up by a volunteer who was a friend of Rob's, change my socks, and restock my bike with food and batteries from my drop bag. The volunteer made me a second sausage after I admitted to feeling ravenous. Bartosz walked into the tent and minutes later had passed out with his boots on while lying on a pile of spruce branches. When I left, the sun was gone and the whole sky was a bright shade of pink. Bolstered by a stomach full of protein and a bike full of everything I needed for days in the wilderness, I pedaled across the well-frozen Kuskokwim River with a grin that no doubt could still be seen from Rohn.

How did this become my life? I'm just extremely lucky, that's all.

The Boundless Night

Even on the first day of March, night in Interior Alaska feels boundless. Darkness is crushed into every horizon without a hint of light pollution to look to for comfort. As much as I enjoyed my solo push over Rainy Pass, solitude became a menacing phantom after sunset. In these rolling hills that border the South Fork of the Kuskokwim River, the forest had been scoured by wildfires. Charred and twisted tree skeletons leaned into the trail, which was a patchwork of dirt, matted yellow grass and amber sheets of ice. Snow was again absent in this valley, located on the dry side of the Alaska Range. What little precipitation falls here is quickly scattered by incessant winds. Without snow to reflect a headlamp beam, this particular night seemed enormously dark. I couldn't see anything beyond a table-sized circle of dim light, and this blindness illuminated how alone I was out here. Bartosz remained at Rob's Roadhouse to sleep off his soothing delusions. As brief and strange as our partnership had been, I already missed him.

I hadn't yet connected with Beat on the satellite phone. Based on memories from our walk together in 2014, I imagined him approaching Winter Lake

Lodge at that moment. There, the trail zigzags between forests and swamps. Reflective trail markers can capture light a half mile away, deceiving travelers into believing they are closer to something resembling civilization. Out here, in the burned hills west of Rohn, permanent trail markers were dulled with dirt and soot. Thin clouds dimmed the stars, and black ice entombed the trail in fathomless reflections.

Pedaling over frozen dirt felt like real mountain biking, with grass clumps — called tussocks — adding fun technical features. The ice, however, became infuriating. Most of it had formed from water seeping out of the ground rather than snow melt, and it was the same color as dirt, only slippery. In the low light I couldn't discern patches of ice from anything else, and made numerous steering errors that sent me skidding toward skeleton trees. When I went to grab the brakes, my numb right hand had no strength. I began to use only my left (front wheel) brake to arrest skids, which eventually caused the bike to flip forward, tossing me onto the hard ground. There were other crashes, too, when I tipped over on off-camber ice or instinctively bailed when I lost control of the bike.

I don't think I've ever — even as a small child — ridden a bicycle so badly. I had no idea what was wrong with me. Studded tires should have offered more solid traction, if I wasn't steering so spastically. The crashes prompted me to ride slower and hit the front brake more often, which only made my handling worse. My arm was still throbbing and swollen from the crash earlier in the day. Combined with a numb hand and shoulder pain from the previous week, it seemed plausible that I'd lost the majority of my strength on my right side, causing this imbalance. Perhaps poor visibility also contributed. Perhaps I was just tired. I still felt wound up, but endorphins have that effect. When I looked at my phone, it was 10:30 p.m., which was the same time I stopped the previous evening.

"I'll bivy here and ride the rest in the morning," I decided. I believed the worst of the bumpy ice would end where the trail dropped out of the foothills at the Farewell Lakes, still about fifteen miles away. All of the crashes had rattled my morale, and I was walking more than riding. Fifteen miles might take me as many as five hours at this timid pace. Daylight and more confident riding could reduce that distance to two hours.

It was a wise decision, but the burned-out forest wasn't the best place to bed down for the night. Snow only covered the tundra in small, petrified patches. The rest of the ground was tangled with berry bushes and basketball-size tussocks. A stiff breeze made the moderate temperature — fourteen degrees — feel much lower, and the toothpick trees provided no shelter from the wind. Still, this was a nice campsite compared to others I'd no doubt encounter if I ventured beyond McGrath. I knew I could use the practice.

I ventured through the brambles until I found a patch of concrete snow large enough to lay out my bivy sack. Propping the bike against a toothpick tree, I stuffed my coats in a sack to use as a pillow, buckled my overboots around the bike frame so the wind wouldn't blow them away, and wedged my boots against the rear wheel for the same reason. Hunkering into my billowing sleeping bag, I felt a wash of tranquility, as though I was being tucked into a warm bed by someone who loved me.

"It doesn't get better than this," I whispered hoarsely as I watched the sky for Northern Lights, until my nose tingled with the cold. I slipped deeper into the bag and drifted to sleep.

The phone, with no reception but an alarm set for five in the morning, rang loudly inside my bag. I sat up and blinked in confusion, understanding where I was but without a concept of time. Did I really just sleep uninterrupted for six hours? Here in this spooky burned forest? And why was it still pitch dark outside? Shouldn't it be morning?

Crawling out of a warm sleeping bag is harsh in any weather, but subzero wind chills and pre-dawn darkness have a way of making this feel suicidal. I shivered violently as I packed up my gear. My right hand and arm were still deeply sore, and my feet felt like they were encased in ice — which they were in now-frozen boots. Even though I could barely feel my extremities, I decided breakfast was in order. I was standing next to my empty campsite and gnawing on a frozen Snickers Bar when an Italian cyclist passed on the trail. He shined his headlamp toward me, and I shined mine back on a concerned face.

"You are okay?" he yelled loudly.

"I'm fine," I said, with a more exasperated tone than I intended. "I'm just getting up for the morning. I'll be right behind you."

It was certainly nice of this man to check on me — and I would have done the same — but the alarm in his voice revealed an attitude common among Iditarod cyclists: that stopping was something we did only in emergencies. Otherwise, we just raced until we reached outposts of civilization, then raced some more. These quiet moments — not racing or recovering, but simply existing in rare spaces — were often overlooked entirely. Sure, camping on an ice slab in a burned-out forest, in Alaska, in March, wasn't a typical pastime. But it had been a wonderful respite.

Morning riding was not better than night riding. Even well rested, I was still terrified of slipping on ice and overreacted to obstacles, which ironically caused more crashing. If I had to guess how many times my body hit the ground in the fifteen-mile segment between the Post River crossing and the Farewell Lakes, I would say at least six, with a dozen more near-misses. Luckily none of these crashes led to new injuries, but it had gotten to the point where I was resigned to walking my bike the next fifty miles to Nikolai. Finally, purple hues began to spread across the sky. The flat light of dawn proved to be better for depth perception than the harsh contrast of the headlight, and my handling improved.

Near the first Farewell Lake, evidence of the trail largely disappeared beneath bison-stomped swamps. I followed faint scratches in the ice to a well-defined trail that snaked up a hill. I labored up the trail for a half hour before memory kicked in and reminded me that there were no big climbs before the Farewell Lakes. I was off route. Exasperated, I rocketed down the hill and encountered two other racers, Amy and Cody Breen, a couple from Anchorage who were racing to McGrath. As I explained why I believed this was the wrong way, they both looked at me like I'd been up smoking crack all night.

"What other trails are there?" Amy asked.

"I don't know, maybe someone has a vacation home," I shrugged. "I only know that there are no climbs near the Farewell Lakes. The Iditarod Trail stays low."

It was clear they didn't believe me. My vacation home theory was pretty ridiculous, given there were no roads, airstrips, or anything else nearby. I turned and continued backward on the trail, and Amy and Cody didn't follow. After several minutes of picking my way around open leads in a stream and finally crossing a narrow ice bridge, I finally located a yellow triangle indicating the Iditarod Trail.

"It's here!" I called out to them. "I see a marker!"

The three of us shadowed each other across the glare ice of the first Farewell Lake, where we encountered Bartosz, again riding backward on the route. He must have passed while I was sleeping. Given how long it took me to pack up camp, crash my bike a bunch of times, and wander for forty-five minutes off route, it was strange he wasn't farther ahead.

"I can't find the trail," he announced. "Where is it?"

Amy pointed to a line of wooden lath that had been hammered into the ice by Iron Dog trail breakers. I also thought they looked fairly obvious, but Bartosz remained skeptical. Still, he maintained a jovial demeanor, and I found it humorous — with dashes of both pity and admiration — that a Polish man who lived in England was so happy to bumble around haplessly in remote Alaska. He latched onto our group and shadowed Amy and Cody as they quickly outpaced me on the lake. The surface was so clear that I could see blades of grass and what I convinced myself were fish on the shallow lake bottom. My own anxiety from bumbling around haplessly had significantly abated, but I was still terrified of falling through thin ice.

As the day brightened and warmed, the four of us tackled the rolling hills beyond the Farewell Lakes, a deceptively tough section of trail rippled with seemingly endless hundred-foot climbs and descents. Although we drifted apart, I could occasionally see Amy and Cody on the crest of the next hill, and Bartosz one or even two hills behind. Whenever I looked back, the jagged crown of the Alaska Range stretched across the horizon — a stunning landmark demonstrating how far we'd traveled.

Almost exactly halfway between Rohn and Nikolai, the trail crests one last forested ridge and drops into a sweeping, swamp-inundated valley called the Farewell Burn. The Burn earned its name when a massive wildfire raged through the area in 1978. Nearly four decades of regrowth have restored the landscape, in a unique way. With spruce trees that are all roughly the same age and height, the boreal forest resembles a Christmas tree farm, only haunted. The trees have grown so closely together that twisting branches weave an impenetrable wall on both sides of the trail. Branches that lean away from the prevailing wind form a menacing canopy. When the wind moans overhead, the spooky vibe of this claustrophobic corridor is overwhelming.

Riding through the revitalized Farewell Burn on a sunny Wednesday afternoon dimmed its ghostly effect. This was surprisingly disappointing. I'd first experienced the Burn at thirty-five below zero, wracked with violent shivering while ducking hurricane-force wind gusts. The second time I visited this place, Beat and I walked through the night as subzero temperatures coated the conifers in wraithy frost. This time around, the afternoon was warm and bright, and I could see this forest for its trees, stunted and benign as they were.

When thrills abate, tedium fills in the empty space. Adding to the slow grind was the state of the trail, which was rippled with snowmobile moguls. Different from the pump track before Winter Lake Lodge, these moguls were more solid, taller, and spaced closely together. It was impossible to achieve any sort of flow. Instead, riding this undulating trail felt like climbing hundreds of tiny hills, mashing the pedals up and coasting down. Despite my best efforts, I couldn't boost my average speed above five miles per hour. Although I acknowledged this was the Iditarod Trail and I couldn't complain about any trail conditions solid enough to support a bike, the back-wrenching fluctuations left me feeling grumpy. With no imaginary zombie trees or deadly cold to distract me, only hard work remained.

Sullivan Creek is a spring-fed stream that never freezes, so the Bureau of Land Management constructed a bridge. It's a rare piece of infrastructure in the uninhabited Burn, and lends some assurance to weary travelers that we haven't teleported to an alien planet. A rusty coffee can on a string allows bridge-crossers to collect water without treading the thin ice along the river bank, so I decided to hunker down here and cook a hot lunch. Three days of racing with no major health problems made continuing beyond McGrath seem more plausible, and I knew I needed to complete at least one more test of wilderness skills. The previous night had been good practice for setting up and breaking down a winter camp, and this would be a good test of firing up my stove to melt snow. Of course I'd done all of these tasks before, but not with the frequency to inspire self-confidence.

Beat would argue that my lunch stop was not a real test of winter wilderness skills. The wind had calmed to a whisper, and it remained so warm that I kept my hat, coat, and mittens stowed as I scooped water from the stream and pumped fuel into the stove. I fashioned a comfortable recliner from a pile of snow and leaned back on top of my puffy coat, sipping hot coffee as a bag of freeze-dried chicken and noodles rehydrated in the sun. Amy and Cody, who had taken an earlier break, passed one more time. I wished them well in the race, since I clearly wasn't making my best effort to compete. Although I normally strive to perform as well as I can in a race setting, at this point I'd started focusing on the bigger picture. McGrath wasn't a finish line; it was just a checkpoint, and an early one at that.

The relentless snowmobile moguls continued beyond Sullivan Creek. The only respites were wind-swept swamps, where snow gave way to glare ice and tussocks. Miles of this were so exhausting that I slipped into sleepy daydreams without realizing my lack of presence, until a gust of wind hit my face and suddenly the distant profile of Denali was in view. It was stunning, and it had been there all along.

I reached the village of Nikolai later than I hoped, but it wasn't yet dark. Nikolai is a rare full-service checkpoint, provided by a local family in their modest home. I arrived during a strange lull in the race, when the competitive end of the mid-pack had already left to make the final push for McGrath, but the back-of-pack had not yet arrived. The home's residents were exhausted from staying awake for two days and already in bed, so I was all alone in the front room. If I was a rookie in the race, I would have been terribly self-conscious about helping myself in a strange house. But I appreciated the lack of distractions. There was a cold pan of spaghetti on the stove, so I heated it up in the microwave and showed myself to an empty bedroom. I didn't feel particularly tired at eight in the evening, but wanted to prioritize rest when opportunities arose.

Instead, I tossed and turned in the overheated room until I heard voices outside. Since I wasn't sleeping anyway, I decided it was time to pack up and leave. Bartosz had finally found his way to Nikolai, along with Lars and another man, Bob May. With a crazy-eyed twitch that made it seem like he'd ingested too much caffeine, Bob shared a hilarious tale of following the wrong trail sixty miles out of the way on the first day. I organized my things and guffawed as Bob shoveled spaghetti into his mouth and described wandering aimlessly through the woods along an apparent trapper trail until he found his way to Skwentna, having missed the first checkpoint entirely.

"They're probably going to disqualify you for that," I said sympathetically. "You can take any route you want, but you have to hit all the checkpoints."

Bob seemed to bristle at this statement but then shrugged. "Well, no reason to travel at night now. I'm going to get some sleep and see the rest of the trail in daylight. You heading out?"

"Ah, I've been here too long already," I answered. "Yeah, I should go."

It was one in the morning. Outside, my thermometer said it was thirteen degrees, but the air felt much colder as I pedaled away from dim electric lights and dropped onto the Kuskokwim River. I left Nikolai wearing layers that earlier had been sufficient for temperatures in the teens, but kinks in the armor revealed themselves when my toes, neck, and lower back began to tingle and go numb. Rather than stop and add more clothing, I made the strange decision to tough it out until sunrise — which wasn't coming for eight more hours.

Green aurora rippled overhead, and the smooth expanse of the river allowed me to crane my neck upward for long seconds, absorbing the light dance as I pedaled. It was too cold to stop. When did Alaska become so cold? The trail veered away from the river and cut a straight line across woods and open swamps. With the sky obstructed by trees, I spent more time looking at the trail, observing the tire tracks of others. There was a fresh set of footprints at regular intervals, and whenever I saw boot marks in the snow, I got off the bike and jogged to warm my toes.

As darkness wore on, I began to see occasional and then frequent canine tracks pressed into the snow, both over and underneath tire tracks. At first I believed the tracks belonged to dog teams, but they were too large for Alaska huskies, and too dispersed for a tethered animal. No, these were wolves, clearly prowling these same corridors. I pointed my headlamp beam where the tracks veered off the trail, and became convinced that I could see the yellow reflections of eyes staring back at me.

I already had goosebumps from the subzero darkness, but now all of my body hair stood at attention. Wolf attacks on humans are exceedingly rare. Bikers had passed by this spot before me and the wolves left them alone — at least I hadn't noticed any blood on the snow. And yet, why wouldn't a pack of wolves take advantage of this situation? We cyclists were meals on wheels out here, doughy and warm and far too slow to run away.

I continued to shine my headlamp into the yawning darkness, scanning for yellow eyes. Overhead the sky was radiant with green and purple light, but an odd sort of apathy had taken over, muting both fear and wonder. When I stopped to fish a peanut butter cup out of my feed bag, the fingers on my perpetually numb right hand wouldn't work at all. Suddenly panicked, I shoved my hand down my tights into the warm space between my thighs. I must have looked like a child desperate not to pee her pants as I sprinted back and forth to generate heat. The adrenaline rush sparked renewed lucidity. Finally, I looked at my digital thermometer.

"Geez, it's minus ten," I said out loud. I was wearing the same layers that I'd worn at the start of the race, when it was nearly fifty degrees warmer. The cold creep had been insidiously gradual, pulling me almost imperceptibly from a mild state of discomfort into hypothermia. No wonder my head had gone foggy, my hand entirely numb. I pulled on a balaclava, puffy shorts, and a thick fleece jacket. Although tempted to put on my down parka, I maintained that it was only to be used during stops or extreme situations. Minus ten couldn't be extreme, or I'd never make it to Nome.

I pedaled away feeling renewed vitality, but the cold continued to bite at my shoulders and backside. Starting out cold meant I had to pedal hard to maintain body heat, and stopping for any reason invited a shivering chill that took as long as a half hour to recover. Minus ten was a tiptoeing phantom, shadowing me even closer than the wolves whose tracks continued to proliferate along the trail.

This is the edge we skirt out here, in these inhospitable places beyond the safety nets of modern life. It takes only one overlooked detail to slip into a potentially dangerous hole from which it can be impossible to emerge. Not anticipating a rapid dip in temperatures during a deceptively long night had been a mistake. It was a mistake I'd made before, and probably would again.

For now, I anticipated daylight even more than my arrival in McGrath, and continued to scan the sky through frost-caked eyelashes, hoping for hints of pink light. By the time the sun cleared the southern horizon, I'd passed a hand-drawn sign announcing I was ten miles from the checkpoint. This news was surprisingly anticlimactic. Even as I anticipated the journey beyond, I expected to feel something more when I neared the end of the short race after three days and twenty hours — nearly two and a half days faster than my previous finish by bike. I thought I'd feel satisfaction. Elation. But no, as I approached McGrath in the warming sunlight, I felt only the same creeping dread I'd experienced in the days before the race started.

Arriving shortly after ten in the morning, I wedged my frost-coated body into a home filled to the brim with other cyclists. The scene was chaotic, with a dull roar of voices, sleeping bodies draped over the couch, and people crowded around a kitchen table overflowing with breakfast foods. There was a round of sleepy congratulations, and the homeowner, Peter, asked me if I wanted anything.

"Coffee?" I said weakly.

For the past two decades, the center of human-powered Iditarod racing has been the home of Peter and Tracy Schneiderheinze, longtime residents of Mc-Grath. Peter is German with a gruff accent that's difficult to decipher, and Tracy is a sweet red-haired woman with a grandmotherly presence that can be both sympathetic and firm. Every March, the couple selflessly opens their home to offer racers a luxurious finish line complete with beds, fire crackling in the wood stove, and an unlimited, twenty-four-hour smörgåsbord of home-cooked meals. Peter was frying omelets when I arrived, and offered one of his famous "man-cakes" — a kind of pancake on steroids, three inches high, twelve inches diameter, injected with berries, butter, and at least twelve hundred calories. I accepted gratefully and sat down at the table with the other McGrath finishers, answering a smattering of questions and feeling predictably overwhelmed.

After breakfast, my thoughts fixated on chores. I needed to collect the box of supplies I mailed to McGrath, dry out all of my gear, do my laundry, take one last shower, and make sure everything was in place for the seven hundred miles still in front of me.

"I need to get it together," I fretted. My hands were visibly shaking. I looked at others sleeping peacefully on the couch and wondered why I couldn't feel they way they did — that satisfying combination of accomplishment and relief. My dread had only intensified as I glanced out the window at snow flurries and conceptualized the distance beyond.

"I can't believe I came all this way just to feel so bad again," I complained to Leah, who had arrived about nine hours before me.

She and others had words of encouragement to offer, but my gut check was failing. Sure, the ride to McGrath had gone well. And sure, I had promised myself that if I arrived here healthy and strong, I would at least start toward Nome. But dread had eroded my resolve. Wearing a T-shirt and yoga pants that Tracy lent to me so I could wash all of my clothing, I traipsed outside into the overcast, ten-degree afternoon to call Beat on the satellite phone. It was our first voice contact since the start. Beat sounded tired but cheerful. He'd come down with food poisoning at Winter Lake Lodge, and had spent the past day struggling to recover. He was resting near the top of Rainy Pass, where the wind was gusting and skies were gray.

"But it's so beautiful," he said. "I wish you were here."

"I wish I was there, too," I said genuinely. I should have walked with Beat. I didn't want to be alone in the great unknown. I told him about my trepidation, about locking myself in a bathroom so I could cry out of sight from the others, about feeling vastly under-prepared for this monumental task that I'd spent a year convincing myself I wasn't fit to attempt.

"How would you feel if you got on a plane right now?" Beat asked.

"I'd feel terrible," I sighed. "I'd feel disappointed."

"So I guess you know what you want to do."

Previously I'd intended to take a shower and a nap, then leave McGrath that same day. After all, I'd arrived early in the morning, and one piece of advice every veteran shared with me was, "Get out of McGrath!" The longer you stay in this warm haven of abundant mancakes, they warned, the less likely you are to leave. As the hours dragged on and my gut check continued to fail, I convinced myself that one last full night of sleep in a warm house would make everything better.

Mike showed up in the afternoon, and spent most of the remaining daylight hours tinkering with his bike outside. His knee was bothering him, but he also planned to pedal away from McGrath the following morning as long as the pain was manageable. When I admitted my own reservations, he told me he was a pharmacist and had an assortment of asthma medications in his possession. We agreed to set out together, but he warned me that he doesn't "like to get up early."

Five men had gone on to Nome ahead of us: Phil Hoefstetter, a hospital administrator who lived in Nome, was far off the front and nearly halfway across the two hundred miles of utter emptiness that separated McGrath from the Yukon River. Three others — Jay, Kyle, and Bill — appeared to be traveling together about a day behind Phil. Robert Ostrom left just an hour before I arrived in McGrath, but our long stay would put Mike and me a day behind him. It was unlikely we'd ever see any of those guys. Still, there were others coming from behind, including Tim Hewitt and Beat. Relative to previous years on the Iditarod Trail, this was a crowd.

Just before I went to bed, I sat down at the kitchen table with Bill Merchant. Bill set out a couple of days before the race to drive a snowmobile all the way from Anchorage to McGrath, and planned to leave that evening to return. He took pity on my bruised and swollen right arm — an injury that I'd barely considered amid all of my emotional fretting — and offered his own supply of lidocaine patches to ease the pain. While telling the story of the crash, I mentioned my numb hand, and Tracy Petervary offered up her own padded bike gloves to help relieve pressure.

Throughout the ride to McGrath, I promised myself that if I failed to reach Nome, I was going to be brutally and publicly honest about the reasons. So without a hint of intimidation, I unabashedly admitted to Bill — who in 2010 told me outright that we needed to discuss my place on the Iditarod Trail, and who had seen me at my worst two months earlier — "I'm not sure I'm brave enough to do this."

"You're braver than you think," he said, with a sincere grin spreading across his face beneath a handlebar mustache. "Tell you what. All you need to do is go to Ophir. It's a beautiful ride. Eat something, get some sleep. Do your gut check there."

Bill may have been a grizzled Alaskan, but at heart he only wanted others to have the same incredible experiences. I beamed back at him.

"One day at a time."

Bumps Along The Way

At 10:30 Friday morning, after spending twenty-four hours in the lavish oasis of McGrath and finally not able to stand it one minute longer, I made my break for the unknown. Mike wasn't being facetious when he told me he didn't do early starts — he was still grazing from the breakfast table when I announced that my pent-up anxiety would explode if I didn't get out of there. Two other cyclists who had laid over in McGrath — Sam and Katie, a couple from Durango, Colorado, who were not part of the race but were planning to tour the entire Iditarod Trail — also were in no hurry to leave.

Remounting my bike after a full day felt like prying open rusty hinges in my joints. I pedaled through a maze of snow-covered streets, following Peter on his snowmobile. He hopped off at a crossing of the Kuskokwim River and pointed to a lone pyramid-shaped mountain to the west.

"Stay to the right of the mountain, and you'll be fine," he said gruffly. I reached out to give him a hug.

"Thanks for everything you do," I said. I figured his was the last friendly face I'd see for a while.

Pedaling away from town, I assessed my physical state. The injured arm and hand were tender and numb, but the rest of my body was surprisingly nimble. My butt wasn't sore, and my legs felt strong. During my two previous 350-mile finishes, I arrived in McGrath sufficiently broken. In 2008, I struggled to drag myself up the stairs after the six-day bike ride. In 2014, a week of dragging a sled for eighteen hours a day left me with painful shin splints and crushing fatigue. Those experiences made Nome seem physically impossible, and it took a big leap of faith just to challenge the notion that 350 miles of the Iditarod Trail was truly all I could handle. Even though I believed I could surmount pain with mental toughness, I continued to be astounded by how efficiently a focused mind can drive my body. Simply by deciding that I wasn't close to being done, my body wasn't close to being spent.

Despite feeling fresh and strong, the tears started to flow when I looked back toward McGrath's radio tower and remembered what I was actually doing. The village of Takotna was just fifteen miles away, and beyond that was a depth of remoteness I had not yet experienced. The two-hundred miles separating Takotna from the Yukon River were inhabited by no one. There were a few abandoned mining camps, but this swath of the Interior saw no winter travel beyond the Iditarod races and the occasional snowmobile-driving tourist. The land was so desolate that even hunting and trapping were infrequent, because there were few animals. It was, I reminded myself, the kind of place where one could wallow in deep snow and minus-fifty temperatures for ten days without encountering anyone.

This day was gray and mild, with temperatures around twenty degrees and intermittent snow showers. I fell into a quiet rhythm, climbing along the base of the pyramid mountain and descending into Takotna. The village was eerily quiet for the early afternoon. Chained dogs slept in front of shuttered homes, not even barking at me as I passed. Beyond Takotna, the trail veered back into the hills, rising more than a thousand feet on an old road bed, then traversing a ridge beside the fog-shrouded peaks of unnamed mountains.

Forty miles passed quickly, and I didn't even pause until I reached the ghost town of Ophir. This cluster of uninhabited log cabins left over from the Gold Rush was used as a checkpoint for the sled dog race, but sat empty the rest of the year. Ophir was the landmark where I intended to camp for the night and ponder whether I was ready to make the full commitment. The first Iditarod mushers wouldn't pass through for five more days, so I hadn't expected to see anybody, but smoke was billowing from one of the cabins. A woman emerged from a barn-like building next door and waved at me.

"Do you need anything?" the woman called out. "Do you want coffee?"

At the place where I was supposed to do my solitary gut check, this unexpected offer caught me off guard, but I nodded gratefully. She directed me toward the wood-heated cabin. The woman and her husband were Iditarod volunteers, preparing the checkpoint for mushers' arrivals. She heated up water for instant coffee and told me about the origins of the cabin, which was built in 1910. As I gulped down scalding coffee, she offered up a bag of cookies, then encouraged me to take two extra for the road.

"You need the calories more than the volunteers," she said.

"I don't know about that. I have a ton of food." In anticipation of potential storms and becoming stranded in three feet of snow like Beat had the previous year, I'd left McGrath with nearly twelve pounds of food — about five days' worth — which was everything I could fit on my bike. But I gratefully accepted the cookies and then surprised myself when I turned down an offer to sleep in another unheated cabin.

"I'm hoping to make it to Carlson Crossing," I said, referring to a public shelter cabin maintained by the Bureau of Land Management. "It's what, about twenty-eight miles from here?"

"We saw Phil on Wednesday. He told us it's sixteen from the airstrip, and that's only a mile from here."

"Oh wow, seventeen miles would be fantastic," I said, even though I didn't remotely believe her. I may have been a Nome rookie, but I knew not to invest too much trust in any information regarding weather or distance, no matter how well-intentioned it was.

Mike still hadn't caught up as I pedaled away from Ophir an hour later, and I was beginning to wonder whether he had decided to leave McGrath at all. He'd been hedging over his sore knee, and he did look particularly comfortable when he was sitting down to a big plate of mancakes at ten in the morning. Sudden loneliness struck, because although Ophir's coffee and conversation had been unexpected, it was truly my last chance for outside interaction.

Twilight descended in darker shades of gray as I pedaled past collapsing cabins, skeletal frames of old front-end loaders, abandoned 1970s-era trucks, rusted barrels and piles of twisting metal — all remnants of the mining activity that proliferated in this region during the past century. Gold mining hadn't been all that lucrative for a few decades, advancing the state of decay. I peeked inside one of the cabins, which looked like a time capsule from 1978, with moldy upholstered furniture and labeled canned goods sitting on shelves. I questioned what was more unnerving — a pristine wilderness ruled by wolves, or a blighted one that had been abandoned by humans in a hurry. Either way, I was entirely at the mercy of the elements in a place so harsh even animals stayed away.

For twelve miles after Ophir, the route contoured hills above a narrow river valley. The trail followed the bed of an old road, complete with concrete bridges across what might otherwise be treacherous ice crossings. I was making great time and anticipated reaching the cabin for early bedtime, until the trail veered around a steep mountain and split at a junction. To the left was the Iditarod Trail's southern route — used during odd-numbered years by the Iditarod Sled Dog Race, this equally remote trail was put in place solely to guide mushers to villages at the southern end of the Yukon River. To the right was the northern route, used during even-numbered years by the sled dog race, every year by the Iron Dog snowmobile race, and the one we'd follow this year as well.

I walked a short distance out the southern route to appease my curiosity. It wouldn't be traveled by any racers this year, but there was a smooth and fairly hard-packed trail broken by unknown snowmobilers. The northern route, conversely, was an utter mess. As soon as the road bed ended, the smooth base and any use by sane snowmobile drivers disappeared. What remained was the result of two-hundred Iron Dog racers tearing up the trail at more than sixty miles an hour, after two feet of snow fell onto bare, partially thawed ground. Their hard accelerations and aggressive turns dug into the powder and tossed it in every direction. Now that two weeks of hard freezes and occasional thaws had passed, the trail had solidified into a bumpy disaster — ridges up to two feet high and sheer drops into exposed tussocks and frozen mud.

As a mountain biker, I'd compare this terrain to riding over the dry bed of a mountain river, with endless finessing over and around large boulders. For snow biking, it was exceedingly technical — fun when you're looking for a challenge, but less fun when you're tired and hungry and just want to be somewhere. The sun set, and temperatures quickly plunged below zero. I was working so hard to navigate the moguls that I felt no need to add layers.

Even though I was sitting in the saddle and pedaling the entire time, the first four miles of this frozen-boulder trail took nearly an hour to complete. By the end of that hour, my leg muscles were in knots and my emotions were nearing a full-tantrum meltdown. Much of this frustration stemmed from misdirected expectations. I anticipated being alone in a wasteland, facing forty-below temperatures, powering through steep climbs and descents, and managing complete self-sufficiency for the next two-hundred miles. I didn't anticipate a strenuous technical challenge that was going to demand more strength and patience than I had to spare.

Just as I stepped off the bike and held gloved, clenched fists against my ice-encrusted eyes, I noticed a headlamp beam approaching from behind. I turned as its source called out an enthusiastic "Wooooo!"

It was Mike, of course. The dude's body language was exuberant, with shoulders raised and a grin visible from a distance, even in the gray twilight. He barreled over the snow boulders like a teenager in a terrain park.

"How are you doing? How's your knee?" I asked as he pulled up behind me.

"It's okay," he said. "A little stiff. Hey, you don't have any KT tape on you, do you?"

I shook my head. "I have some Leuko tape that I use for blisters. Might work. Do you want some?"

"I'll wait until we get to the cabin. We're almost there."

I shook my head. "It's twelve miles away. Could be three, four more hours if these bumps continue."

"No," Mike said with over-exaggerated indignation. "The lady said it was sixteen miles from Ophir. That's what Phil told her."

"You believed her? We've already gone sixteen miles since Ophir. It's twelve more. Trust me. I wish it were anything else."

Mike considered this. "I'm not even sure I can make it tonight," I continued. "I'm exhausted. I may need to camp before Carlson Crossing. You go. You're faster than me."

"We'll make it. We'll make it together!" Mike yelled, his exuberance returning.

Mike launched ahead and I shadowed closely behind, attempting to mimic his maneuvers because he seemed more technically skilled than me. His overstuffed seat post bag swayed in a humorous fashion, and I lost concentration and toppled over onto an exposed patch of tussocks. He didn't notice and pulled away. I thought he was gone, but five minutes later, I found him leaning against his bike next to a stream bank, waiting for me.

"How far do you think we've gone?" he asked.

I looked at my GPS. "Three quarters of a mile."

"No. Is that all?"

"Sadly."

When we rode together on the first day of the race, Mike and I discussed some of the races I've run. After I vehemently defended sled-dragging, he assumed I was primarily a runner who only occasionally rode bikes. As we resumed bopping along the bumpy trail, he asked, "How fast do you think you could run this stuff?"

"Probably same speed, four or five miles per hour," I said. "But not with a sled. With a sled, I'd be ridiculously slow. And even more grumpy."

"I bet we can do ten-minute miles," he said, turning the comparison back to running vernacular. "Two more hours."

The pedaling effort was already more strenuous than any ten-minute mile I had ever run. Enduring twelve miles at that pace would be like running a half marathon up a steep and rocky mountain, with a heavy pack. Mike surged ahead and I summoned all of my reserves to keep up.

"I might need to let you go ahead," I gasped. "I'm having trouble breathing."

He slowed again. We resumed the fifteen-minute-miles as I concentrated on taking deep breaths through a face mask that was soaked with respiration. After a few more trundling miles, I wasn't entirely sure his slow speeds were for my benefit. His body language was decidedly more subdued. Conversation ceased. Mike stopped in the middle of the trail to shovel food in his mouth, so I did the same. He handed me a log-sized frozen sausage stick from which I gnawed little chunks, and I shared handfuls of M&Ms. Mike and I could make a good team, I thought, like the odd couple — Mike being the eternally optimistic, goofy young guy, and me being the pessimistic, realist old guy.

Nearly two hours later, after covering a blistering six miles, I announced we were halfway there. Mike was incredulous.

"I don't like that GPS," he said.

"I love GPS," I countered. "GPS tells me the truth, and it never lies. I'd probably go crazy if I let myself believe the cabin was sixteen miles from Ophir. By now it's been five hours, so it must be right around the next corner. How do you cope when it's not?"

Mike shrugged. "I'd get there eventually."

The truth can be its own burden, though, when the night stretches out indefinitely and fatigued concentration pulls thoughts into a place where time and space are fluid. After days had passed and GPS still displayed a three-mile gap, I was beginning to wonder if I was losing my mind.

"Maybe there is no end," I whispered into a cloud of my own breath. Mike was a hundred feet ahead, head lowered and shoulders hunched as his bike bucked and swayed through the yawning darkness. "Maybe this is all there is."

This would be a proper purgatory for me — seeking respite that never comes, with a companion in sight but too far away to feel connected, riding a bicycle at my physical limit to achieve walking speeds, in the dark, in the cold, on terrain so technical that I could focus only on pedaling and steering, and couldn't retreat to deeper thoughts or happier memories.

Still, when Mike stopped and pulled out his sausage log and a bag of crushed potato chips, the angst momentarily faded. We'd fill our mouths with salted satisfaction and stare up at waves of green light making their way across an unobstructed sky.

"Maybe this is heaven." I always suspected that if there is an afterlife, the contents of it will reflect life experiences — a sort of ongoing consciousness rather than physical existence. Maybe heaven and hell are not only individual, but one and the same.

It wasn't our turn to slip into eternity yet, although it felt that way by the time the cabin finally appeared around the next corner. It was well beyond two in the morning. The cabin stood on a wind-swept bank at the edge of the Innoko River, flanked by birch trees and barren ground. Mike and I propped our bikes against the porch and robotically launched into a flurry of chores. I hauled a pot and empty dry sack out to the river to skim snow off the ice, then fired up my stove to make drinking water. Mike found a couple of big logs and dragged them to a clearing to split them apart while I stripped to my base layer and hung sweaty jackets and socks on the wall, anticipating the drying warmth of a fire.

With the fire started and our bagged meals rehydrating in hot water, Mike again went outside. He was still absent ten minutes later when I realized the snow sack was empty, and left the cabin to collect more. Out on the river, a hundred yards upstream from where I crouched without a headlamp, I saw Mike. He was standing on the ice wearing only boots and bike shorts, rubbing snow into the bare skin on his scalp and chest. As best as I could tell, he was bathing, which I thought was an impressively brazen act in a place far beyond the sensibilities of civilization ... a place where truly no one cared if we smelled like sweat and sausage log ... a place where taking a shower meant dousing one's naked body in snow when temperatures were below zero. We'd just left McGrath that morning, so I still felt relatively clean, but I could hardly imagine ever feeling so wretched that I would endure the cold to that degree.

I didn't tell Mike I had caught him bathing when he returned to the cabin, smiling and shivering. "There's some hot water," I said, pointing to his Nalgene bottle.

"Oh great, I've been out of water for a while." I also found this statement interesting — he was out of drinking water and no doubt was as hungry and tired as I was, but his first priorities were fire and personal hygiene.

Mike took the water and produced a small bottle of Fireball — cinnamon whiskey. At this point I was incredulous. Did this guy take anything seriously?

"It's great in hot chocolate," he said. "Try it."

"Oh no, no, whiskey is the last thing I need," I said. "I'm about to lose consciousness as it is."

"Just try some," he urged.

I reluctantly poured a few capfuls into my own mug of hot chocolate and took a sip. The cocktail was a taste sensation unlike any I had experienced — a sharp injection of warmth and vitality infused with sweet and spicy richness. "Wow ... that's just ... amazing," I stammered, genuinely floored.

"Told yah," he said. "It's extra weight but worth it."

We finished up our bagged meals and settled in to sleep in the lap of luxury — the musty interior of a log cabin that smelled of pine wood and gasoline, with dust clouds swirling near the windows, capturing the silver moonlight.

✳ ✳ ✳ ✳ ✳

I made the mistake of not setting an alarm, justifying this with the excuse that I needed sleep to recover from our hard ride. Mike, of course, didn't stir all morning. By the time I hobbled outside to pack up my bike, the winter sun was high in the sky. Sam and Katie — the touring couple from Durango — rode up to the cabin just as I was pulling away.

"Did you guys camp last night?" I asked.

Sam nodded. "About ten miles back. We're just thinking about stopping here for lunch."

"Lunch? What time is it?" I asked.

"12:30."

"Oh," I said, feeling deflated. Lazing around past noon was not an ideal approach to any race. "We got in really late last night. I had no idea it was after noon. Oh. Shoot."

"We hoped to make it here last night too, but it was getting too late," Sam said.

"The trail got slow, didn't it? Are you shooting for Innoko tonight?" I asked, referring to the next shelter cabin.

"Yeah. It's probably going to be a late night for us."

"Us too, I suppose, now that it's past noon. It's forty-five miles to Innoko. I'm thinking ten, eleven hours."

"Sounds about right," Sam said. It was gratifying to hear someone else confirm my pessimistic projections. Mike was no doubt snoozing peacefully on his cot, secure in the hope that trail conditions would suddenly transform to smooth, fast ice that we could blast through the Innoko Valley at ten miles per hour.

Mike would have to rejoin reality eventually, and I figured I'd see him by nightfall. The one shred of optimism that I clung to — a hope that the trail would ride better in daylight — was shattered when I crossed the smooth river and returned to the bone-jarring grind. The valley's snowpack had thinned considerably since Ophir, and beside the route there was only a thin layer of sugary snow mottled with bowling-ball-sized tussocks. Tall moguls still rippled across the trail where hard-packed snow had resisted recent thaws. I bobbed along at my predicted four and a half miles per hour, examining the tracks of the cyclists who were now two to three days in front of me. No one had used this trail since, and the cyclists' perfectly preserved tire and boot marks told stories of swerving struggles and hopeful surges.

The area had recently burned, and the charred toothpick forests opened views of domed mountains surrounding the valley. I'd imagined this land as flat, with geography to match its blankness on the map. But the reality was as undulating as the trail, with seemingly endless drainages to climb and descend. At the bottom of every drainage was a creek. Some were wide and frozen solid. Others were narrow and flowing, with unstable ice bridges spanning the frigid water. Others were inundated with slushy overflow, with no guarantees of solid ice underneath. Each crossing spiked my heart rate, and adrenaline carried me up the next hill.

It was still early in the afternoon when I passed a cluster of burlap sacks next to the trail on an open slough — the supplies we had prepared for ourselves, which were air-dropped by the race organizers. It was only about eighty miles from McGrath, and I'd consumed fewer than two of the twelve pounds of food I'd carried from town. Briefly embarrassed by this excessiveness, I still sat down and sorted through my bag, restocking anything I could cram into empty spaces. There was no way to predict the next hundred and twenty miles, and I knew a storm could pin me down for days without warning. This is the burden of the pessimist — I'd rather endure slowness and fatigue than the misery of fretting about what might happen if I didn't have enough food or gear.

Darkness arrived soon afterward — the burden of sleeping in. My necessary focus waned, leading to more crashes. Across burned and treeless hillsides, the Iron Dog trail was often more than a hundred feet wide. It became impossible to find a consistently rideable line. I'd bounce and swerve and plant my front wheel in a hollow, or veer off the trail into unconsolidated snow. Even pushing the bike was an ankle-rolling affair, and frustration bubbled to the surface. I decided I could no longer handle the truth and switched off the screen on my GPS, so there was no way to monitor my slow rate of progress.

Eventually I rounded a corner, and there was the Innoko shelter cabin. The log building was hidden in a tall birch forest that itself was a surprise after so many miles of burned spruce. Sam and Katie were already there, having passed me while I sat next to the drop bags and stuffed my face and bike with candy. They had arrived at the cabin fifteen minutes earlier and were busy collecting branches from the surrounding forest.

"The stove here doesn't really work," I said to Sam. This was information I received from Beat, who spent a night in this cabin the previous year. Saying this made me imagine Beat hovering over this glass-doored stove, back when Innoko was a considerably more sinister place. "Yeah, Beat told me the heat goes up the chimney or elsewhere, and doesn't warm the cabin."

Sam's expression told me he didn't care to hear this truth. "We'll see," he said. Sam had ridden the entire Iditarod Trail before, back in 2000. At the time, Sam was only nineteen years old, fat bikes had not yet hit the market, and only four men had ever completed the trip to Nome on bicycles, eleven years earlier. It was an impressively bold undertaking for a teenager in an era of limited information and technology. I viewed Sam as a pioneer, but he self-depreciatingly wrote off his adventure as the folly of youth. Still, he returned sixteen years later with his girlfriend to rediscover a trail that was both unchanged by progress and deeply affected by climate change.

Sam and Katie had a unique travel style — lightweight for non-racers, although their background was endurance racing and they had finished the Tour Divide on a tandem in 2014. They shared a double sleeping bag that was rated to a paltry ten degrees, with a thin liner sack that they insisted kept them comfortable to forty below, thanks to shared body heat. I was unconvinced, and their insistence on building a twig fire in the nonworking stove didn't lessen my skepticism. They carried low-sugar, organic food that included homemade dried vegetable soup. I wasn't proud of my diet, which consisted mainly of nuts, chocolate, and gummy candy, but I was confused how they derived enough energy from theirs. I was eating as many as six thousand calories a day — not because I found this kind of gluttony fun, but because I felt chilled and faint whenever my blood sugar dipped too low. Foods with low moisture content and high calorie density that were quick to ingest were the only fuel sources that had ever worked for me in winter conditions. But I had to give Sam and Katie credit — they were moving as well as I was.

Mike showed up as the three of us were digging into our dinners. Talking, laughing, and sharing stories carried us late into another already late evening. I was both grateful for and amused by this atmosphere — here we were, in the middle of a combination adventure race and survival situation, in what was absolutely the middle of nowhere, carrying on as though we were on a pleasant camping trip with friends. It certainly wasn't what I expected, and I was sure there were more surprises to come.

Somewhere In Innoko

I managed an earlier escape from the Innoko shelter cabin, which is to say it was half past nine. Sugary snow sparkled in the morning sunlight. It was eight degrees, which felt so warm that I removed my jacket. I'd indulged in three long nights of rest, and despite the hard miles behind me, my body felt strong. Actual protein for breakfast — in the form of freeze-dried eggs — put me on an incredible high. I was unstoppable, mashing pedals and singing along to my iPod with slightly modified lyrics from a song by Ace Reporter, "Into Chicago."

"Carry me into Innoko. Chasing my whiskey with Skittles. Losing it all just a minute from the hotel. I think this biker's been drinking. The heat is on and I'm roasting. Maybe the ice is affecting my head. And I'm alive, but I'm quite surprised! I thought we would die, somewhere in Innoko."

North of Innoko, the landscape became much hillier. Sam warned of this, and I confirmed the topography with my truth-telling GPS. The previous section featured steep but short climbs in and out of drainages. Now we needed to make our way out of the river valley over a series of progressively larger hills, with crests over a thousand feet high. On an eighty-pound fat bike, crawling over a virtual rock garden, just one or two hundred feet of elevation gain becomes Everest.

The forest in these hills had been ravaged by beetle kill, and many of the trees were an electric shade of reddish orange. I found this unsettling but beautiful — a kind of inauspicious cheeriness that reflected my mood. By midday, signs of civilization began to reappear: more rusting barrels, dilapidated cabins, and the three-story remnants of a massive gold dredge on Poorman Creek. This was the ghost town where Tim Hewitt holed up the previous year during the deep snow fiasco. He pushed his bike to the site of an old airstrip and stayed put for nearly two days before he turned around and encountered Beat. As a spectator, I watched his GPS tracker's lack of movement and fretted that Tim had crawled up the hill to die.

Now that I knew the outcome of that story, it was entertaining to stand at the base of that hill and imagine what Tim saw and felt at the time — hoisting his bike over chest-deep drifts, shivering in his thin sleeping bag, waking up to somebody screaming about the cold, only to realize it was his own voice. Poorman is sixty miles from Ruby, a distance that took Tim, Beat, Steve, and Loreen six days to travel last year. I was in disbelief how painless our passage was this year. The only descriptions I'd heard of this region emphasized frigid weather and remoteness, along with a sinister solitude that could drive a weak-willed person mad. This year brought sunshine and warmth, difficult but rideable trail, and enjoyable company. I was even the unlikely early riser in the group. I held warm bare hands to my cold cheeks and wondered if this was even real. There's always some amount of cognitive dissonance when life doesn't mimic our expectations.

According to Sam, the trail joined an old road bed just beyond the ghost town, and I anticipated a return to the smooth surfaces we enjoyed before Ophir. Instead, snowmobile moguls became even more pronounced, the trail launched up a climb to eight-hundred feet (which felt more like eight-thousand), and all of my good will unraveled. This is the adventure life — it wouldn't have the same lasting effect if everything was easy and fun all of the time. I even reminded myself of this as I plodded up the hill, but my sore legs did not want to hear the truth. GPS offered no better promises, as according to it, the intersection with Poorman Road was already behind me.

Still, I was not so jaded that I couldn't concede to beauty as sunset drew long, gold-tinted shadows through the spaces between scrawny spruce trees. Anger melted into awe, and purple twilight softened what had previously been frustrating views of hills rippling beyond the horizon. A steep descent brought me to a concrete bridge, where the Iron Dog moguls faded into a smooth, wide strip of packed snow. It also brought another long climb, but I breathed a sigh of gratitude that for now at least, I could both pedal and look up at the sky.

Nighttime, in turn, brought a strong wind. Gusts tore along the high ridge and sent me scrambling for my sturdier layers before I'd crested the climb. A headwind had been present all day, but wasn't as noticeable while pedaling four miles an hour with my head down beneath warm sunshine. As the trail neared the Yukon River, the wind gained ferocity, and gales occasionally brought me to a standstill. This development was discouraging, as I'd hoped to find a place to bed down for the night. Although I'd harbored ambitious hopes to reach Ruby before daylight, exhaustion was compounding by the mile. Setting up my bivy in this wind was going to be uncomfortable at best. If I stopped for a moment, wind needled through my clothing and rapidly chilled my core. Digging a hollow in the snow and anchoring every errant piece of gear would be an arduous task.

The trail continued to undulate along these true mountains. For hours I labored upward to wind-blasted ridges and coasted down into frigid drainages, where wind-protected canyons held air inversions that lowered the temperature by fifteen degrees. Skeletal birch trees swayed and popped. When the breeze calmed, I could hear wolves howling. My entire lower body became unnervingly weak, as though fatigue would soon consume my legs and leave me crumpled on the trail. I opted to hike the steepening climbs, listening for animal sounds as my core temperature cooled to an uncomfortable degree. Everything was so difficult to balance out here. I didn't want to admit it to myself, when logically my menace was just a typical wind, but I was intensely frightened.

"And why shouldn't I be afraid?" I thought angrily. "I'm just a Mormon girl, alone in the Alaska wilderness with a bicycle."

Often when I am struggling, I revert to my cultural background as a kind of excuse, because I was raised in a culture that praised submissiveness and taught girls to rely on the men in their lives to do the heavy lifting. That's an oversimplified description, of course, and Mormons also promote work ethic and pioneering spirit in both men and women. Still, when I was a devout child, adventure was not on my radar. I assumed I would toe an entrenched line of marriage, homemaking, and children, finding meaning in quiet communions with God. As I grew into a teenager, God only became more distant. Time on my knees brought more silence, and the violence of the world was substantially louder. By age fifteen I'd neared a fever pitch of confusion, ready to lash out in the ways teenagers often do.

It took my devout Mormon father — unintentionally, and perhaps ironically — to show me the path out of spiritual confusion and worldly despair.

This happened a few weeks before I turned sixteen. I remember the date. It was August 2, 1995, a sweltering summer day. My dad invited me to join him on a climb up Mount Timpanogos, a prominent peak above the Utah Valley. The trip required eighteen miles of difficult hiking with more than four-thousand feet of elevation gain, topping out above eleven-thousand feet elevation. I wasn't an athletic child and my hiking resume was thin, but I loved my father and was eager to do something that might make him proud.

My heels bled in my brand-new hiking boots and my legs hurt in a way that I can still recall, to this day, as an exquisite pain. But when I stood on a chunk of granite at the top of Timpanogos, looking out over the grid of the city far below, eyes wide and jaw unclasped at the expanse of mountains beyond, everything changed. It was then that I first understood there was so much beauty in the world — more than I could ever see. There was so much truth — more than I could ever know. But I could continue to seek both — not in the dark corners of my bedroom or musty pews of my church, but out in the limitless world.

Twenty-one years later, this journey brought me to a landscape that resembled the alpine valleys beneath Mount Timpanogos. Birch and black spruce bear strong resemblance to aspen and subalpine fir. Snow-covered meadows glowed in the moonlight, not unlike the granite cirques of Utah's Wasatch Mountains. Steep slopes obstructed the sky, and I had only my truth-telling GPS to remind me that these peaks were eleven-hundred feet, not eleven-thousand. When fear started to take over, I looked to these memories — places of similar beauty where I found peace.

"The world isn't against you," I whispered.

Wind pummeled my masked face as I plodded up another nameless Alaska mountain, reaching gale force on the bald ridge. Fatigue had wrapped itself around me like a blanket, so tight that I felt smothered and helpless to fight it. I scanned the lower slope for any kind of protective nook. The forest was anemic at this modest altitude, and tangles of alder were the best I could find. The trail crested a saddle and plummeted down the other side. Too tired to even process that the climb had ended and it was time to descend, the sudden blast of speed caught me by surprise. Tears streamed down my frozen cheeks as I rocketed downhill.

The descent bottomed out at a large creek, where flowing water roared beneath a thin layer of ice. I'd heard the rapids from a hundred yards away, and worked myself into such a panic over the crossing that I stopped the bike in disbelief when I reached a snow-covered concrete bridge. Did that bridge really exist? Was it really that easy?

Now paused, I realized the wind was absent here. I could still hear gusts whistling above, but this was a narrow canyon with thick tree cover. Elated, I pedaled across the bridge and ascended a small rise. The road bed went around a sharp curve, and there was an old pullout — a perfect clearing, surrounded by a robust forest and protected from the wind.

Adrenaline from the stream crossing had remedied my sleepiness, but I wasn't about to reject what might be the last sheltered spot until Ruby. I rolled out my bivy and sat at the foot, heating water for dinner and hot chocolate. My thermometer registered minus five. Without a wind chill, this was pleasantly comfortable.

Just as I was finishing freeze-dried spaghetti with meat sauce, the sky lit up with waves of green light. I positioned my sleeping bag so I could wrap myself in this cocoon of my own body heat and stare up at the sky. It was cold and indifferent and burning with the beauty that I spent most of my life seeking — twenty-one years of motion to arrive in this place, in this moment.

I'm no longer a religious believer. I consider myself an agnostic, whose only conviction is that humans have only seen and can only understand fragments of the truth. But every so often I revisit the God of my youth, in a quiet prayer, always to say, "Thank you."

✳ ✳ ✳ ✳ ✳

Morning was rose-tinted and cold, so cold — which is always the case when transitioning from a billowing down cocoon to the white, frozen world. I did jumping jacks between frantic motions to pack up my belongings, and took off in a sprint when I finally had everything more or less strapped to the bike. I was grateful for the early climb, but as soon as I generated enough heat to feel lucid, the weight of my fatigue clamped down. Why was I still so tired?

Breakfast on the bike was a difficult affair — steering with a balled-up mitten beneath my numb right hand while scooping trail mix out of a "gas tank" top tube bag with my left hand. My body still wasn't warm enough to stop for long, but I suspected my low energy level was the result of a calorie deficit. Although I needed to consume more than five thousand calories a day, the technical terrain didn't allow me to eat on the bike, I didn't take many breaks, and my six-hundred calorie breakfasts and one-thousand-calorie dinners weren't quite filling in the gaps. The sheer bulk of food still weighing down my frame bag proved I'd been on an unintentional diet. No wonder I was tired and cold.

Three miles past my camp, I approached a cluster of dilapidated cabins. Mike's orange bike was propped against one of the buildings — he must have passed me while I was sleeping. I peeked inside the shack, which had no door. One corner held a few dirty plastic barrels, and the rest of the interior was piled with paper and garbage. A down sleeping bag was spread across the only bare spot on the floor. Mike's nose poked out from a small opening. I didn't intend to wake him, but he spoke without even stirring.

"What time is it?"

"About eight o'clock," I said. "What time did you get here? I never heard you pass, and I was up past midnight."

"Maybe two a.m.," Mike said. "I saw your camp spot. Almost stopped, but I thought I might find a cabin if I kept going."

His shelter wasn't much — particle-board walls and a sagging roof, missing both windows and the door. But it did block the wind.

"It was a nice night," I said. "Did you see the Northern Lights? I must have spent a half hour watching them."

"Mmm hmm," Mike hummed. He seemed to be drifting back to sleep, but then said, "Galena today?"

"I don't know. It's thirty more miles to Ruby, and I think it's going to be hilly the whole way. Then it's fifty more to Galena. That would be a really long day. Too long. I feel awful this morning."

"Mmm hmm," Mike hummed again.

I left Mike to let him snooze until what would almost certainly be an afternoon hour. He'd still probably catch me before Ruby. Mike was strong, but he was clearly on vacation. I envied his happy-go-lucky attitude, but if I slept as much as he did, spring would probably beat me to Nome.

The sun rose in sync with the long climb, pulling back a curtain of forest shadows to reveal a bright, warm day. Only it was still ten degrees, and my body fluctuated between shivering and sweating. I felt dizzy and flush. Something was clearly wrong with my system. Electrolyte imbalance? Potassium? I realize it's not healthy to subsist on nuts and candy, but a body doesn't become malnourished in three days. I tried to shake off this gnawing fatigue by focusing on my immediate surroundings.

Human debris became increasingly more frequent past Mike's cabin. A surprising number of abandoned vehicles sat rusted and half-buried in snow drifts. Although the lightly traveled trail revealed little evidence of a road bed, there were actual mile markers — numbered green signs sticking a few inches out of the snow — that clicked slowly backward. These sprinkles of civilization were oddly fascinating, and I rubber-necked every rusted rim and detached snowmobile windshield that I passed. Each one caused a pang of sadness, and I wondered why I felt so lonely. Only three days had passed since I left McGrath, which is not even close to the longest I've gone without outside human contact. When I was twenty-two years old, I spent nine days backpacking in the Utah desert with only two friends for company. We didn't even follow trails — we wound our way along a shallow river at the bottom of a sheer canyon, where there was no human debris. I recall jumping in surprise when a jet flew overhead on day seven.

Still, there was something about this no-man's-land that felt even more isolating than the desert. During that ninety-mile backpacking trip, I understood that we had sequestered ourselves in a narrow crack in the Earth. Above us on the plateau, cattle were grazing, ranchers were herding their stock, and cars were streaming along a smooth highway. The corridor along the Innoko and Poorman rivers was a hundred and fifty miles long, surrounded by thousands of square miles of nothing. The wind blew incessantly and ten degrees was a hot day. The fact that anyone ventured here at all remained fascinating.

Four miles from Ruby, the satellite phone finally patched through a call from Beat. He was just about to leave McGrath, he said, and was traveling with Peter Ripmaster — the man who fell through the Tatina River ice — and the physician from Utah, Eric Johnson. Beat had the usual foot and leg pain, but he was finally starting to feel strong. It was just like Beat to take three hundred and fifty miles to warm up.

"I'm so tired today," I admitted. "I've been getting a ton of sleep — you'd be ashamed — but it's still catching up to me. I don't know. Maybe it's the cold, or not enough food. Maybe it's just living out here, just keeping myself warm. It's hard."

"It is," Beat agreed. "Get some rest in Ruby. That's a long section you went through, and you still have lots of time."

As much as I anticipated conversations with Beat, I always hung up the phone feeling acutely lonely. These calls were so brief that they left many questions unanswered, which in turn emphasized our absence from each other. I missed Beat, but I didn't feel truly alone until I heard his voice crackling over a connection that was tenuously held together by a distant object hurtling through space. This yearning wasn't unlike the wistful sadness I felt while staring at a piece of trash alongside the trail. I realized the reason this wilderness felt so isolated was because it was littered with remnants of humanity. Relics, like too-short phone calls, are only reminders of companionship, displaced by time and distance. I longed to see Beat again, but Ruby would come first, so I anxiously anticipated that.

Mile-marker three brought a four-hundred foot climb. The effort bolstered my angst, as it took my ragged legs a half hour to make the mile-long ascent. At the crest of the hill I could see Ruby, nestled against a steep river bluff, with homes built most of the way up the hillside. The village wasn't what I imagined — I'd pictured something flat and sprawling, a settlement to match the expansiveness of the Yukon River. Beyond Ruby was a white strip of ice, at least a half-mile wide. On the far side were more domed hills, interrupted by sheer limestone cliffs.

"The mighty Yukon," I breathed out. The statement sent a chill down my back. I did this — I actually pedaled a bike to the Yukon River.

One last frigid descent brought me to the River's Edge Bed and Breakfast, where I'd sent my supply box. The proprietor was a Native woman with a number of children in the house — I counted at least four. She hastily showed me around then apologized when she had to go back to work. This also didn't match my preconception of Ruby, as I imagined a slower pace of life on the Yukon. I was impressed that a woman with multiple children and a day job also ran a B&B.

She asked if I was staying for the night, and looked surprised when I answered yes. I suspected she disapproved of my own relative laziness. It was an embarrassingly early hour to stop for the day in the middle of an adventure race — two in the afternoon — but I made the usual justifications. I'm tired. I'll put in a long day tomorrow. Beat agreed it was a good idea.

The hot shower was sublime, even on wind-burned, chafed skin. My appetite soared. I didn't want to go rifling through a stranger's kitchen, so I gnawed on an astronaut ice cream sandwich from my box, and a bag of beef jerky left over from one of the cyclists who had been through Ruby two days earlier. The jerky tasted particularly amazing, and I wondered if not eating enough protein was partially to blame for my fatigue.

The afternoon dragged on as I fiddled with my gear and grappled with the inevitable onset of town anxiety. Comfort was something I wistfully anticipated, but once removed from the trail, down time proved to be more nerve-wracking than relaxing. Eventually I'd have to return to cold solitude, and this knowledge kept me on edge. I sorted my food, then laundered my clothing and arranged it in piles. My gear looked simultaneously inadequate and burdensome. How would I coax myself back out into the cold, yet again?

Sam and Katie arrived at sunset, and stepping outside to greet them brought a shocking chill. Sam had stories to share about breaking creek ice to collect drinking water and finding their own perfect campsite, but I could only handle the cold for a few minutes. I mumbled an excuse, then rushed back into the heated house and climbed into bed.

Mike arrived about an hour later. Unable to sleep, I ventured back outside to fiddle with my bike bags one more time. The temperature had fallen to five below zero, which burned on my bare hands. It would take a few more minutes before convulsions started, so I worked quickly, reminding myself that an afternoon of acclimating to indoor temperatures — rather than weakness or fear — was to blame for how sinister subzero air suddenly felt. Sam and Katie were still sitting on the porch in their down coats, sipping on tea that they heated on their camp stove.

"Are you guys staying here tonight?" I asked.

"Maybe," Katie said. "We haven't decided yet."

I turned to face their view of the river. There were still wisps of crimson light to the south, and a purple curtain of stars to the north. The river ice reflected moonlight that was still hidden behind towering river bluffs, and silhouettes of cliffs on the other side of the river created a spooky contrast.

"The Yukon River," I said. "Can you believe it?"

"It's beautiful," Katie nodded. "We were just talking about spending the night out on the ice, under the moon."

"Huh," I said. If it was five below on this hillside fifty feet above the river, it was probably fifteen or twenty below down on the ice. "That would be amazing," I agreed. "Tomorrow night, maybe."

The chill cut deep by the time I retreated indoors, and I was shivering profusely when Mike approached to ask when I was leaving in the morning.

"First light," I said. "I set an alarm for six."

"Six? Why not eight?"

"Ha! If you want to leave with me, great. Otherwise I'm sure you'll catch me somewhere on the river tomorrow."

This night, even more so than my nights in Anchorage and McGrath, I wondered where I'd find the courage to leave comfort and safety for the ever-widening jaws of the unknown.

The Mighty Yukon

At first light, I ate breakfast alone. The man who co-owned River's Edge Bed and Breakfast cooked a plate of potatoes and eggs, then sat on a couch while I awkwardly picked at food I was grateful to receive, but had no appetite to ingest. Instead I peppered him with questions about the trail. Were Iron Dog markers still in place? How much of the trail was glare ice? Where was the danger zone where a snowmobiler broke through the ice and drowned a few weeks earlier? Were there new open leads on the river?

It must have been clear that I was nervous about the prospect of traveling on the Yukon River. Even though it was early and we'd just met, the B&B owner was polite and generous with information. He pulled up a map on his phone and described the fifty-mile trail to Galena in such detail that I could imagine the scenery.

There was a thirty-mile detour around open water after the village, but he didn't have first-hand experience to offer further details. I asked him whether he traveled to Galena often.

"About once a month, to see my sister," he said. I imagined what such a trip might be like in the summertime. Folks would load up an aluminum skiff with supplies and steer an outboard motor into the blue current. Along the banks there would be grizzly bears grazing on sedges, moose wading in the shallows, black clouds of mosquitoes, and the sun making its wide arc around the sub-Arctic sky. What a contrast that would be to March, when travelers suited themselves in full-body, insulating armor and drove snowmobiles up a natural highway of ice. Then contrast that to the way most Americans travel to visit their families — inside a climate-controlled vehicle over smooth pavement lined with strip malls and gas stations. As one of those Americans, my adventure of a lifetime was this man's monthly routine.

As anxious as I'd been, the act of coasting down a snow ramp onto hard, blue ice was thrilling. The Yukon River! I thought back to my first glimpse of this mighty river's source. I was pedaling the Klondike Highway over White Pass, which is on the border of southeastern Alaska and northern British Columbia. Below the pass was an overlook, where I stood watching white cataracts course down a narrow ravine. That Yukon River seemed so far away, and so removed from this silent, frozen expanse. It was gratifying to imagine these two places as the same tributary. That somewhere a thousand miles away, water was cascading out of glacier-capped mountains on a journey to this wide channel. Eventually this water would flow a thousand more miles to the sea, where ocean currents would carry it around the globe. How incredible would it be to experience life in a droplet of water, riding the pulse of the world?

For now I was a mere traveler on the river, pedaling downstream in a wash of pink light. The surface had been swept clear of snow, revealing fissures, exposed gravel, and pressure ridges where ice plates fractured and buckled. On smooth surfaces I could pedal twelve miles per hour with ease, but fear of falling onto hard ice or losing the trail held me to a more conservative eight or nine miles per hour. Irregular Iron Dog stakes and faint snowmobile scratches were all I had to distinguish the trail over a mile-wide sheet of ice.

Often I stopped to scrutinize the path ahead, knowing any ventures off the established route could dump me into a human-swallowing hole in the ice. This already happened to a couple of snowmobilers earlier in the year, and they were never found. Although my slow speeds made it easier to spot danger, they also put me at higher risk of breaking through thin ice. Frequently I encountered unnerving disruptions — patches of ice as clear as glass, and others blackened with sand — that were difficult to discern from open water.

It was a beautiful morning, though, with only a light breeze and temperatures around eight below zero — at this point, perfect cycling weather. Two state troopers were traveling on snowmobiles down the river, and stopped to warn me about the detour out of Galena. One brought up the recent death of a snowmobiler from Ruby.

"Yeah, I heard about that."

The trooper appeared surprised when I spoke. My face was fully covered in a fuzzy blue buff and sunglasses, so I guessed that he hadn't expected to hear a woman's voice. It occurred to me that the state troopers were the first non-cyclists I'd encountered on the trail since McGrath.

"Be careful out there," he warned, and reached out to shake my hand. As I pulled my bare right hand out of my pogies, he audibly gasped. "Where are your gloves?"

"Not quite cold enough for gloves," I said. "It's a great day for riding."

Fifty miles passed quickly, and by Galena I felt fully recharged. Once the site of an Athabaskan salmon camp, the local population grew after Galena picked up a Cold War-era military base. Even though the base is now closed, the town remains one of the largest on the Iditarod Trail, with a population of 470. The village was bustling on a Tuesday afternoon; I watched two planes approach and two depart as I pedaled from the far side of the river.

A few months prior to this race, a Galena resident who owned a summer-time bed and breakfast beyond the edge of town caught wind of the event. Captivated by the idea of oddball outsiders pedaling bicycles and dragging sleds to his remote hometown, Larry appointed himself the official Galena liaison, and the most helpful resource on the Yukon River. He sent a brigade of e-mails with hand-drawn maps, descriptions of the post office and two stores in town, opening times, suggestions for resupplies, and directions to a bed and breakfast that his daughter owned, which was closer to the trail. The three-story building was difficult to miss. I promised myself I'd rest for only an hour in Galena, just long enough to sort through my box and eat some lunch. Within five minutes of showing myself into the big blue house on the river bank, a tall white man wearing a baseball cap in the sub-freezing afternoon arrived at the door. He introduced himself as "the e-mail guy, Larry" and asked if I needed anything.

"There's nothing I absolutely need, but I'm curious whether I can buy white gas somewhere in town. Like Coleman fuel," I said. White gas is the fuel most cyclists use in camp stoves to melt snow and cook meals. The fuel is light and efficient but exceedingly difficult to find in rural Alaska.

Larry shook his head, and then his face lit up. "I think I know someone who might have some."

While Larry went on a mission to find elusive white gas, I dug into the stack of post office boxes. Before I even opened mine, I noticed piles of rejected supplies left behind by the riders in front of me. Phil Hoefstetter in particular abandoned a treasure trove — packets of tuna, beef jerky, and dried bacon. Ten days of subsisting on nuts and candy had finally gotten the better of me, and I craved meat protein like it was heroin. The Jill who packed these boxes never thought I'd make it this far. Unappetizing stacks of Snickers bars, sour gummy bears and honey-roasted peanuts – food even Beat had rejected — reflected that skepticism. Now that I was actually going through with the ride to Nome, I would have to forage for edible food. I scavenged all of Phil's protein, some fancy chocolates, more beef jerky from the bottom of the pile, and a nut mix that was somehow better than my nut mix — because it wasn't mine.

Although tuna was more valuable than gold, it was still heavy, so I opened three packets and mixed tuna with instant mashed potatoes for lunch. This was another taste sensation that can't be adequately described. After the overwhelming anxiety of Ruby put me off breakfast, I was ravenous for lunch. The tuna and potato dish had more than fifty grams of protein. Flavored with four-cheese powder, a dash of black pepper, and a king's dose of sodium, this microwaved bowl of mush was the best meal I had eaten, ever. At least in recent memory.

Larry returned within a half hour, as promised, toting a gallon container of Coleman fuel. The can was nearly empty, but held exactly what I needed. I had just ventured outside to pack up my bike — barefoot, sunburned, gloveless and hatless. The afternoon temperature had risen to twenty-three degrees. Larry snapped a photo for the race's Facebook page, then wished me well before I went back inside to put all of my clothes back on and leave a large tip.

The trail veered back onto the river for ten miles before cutting inland on the detour. Knowing there were unbridgeable gaps of open water nearby, I expected the river ice to become more tenuous. Instead, the ice beyond Galena was snow-covered and soft. The morning's effortless ten miles per hour became a strenuous five or six, but I couldn't complain — soft snow was still faster than the tussock minefields of the Interior. The sun slipped beneath wispy clouds, and peach light spread across the horizon. Away from the high bluffs of the river, most of the landscape was a wide-open plain of what were likely marshes during the summer. These flat, white expanses were occasionally interrupted by tiny rises that allowed spruce to grow. The forests were brief and sensory-loaded, with the newly built trail smelling strongly of pine as it wound through a corridor so narrow that my handlebars barely cleared the tree trunks. The marshes, in turn, were long and reflective. Under the violet sky I slipped into subliminal contemplation, until an unexpected tear rolled down my cheek. I was crying to a folk song playing on my iPod, which I didn't even register before strong emotions trickled to the surface:

"I stood above the Rocky Mountains, where Colorado touches New Mexico. And I could see a hundred miles, but I was many thousand miles from home."

Colorado had been on my mind frequently, as Beat and I were preparing to move from California to Boulder the following month. We had purchased a home in the mountains, nestled beneath craggy peaks in a forest of Douglas fir and ponderosa, yet close enough to town that Beat could commute to work by running on trails. It was a big leap away from our life in the Silicon Valley. We were moving from a small apartment in a metropolitan area to a house on a dirt road with snowy winters, property to manage, and wild animals as neighbors. Beat was thrilled to finally have his own space. I was excited as well, but concerned that working from home in the mountains would leave me feeling more isolated. I worried about the altitude's effect on my lungs. Although I never set out to become a Californian, I'd lived there for five years, and developed affection for my surroundings. Change, even positive change, can be difficult. Sometimes I wonder if my dedication to staying in motion is my own way of coping with the inevitability of change.

This year's journey on the Iditarod Trail just happened to fall into the calm before that storm. As soon as we returned from Alaska, Beat and I would pack up our belongings and uproot our lives. That is, if we survived this race. While grappling with the recent health concerns, I harbored strong doubts that I'd live through this. These thoughts were pressing enough that I secretly questioned the point of making plans for Colorado, since I might be dead by April.

Now I was pedaling across expansive marshes where the Koyukuk River touches the mighty Yukon, and subsequent chapters were becoming more real. I was still breathing, and those breaths very well might take me to Nome, and then beyond Nome to the Rocky Mountains. It was a beautiful thought, full of uncertainties. The salmon-hued sunset revealed no promises. I repeated the song again and again, whispering lyrics through a lump in my throat.

"I was many thousand miles from home."

Sleepiness settled in with the rising moon, unraveling my determination to pedal late into the night. A strong breeze had returned, and I knew that as soon as the trail veered back onto the Yukon River, I'd be viciously exposed to the wind for the next sixty miles. Koyukuk was just six miles away. I'd heard stories about unfriendliness in the village and expected it to be shuttered at this hour, but figured I could find shelter in the surrounding forest. The trail dropped onto the Koyukuk River, again swept clear of snow. The ice was the same color as the nighttime sky, and its bottomless appearance was unsettling.

I pedaled timidly as the wind blasted my side with shards of snow. Feathery drifts swirled over the ice. A chill needled into my face mask, so I stopped to adjust it. When I looked up, I saw the silhouetted profile of a mountain so eerily familiar that the chill rippled through my spine, because of course I hadn't been here before. It was a broad peak with sheer cliffs that plummeted directly into the river, rendered by the moonlight in high-contrast silver and black. Was this spooky recognition something from a dream? A dark premonition? And then the memory came to me. It was Steve's photograph. This was the place where he learned his wife had died.

Mystery dissolved into sadness, which bubbled over into more tears. I was ashamed. Similar to my experience at Little Mountain a year earlier, it seemed inappropriate to indulge in such reactive emotions. It wasn't my place to feel so sad. And yet, a large part of the human condition is empathy toward others' experiences. I held my limp hand to my chest and drew a cross over my heart.

"I was many thousand miles from home."

The streets of Koyukuk felt as empty as the mile-wide river stretching beyond the village. Still, I couldn't bring myself to move past the companionship of other people, even if they were strangers, perhaps unwelcoming, and hidden away in their homes. The school was locked, so I pushed my bike into the playground and rolled out my bivy sack on a patch of gravel next to the slide. Electric street lamps illuminated the snow-covered schoolyard, and I felt comforted by the yellow glow.

The temperature was a moderate seven degrees, but I became chilled as I struggled to put on my down coat and pants. The numbness in my right hand was becoming worse, to the point that it was affecting mobility. This sharp reduction in dexterity and strength in my dominant hand was a worrisome injury to incur. Out here, my life might depend on an ability to zip up a coat quickly, start a fire, or fix a broken bicycle chain. Limited use of my hand meant limited trust in my survival skills. My frustration compounded as I struggled to strike a match, and then repeatedly failed to light my stove. I was just lucky it was a forgiving seven degrees, as this kind of delay at forty below could rapidly spiral into danger. Jack London's short story, "To Build a Fire" — in which a series of mishaps causes a man to freeze his hands, leading to his death — came to mind.

Although I managed all the chores of cooking dinner, melting snow, and unrolling my bivy sack, a rigid hand meant everything took twice as long as it should have. After curling up in my sleeping bag, I spent several minutes massaging my hand and wrist. Even warmed up, the fingers refused to clench into a fist.

"We're sure fragile creatures, aren't we?" I thought with disgust. First it was my lungs. Now this. I wondered whether the numbness was caused by vibrations from the handlebars, cold temperatures, or impact from a crash. But it didn't really matter. My hand had undoubtedly gone bad. Now it was just a question of whether I could stay out of "To Build a Fire" scenarios for the rest of the journey to Nome, which was still more than four hundred miles away.

✳ ✳ ✳ ✳ ✳

Dawn's gray shadows cast Koyukuk in a depressing light as I rose to streets still empty at seven in the morning. Many of the homes were windowless, constructed with particle board or logs, with some leaning dramatically over unstable foundations. This is the physical reality of villages where nearly half of the population lives below poverty line, supplies are expensive and difficult to ship, subsistence-based livelihoods have been compromised by decades of cultural suppression, alcohol abuse is rampant, and resources for health and safety are limited. Even before factoring in climate change, challenging weather, and winter darkness, life is hard in rural Alaska. Suicide and domestic violence rates are extremely high, and populations are declining as young people take any opportunity to leave.

I can't pretend to understand what life is like in rural Alaska, but I do wonder what will happen to these communities in the next fifty years. I can only imagine extremes — abandonment after the economics become completely unsustainable, or an onslaught of development after climate change creates a more desirable environment for outsiders. Even if a happier scenario can be realized, dramatic change is inevitable. I felt grateful for this opportunity to experience the Iditarod Trail at what may just be the end of an era.

As I wheeled my bike past rusted goal posts in a snow-covered soccer field, a young man approached from the street. He appeared intoxicated, but in a subdued way. His gaze was piercing and vacant at the same time, and he regarded me — an unaccompanied white woman with a bicycle — with no hint of surprise.

"Are you looking for wash-ateria?" he asked.

"No, I'm just passing through," I said. I didn't want to admit I camped in the schoolyard overnight, although he appeared to be wandering aimlessly and likely already noticed my bike propped against the swing set.

"It opens at eight. You can wash something."

"Thanks," I said. "But I'm good. I'm going to Nulato. Do you know how far away it is?"

He looked thoughtful. "No. Hey, what's your name?"

I told him.

"Are you on Facebook?"

I laughed. This guy was clearly drunk at seven in the morning, but he wasn't threatening and he was friendly enough. "Yes. You?"

He grinned. I noticed he was missing a few teeth, even though he looked to be in his early twenties. "Yeah."

"Well, look me up if you get a chance," I said.

"Okay!" he said excitedly, and took off at a full run up the street. I didn't get his name and felt disappointed that he surely wouldn't remember our conversation. I would have liked having a Facebook friend in Koyukuk.

Back on the Yukon River, the temperature was a brisk eight below zero, with a quartering wind nipping at my nose. During mornings after a night outside, I had a more difficult time recovering. My arms and legs were stiff, and sleepiness cut so deep that for an hour my vision was blurry. While I relished the limitless independence I felt every time I awoke to ice and snow — still alive — the energy expenditure required to survive a subzero campout seemed to take a toll. Although I was technically resting while I set up camp, cooked, slept, and packed up in the morning, my body still had to work incredibly hard to produce the heat that filled my insulated clothing and sleeping bag. The urgency of mornings highlighted just how much energy I was expending all of the time, and this same urgency limited the number of calories I ate as I hurried through my chores. After ten days on the trail, the appreciating energy deficit was becoming apparent around my hips and thighs, where both body fat and muscle protein were being rapidly consumed.

Running a calorie and protein deficit while riding a bike all day in freezing weather generates incredible fatigue. It's difficult to quantify, because after ten days my body was so entrenched in survival mode that it was tapping into veins of energy that haven't been used by a majority of humans since the Bronze Age. Every muscle fiber was engaged, in ways I wouldn't have even noticed were it not for the soreness emanating from inexplicable places, such as my ribs and forearms. Energy is extracted from every available cell because the body has no choice — a halt in heat production would mean death.

My body was still operating well, and yet my mind was unbelievably tired. With shoulders slumped and head lowered, I blinked through frosted eyelashes, straining and failing to sharpen the focus of blurred river bluffs and washed-out marks on the trail.

The Iditarod didn't offer a moment of respite. Back on the river, recent winds had buried the trail in several inches of unconsolidated snow. "Sugar," as this wind-drifted snow is often called, is composed of polished, round crystals that won't adhere to anything else. Increased village traffic only worsened the sand-like surface as snowmobile tracks stirred up the drifts. Uneven mounds made it difficult to steer, requiring extra focus that I didn't have.

Despite this strenuous grind, I made consistent progress to Nulato, covering eighteen miles in three and a half hours. The warming temperatures and hard work drained the last of my drinking water, so I hiked into the village to refill my bladder. As the only public building in a town of three-hundred, the school was surprisingly large — nearly the size of the building where I attended grade school in suburban Salt Lake City, which had more than three-hundred students enrolled. This would be an ongoing theme in villages along the Iditarod Trail

— large, modern schools appeared vastly out of place amid rustic cabins and modular homes.

It was recess time, and dozens of students were playing basketball in the gym. A petite Native woman intercepted me at the front door with an enthusiastic greeting. She appeared to be in her late fifties and introduced herself as "Girlie." I asked her if I could refill my water bladder.

"Oh, I don't know, I don't know," she said, sounding flustered. "Let me check. How much do you need?"

"Only three liters," I said. "It doesn't have to be special water. I can just fill up in a sink in the bathroom." All of these schools had indoor plumbing, which also amazed me, because running water was a luxury in rural Alaska.

"Let me check," Girlie said, and rushed away. I waited and fidgeted with my backpack as children swarmed past, surprisingly uninterested in me. Five minutes later, Girlie returned and informed me the employees in the kitchen said no, but there was a laundry room behind the school. I practically had to run to keep up as she led me through a maze of hallways and outside to another building. This all seemed like a big production for a small amount of water, and I wondered if I should have just stopped on the river to melt snow.

At the laundry room sink, Girlie peppered me with questions. Where was I from? What were the schools like in California? Was I alone? Was I scared? Where was my gun?

"I don't have a gun."

"No gun?" Girlie yelled. "How can you travel without a gun? What will you do about wolves?"

"Actually a guy near Fairbanks once told me about this trick where you grab a willow branch and whip the wolf on the snout to scare it away," I said. The man who told me about that ancient technique was also incredulous that I didn't have a gun. Gun possession is often the first thing local people inquire about in rural Alaska, and their response nearly always contains references to wolves. Although I am afraid of wolves, I wonder how this fear came to be so prevalent. Attacks on humans are exceedingly rare — there have been only a handful of documented cases in a hundred years. Drunken snowmobilers, moose, and even stray village dogs are a far bigger threat. There must be a reason rural Alaskans are so specifically leery of wolves. I suspect this reason has the same primal roots as survival mode.

Before I left, Girlie urged me to meet the principal, who was a young white man with a broad smile. I waited impatiently in his office while he continued an extended phone call. This seemed like a large waste of time, and I regretted stopping in the village. At the same time — how many chances would I have to visit Nulato? I glanced out the small window and watched two children playing a game of tag while driving four-wheelers along a snow-covered street. One looked too young to even be enrolled in school — no more than four years old, driving a vehicle. I smiled. Remove the snow and cabins and frozen Yukon River, and you'd still never see that in California.

The principal finally ended his call and asked whether I needed anything. I asked if he could call ahead to the school in the next village — Kaltag — to let them know I was coming.

"It's thirty-nine miles. Think you'll make it?" he asked.

"I'm doing about six miles an hour right now. Might drop to five. Eight hours?"

He frowned. "Eight hours? That's a little late."

"Well if the school's closed I'll be okay. I camped out last night."

"All by yourself?" Girlie interjected from the hallway.

"Yes, all by myself. It's really okay."

By the time I left Nulato the sun was high and hot over the Yukon River, although my thermometer registered thirteen degrees. A mile and a half away, the village was still in sight, but I was already exhausted and took a break to call Beat on the satellite phone. He was making his way along the bumpy trail north of Ophir, traveling alone but near Pete and Eric, who took shorter sleeps but longer breaks during the day. Even so, he often only rested four hours a night. The trail wasn't as deserted as it was when I traveled through Poorman. The first mushers of the Iditarod Dog Sled Race had already caught him.

"Aliy Zirkle asked 'do you like bacon?' and then handed me a bag of bacon," he laughed, referring to the woman musher who was leading the race at the time. "It was cooked and everything. Delicious." He asked how I was doing.

"I'm so tired. I don't get it," I said. "Trail's been mostly rideable, and I've been eating lots and sleeping full nights. I don't even understand how you keep going on so little sleep. If it's so hard to ride fifty or sixty miles a day — walking must be impossible."

Beat said he thought conditions were good and wished he was moving faster. He regretted that he wasn't in better shape. After the winter's bicycle training and two-month-long battle with pneumonia, Beat was effectively competing in a thousand-mile foot race off the couch.

"You're one of the few people strong enough to do that," I offered as encouragement.

"Dumb enough to do that," he corrected me.

Our call ended and the afternoon wore on. I had jelly legs and ragged breathing, and swore loudly when my strenuous pace fell below five miles per hour. The Yukon River splintered into braids, and the trail followed narrowing channels flanked by golden willows. Just when I began to fret that I was nearing a dead end, the willows parted to reveal the mile-wide main river channel. A village stretched along the far bank, with distant windows reflecting the last glimmers of orange sunlight. I'd arrived two hours earlier than I expected, somehow no more exhausted than I was in the morning.

The Kaltag school principal was a heavyset white man named Doug. He enthusiastically guided me on a tour of every room in the school before offering to put me up in a vacant apartment in the teachers' quarters. This apartment was the height of luxury, with my own bed, electric stove, shower, washing machine, and dryer. I was beginning to feel guilty about these unexpected indulgences on what was supposed to be a soul-rending wilderness adventure. Still, no amount of competitive spirit could inspire my wobbly legs to venture farther into the night.

"The Yukon was almost a breeze," I tapped into my phone as I settled into the open sleeping bag I'd spread out on a bare mattress. "Will the coast grant me the same kindness? Seems unlikely."

My Best Day On A Bike, Ever

The Iditarod Trail connects the Yukon River to the Norton Sound via an eighty-mile overland traverse known as the Kaltag Portage. The geography here resembles a crinkled piece of paper, with small mountains rippling across every horizon. Travelers follow the path of least resistance along the Kaltag River, where the trail wends in and out of steep embankments on a gradual rise to a pass. Beat told me the Kaltag Portage was one of his favorite segments of the Iditarod Trail — high tundra where everything is sparse, except silence.

I rolled away from Kaltag at first light, when the sky was still a gray pall. I struggled to engage even my lowest gears as I pedaled through a suffocatingly thick forest. My breathing was disproportionately labored for this meager effort.

"It's just a morning funk," I assured myself, ignoring the similarities to the early stages of every other physical shutdown I'd experienced in the past year.

Despite the respiratory angst, I felt a thrilling buzz of anticipation. This electric sensation hearkened back to Friday night adventures as a teenager, riding shotgun along State Street and stretching my arm out the open window, as far as I could reach into the summer night. It was the feeling that anything and everything could happen, and not even the stars could predict what life-altering experiences my friends and I would forge before the neon-lit darkness faded to dawn.

My life had changed a fair amount since my greatest adventures encompassed dragging the main strip of downtown Salt Lake City in a Chevy Cavalier, but this adolescent zeal returned each time I ventured beyond the edge of my known universe. I believe outdoor adventures are a fountain of youth for many reasons, but the most prevalent is their preservation of childlike joy.

I'd ventured far beyond my pessimistic expectations, and every bend in the trail was a new triumph. The Kaltag River was laced with open leads that burbled menacingly, but every crossing was spanned by an ice bridge. After pedaling across four of these bridges without incident, I felt invincible. The trail climbed to the cusp of tree line, and the thick forest gave way to spindly black spruce, which gave way to bare, rolling hills.

Each crest brought a steep descent, which I hadn't encountered in days. Now that my numb right hand was almost rigid, I no longer had the dexterity to steer or the strength to press the rear brake lever. As a result, my descending skills were severely compromised. I clasped the front brake and held on for my life as the rear wheel fishtailed dramatically, stirring up clouds of snow. I managed three lucky drops, but on the fourth hill, I lost control at twenty miles per hour. The front wheel plunged into a snow bank, flipping my body over the handlebars and tossing me into a hollow more than six feet off the trail. I was buried face-down in a drift, thrashing violently amid an exhilarating rush of adrenaline. After freeing myself and crawling back to the trail, I shook like a wet dog. My coat, hat, and boots were packed with snow, and the explosion of powder evoked a maniacal laugh. Nothing could touch me! I was unstoppable!

At noon I ate the last of the protein snacks I'd scavenged in Galena. I managed to cover twenty-two mostly uphill miles in four and a half hours, so traveling sixty more to the village of Unalakleet seemed like a feasible goal for the day. It felt unreal — the possibility that later that evening I'd return to the village where I started my ill-fated bike tour a year earlier, and left vowing never to return. Of course, I'd have to put in a hard effort if I wanted to reach Peace on Earth Pizza at a reasonable hour. The carrot of a hot pizza — and even more enticing, fresh salad and fruit juice — pulled me forward. I concentrated on rhythmic breathing and visualized a cartoon-like depiction of proteins replenishing my depleted muscles. This is another benefit of a childlike mind — the uninhibited hope that imagining something will make it true.

In the golden light of mid-afternoon, I descended through a charred forest toward a pyramid-shaped peak known as Old Woman Mountain. Iditarod legend tells the story of an old woman who ascended this mountain against the wishes of village elders, who believed such an arduous task was too dangerous for a woman. Because of her defiance, she was swept away in an avalanche, never to be found. Now her spirit haunts this desolate valley, cursing travelers so they too can never leave.

Iditarod mushers tell of sudden bouts of crushing fatigue and inexplicable urges to slow down or rest when passing beneath the Old Woman's mountain. Legend holds that the ghost also has the power to generate terrible storms. A shelter cabin was built here to protect travelers from weather that reportedly is among the worst in Alaska. According to musher superstition, if an offering is left at the cabin for the Old Woman, she will spare the traveler. Otherwise, she will curse them with bad luck until Nome. Women are said to be especially susceptible to her curse, so I came prepared with an extra Snickers bar to sacrifice.

After several decades, the Old Woman cabin had fallen into disrepair, to the point where it could provide neither shelter nor respite for any traveler. The roof was collapsing, plywood walls were punched full of holes, and the door was missing. The interior was filled with garbage — empty food containers, rusted gasoline canisters, and snowmobile parts. As I approached the cabin with my chocolate offering in my hand, I was loathe to add to the garbage pile.

"Let her haunt me," I thought, placing the candy bar back in my top tube bag. "She can't slow me down."

A few miles down the trail was a new Bureau of Land Management shelter cabin that also bore the Old Woman's name. Although superstition wouldn't allow me to believe that an ancient ghost would just pick up and move to a nicer location, I pondered leaving my Snickers bar there to ensure a smooth trip into Unalakleet. Two men on snowmobiles were just pulling up when I arrived. One introduced himself as Kevin Keeler, a BLM employee whose Facebook page I followed for the latest trail updates. The other was a Native man from Unalakleet who was joining Kevin for a few days of work on the Iditarod Trail. As I paused to talk with them, I mindlessly gnawed on the frozen candy bar I'd intended to leave inside the cabin. This was only my second encounter with non-cycling humans on the trail — my first being the state troopers on the Yukon — and I enjoyed conversing with them. Kevin was particularly interested in my raggedy clothing system. The layers on my legs looked like a homeless person had cobbled together scraps of fabric from a dumpster.

"These aren't pants, they're actually primaloft shorts and homemade overboots," I explained. "I use these detachable knee warmers because my knees are always cold, but I open the zips on my shorts because my thighs are always warm. I have to wear a hood over my balaclava to keep my ears and face warm in the wind, but open up my jacket to vent the heat from my core. Sometimes my butt is cold but my back is scalding. I'm always running both hot and cold somewhere."

"That makes sense," said Kevin, who was thickly bundled up in a one-piece snowmobile suit and full-face helmet. Although driving a snowmobile is far from a sedentary activity, snowmobilers aren't as prone to sweating and can afford to wear heavy insulation. I envied them for this. Human technology allows us to wander through the harshest climates on Earth, but biologically we're built for life on the savanna. Our bodies' ultra-sensitive cooling system remains active even when our survival depends on staying warm and dry. While engaged in strenuous exercise, I needed to somehow vent moisture and retain heat at the same time — an impossible task because it defies the laws of physics. Since there's no way to strike a balance, I was forced to reach compromises. Those compromises took me from overheated to shivering in the ten minutes I spent resting at the new Old Woman cabin.

"Sorry to run, but I'm getting really cold just standing here," I said. "I should go."

Kevin told me Unalakleet was thirty-seven miles away. I looked at my watch — 4:30 p.m.

"I wanted to hit the pizza place by nine," I announced. "I'm going to have to book it."

I bid them goodbye and continued pedaling down the winding trail along Old Woman Creek, with the menacing north face of Old Woman Mountain directly overhead.

"Those avalanche gullies look like they're right on top of me," I thought. Steady wind emitted a high-pitched hum — eerily similar to a siren. I regretted eating the Snickers bar that should have remained in the derelict cabin. But the infusion of sugar and the conversation with real, living people gave me a needed boost. Spinning the pedals faster, I imagined a specter in a tattered caribou-skin robe, floating over my head. My childlike state of mind gave weight to this fantasy, until I was looking over my shoulder every time a gust of wind screeched through the trees.

"Old Woman, go away, go away, go away," I chanted.

The screeching intensified as the valley opened up and the forest again diminished. With no trees to block the wind, whistling gusts slammed into my back and pushed me down the trail. At thirteen or fourteen miles per hour, the landscape suddenly went silent. It's always a little unsettling to hit wind speeds on a bicycle — sounds are muted and the air becomes calm. It feels as though time has stopped. You can see that you're still moving forward, but inside this invisible bubble, everything is eerily still. It's an otherworldly state that can mean only one thing: an incredible tailwind. As it turned out, the Old Woman was trying to push me away.

I pedaled as hard as I was physically able, straining to remain inside this wind-speed bubble. As the valley opened up, snowpack diminished until the ground was a patchwork of brown tussocks and sugary clumps of snow. Wooden tripods marked the trail, which was barely discernible from the uneven landscape, yet felt smooth underneath my tires. Rounded mountains towered over the southern horizon, cast in gold and silver light in the late afternoon. To the north was a thin strip of spruce trees snaking down the valley — the corridor of the Unalakleet River. Exhilaration surged through my veins, and I pedaled until my legs and lungs were searing with hot blood and cold air. I didn't fret because I truly was unstoppable. The Old Woman was on my side.

Progress came to a screeching halt when I dropped onto the river and approached a sheer rise on the other side. The river bank was only five feet high, but so steep that it might as well have been a wall. My numb right hand no longer contributed to pushing efforts, and all seventy-something pounds of the bike pressed against my chest. As I struggled to shove it forward, I heard a loud "Wooooo" from behind.

"I wondered when you'd catch up to me," I said without glancing backward. My poorly anchored left foot inched down as I spoke. "You picked a bad time. This is going to take all night."

Without a word Mike pressed both hands against my butt and shoved, and I was so startled that I lunged toward the lip of the river bank. I might have taken offense, but it was clearly the most logical thing for him to do in that moment.

"Uh, thanks," I said. "These steep banks always get me. If I ever do this race again, I'm going to make sure I get a whole lot stronger." This was a lie on multiple levels.

"No problem," Mike said. "How far do you think it is until Unalakleet?"

"Probably about twenty miles."

"So two hours?"

"Maybe for you," I said. "The tailwind is dying, and so am I. The sun starts to set and suddenly everything shuts down."

"I love riding in the evening," Mike said. "I finally feel awake."

"I don't know about you, but pedaling all day makes me kind of tired," I said. "Did you make it to Kaltag last night?"

"Yeah. I got in around midnight. I followed bike tracks to that apartment and knocked on the door, but no one answered. I looked through all the windows, but all I saw was this big dude in his underwear, and decided to get out of there. Luckily Doug got up and let me in the school."

"Oh, I'm sorry," I said. "I did not hear you at all."

Mike shrugged. "It all worked out. I checked out the place in the morning. Looked nice in there."

I blushed. "It was pretty decked out. Too bad you didn't get there earlier. I went to sleep around ten thirty."

We remounted the bikes and started pedaling. "You go ahead," I said. "I started before eight and I'm guessing you left around noon … so yeah, tell the pizza guys I'll be there in an hour."

He passed with a devilish grin on his face. "Race you?"

Mike was strong and highly food-motivated. I doubted I could hold his wheel for a minute, but sprinted toward him anyway. Beside the trail, wind had carved intricate designs in the snow that reminded me of a plaster mosaic. The sun lingered just over the horizon, casting a metallic glow across the valley. A long shadow stretched from Mike's silhouette, until it looked like I was chasing a phantom. The Old Woman's wind had become a gentle breeze, caressing a patch of skin on the back of my neck. Mike and I raced as though Unalakleet were the end of the trail. We strained as though pizza was the ultimate reward. And we smiled as though the coast — the brutally exposed sea ice, the North Wind, and all of the hardest parts of the Iditarod Trail — was behind us, not ahead. Fatigue was consumed by fire, until everything about this evening was intoxicatingly perfect. I decided this was my best-ever day on a bike. I say that frequently, but this was truly it.

Mike still beat me to Unalakleet by more than twenty minutes. I lost ground after the trail meandered onto purple river ice, where I pedaled delicately and watched a salmon-colored sunset fill the entire sky. Three miles from Unalakleet, I descended a final hill and saw a twinkling strip of lights strung along the black, open ocean. "The Coast," I breathed out. I'd returned.

With nearly seven hundred residents, Unalakleet is not only large enough for a real airport, but also several restaurants. Peace on Earth Pizza had taken to supporting the Iditarod races by offering floor space and pizzas any time of the day or night. Fresh ingredients are expensive out here. Large pizzas cost forty dollars for the works, but are worth every penny.

Thanks to Mike's and my impromptu race, we both arrived during proper business hours and put in an order for a large vegetarian, two full-plate salads, and Odwalla smoothies. I took the rare Wi-Fi opportunity to pull out my phone and check e-mails, making it through two before I forgot how to read and mindlessly clicked on bookmarks. I announced to Mike that I was checking the weather.

"Friday in Unalakleet," I read out loud. "Highs around five above. Northwest wind twenty to thirty miles per hour. Shaktoolik. Highs zero to five above. North wind thirty miles per hour."

I looked up and let my jaw quiver for a few seconds.

"So that's good?" Mike interjected.

"That's bad!" I yelled. "I saw a better forecast in Unalakleet last year — remember I told you about the short trip where I almost got mowed off the sea ice? If they say it's blowing thirty in town, it's gusting to fifty on the ice. And a northwest wind is going to be right in our face all through the Blueberry Hills."

"After the last few days, I'm getting pretty used to headwind," Mike said.

"Those were like ten miles an hour, gentle breezes," I said. "This is like … we're going to die."

"Ah, it will be fine," Mike said. "Don't be such a pessimist."

"It's best to be a pessimist," I said. "I'm either right, or I'm pleasantly surprised."

We polished off our pizza while continuing to surf the Internet on our phones. I don't recall reading anything or enjoying a single bite of the formerly anticipated pizza and salad. All I remember is the leaden taste of doom.

✳ ✳ ✳ ✳ ✳

Mike and I set up nests with cushions from the old church pews in the back corner of the restaurant. Before bed, Mike prodded me to consider pedaling all of the ninety miles to Koyuk in one day. He thought this goal was doable, based solely on our flawless eighty-mile ride from Kaltag. He even set an early alarm, despite my insistence that his target was impossible. I reiterated my view that the Blueberry Hills were "real hills," that the North Wind was "real wind," and riding the sea ice at night was a death wish. I planned to sleep in and eat a proper breakfast, aiming only for Shaktoolik. Even then, I didn't expect to arrive until late.

"It took me four days to reach Little Mountain cabin last year," I reminded Mike. "That was the hardest sixty miles of my life."

He either didn't believe me or didn't care, exclaiming triumphantly that an early start would ensure success. Still, I wasn't surprised when he was snoozing on the floor as I packed up to leave at nine the following morning.

Dawn was bright and relatively calm, with one of those ten-mile-an-hour baby breezes caressing the jumbled ice along the shoreline. During the 1925 serum run, mushers traveled directly over the ocean between most of the coastal villages, but it's been decades since the Bering Sea froze solid enough to allow this. The modern Iditarod Trail contours steep headlands that parallel the coast, contributing to the bewildering difficulty of this section.

The Blueberry Hills rose abruptly out of the Unalakleet River Valley, forcing me off the bike as I clawed my way up another vertical headwall. Wind and warm temperatures had scoured the hillsides of most of their snow, and the trail was a bumpy four-wheeler track riddled with tussocks and glare ice.

"Beat is not going to like this," I thought, imagining the maddening effort of pulling a sled over bare dirt. Riding a bike was wholly enjoyable, with steep climbs, technical maneuvering, but enough smooth descents to maintain a consistent speed. I still viewed these hills through the lens of the previous year, when the wind was blowing so hard and ground blizzards were so intense that I couldn't see beyond my handlebars. Any trail condition that didn't force me to stumble through knee-deep snow drifts was unbelievably good.

Shortly after maneuvering around a maze of open stream crossings, I was approached by two snowmobiles. The drivers stopped and offered enthusiastic hugs. The Unalakleet local and his friend from Minnesota were avid cyclists, and followed the progress of the Iditarod Trail Invitational online. They noticed my tracker moving through town in the morning and drove out the trail to meet me — my first encounter with race fans.

"How are you feeling?" the local man, Jeremy, asked. "They say you're on track to beat the record!"

"Really?" I frowned. "I don't know about that. Do you know what the record is?"

Jeremy shook his head, and I returned this gesture. Still, a shy smile curled across my face. Was I really on record pace? There was no way to know. I knew the current women's record was held by an Italian cyclist named Ausilia, who rode to Nome in 2013 and 2014. She broke the record in 2014, during a year of nearly perfect trail conditions that allowed most finishers to complete the race in relatively fast times. Before 2014, the men's record was fifteen days, and had stood since the inaugural year of the Iditasport Impossible in 2000. Jeff Oatley dropped the record to ten days and change — a time that previously had been the realm of the fastest dog teams. I vaguely recalled that Ausilia's record was in the sixteen-day range.

Jeremy reminded me that day twelve would begin at two in the afternoon. "You only have two hundred and something miles left," he said.

"I know, but they're all of the hardest miles."

"You can do it," he encouraged.

"I'll try my best."

After the guys turned around, I dropped into the ghost town of Egavik, where an abandoned three-story industrial building loomed over the shoreline. After winding through a maze of red-branched blueberry bushes, the trail launched into a thousand-foot ascent. Halfway through this climb, there was another BLM shelter called the Foothills Cabin. Since I was making such good progress, I decided to take a long lunch break and melt snow for freeze-dried chicken and noodles and coffee. I'd slept in this cabin the previous year, after spending more than nine hours pushing my bike twenty-three miles from Unalakleet. Wind knocked against the walls all night long. I could only collect enough wood for a small fire, so I burrowed deep in my sleeping bag, reading a somber philosophy book by headlamp and feeling exquisitely lonely. My 2015 entry was still scrawled in the logbook in pencil:

"Riding a bike from Unalakleet, heading to Nome. Hard first day, wind and drifted snow. Hoping for better weather into Shak. If you see this Beat, I miss you. See you soon."

The message to Beat — one he never saw — brought a lump to my throat. I turned to a fresh page to update my entry:

"Jill Homer from California, returning with my bike, this time all the way from Knik. North wind kicked my butt last year, only made it as far as Little Mountain shelter. Hope to see Nome this year. To Beat: I love you."

Beyond Foothills Cabin, the trail followed a direct line along a ridge. I pedaled over the bald spine, high above the Pacific. Dark water sparkled beneath the midday sun, and there was a white shelf of ice that almost looked like marine fog. If it weren't for the snow-covered landscape and searingly cold wind blowing in my face, I could almost imagine a round headland beside the California coast. The geography was strikingly similar — just a few thousand miles north.

The ridge abruptly ended a thousand feet above the sea, and the trail plummeted down the slope on a trail that sliced through thick brush. From the crest of this hill, I could look out toward the last vestiges of forest and the desolate, wind-swept peninsula that was home to the village of Shaktoolik. A thin white seawall split two shades of blue. The ocean was a bottomless indigo, and the land was the same color as the sky — indicating an expanse of glare ice.

My right hand was too weak to squeeze the brake lever, but there was no way to manage this descent with the front brake alone. I shoved my left hand into my right pogie and manually curled each numb finger around the lever until it was fully engaged. I would just have to descend with the rear brake locked in place. Gravity pulled me downward in awkward jerks, digging my right heel into the snow and carving as though the rear wheel was mounted to a ski. It was ugly, but got me down safely. Back at sea level, I pedaled past one final cluster of spruce trees. The forest ended, and just like that, a stiff breeze gave way to a howling gale. I had to put a foot down just to prevent myself from blowing over.

"Hello, North Wind," I said as I turned to face the gale. My eyes were full of involuntary tears, which froze the instant they hit my cheeks. "We meet again."

Sideways snow knifed into my face. I quickly turned away and rushed to dig my goggles out of a pannier.

"You should have done this back in the trees," I grumbled as I pulled the goggles over my balaclava and struggled to adjust the strap as my fingers froze.

I expected the wind to worsen after I ventured beyond the relative protection of the Blueberry Hills. But I could not anticipate how quickly a moderate fifteen-mile-per-hour wind could increase to forty miles an hour. It happened in an instant, like flipping a switch.

There were eight more miles to Shaktoolik, traveling due west with a fierce crosswind. The route paralleled the seawall, which was piled with driftwood and blocks of ice the size of small vehicles. Since the coast was impassable, the trail cut along sloughs and swamps just beyond the beach. Wind had polished the surface ice until it was as smooth and slippery as a mirror. Expecting my studded tires to grip into this hard ice was like asking a fork to hold tight to a plate. Since I had almost zero traction, the wind grabbed my bike like a sail and shoved me toward the seawall. Riding south, out to sea, would have been effortless. Riding west was impossible. I couldn't even imagine turning north.

For now, western progress was necessary, so I stepped to the leeward side of my bike and commenced pushing. The purchase of my studded boots wasn't much better than the tires. The bike pressed into my right hip, shoving me sideways. I slipped and stumbled countless times. If I dropped the bike, it skittered along the ice for several seconds before stopping. Loud swearing and occasional crying followed, but my temper tantrums were short-lived, because what choice did I have?

"Eight miles, two miles an hour, that's only four hours," I consoled myself. Cold wind stabbed at my neck and lower back, needling into my skin through microscopic tears in my clothing. Tears froze to my eyelashes, even though they were protected beneath goggles. The ambient temperature was near zero, which would place the windchill around thirty below. With the wind pushing so hard against me, wrangling the bike became a Herculean task on top of the already strenuous effort of walking. Most of my falls happened when my bad hand gave way. Eventually a gust pushed me over, and my body slid over the ice for two terrifying seconds before coming to a stop. This brief loss of control rattled me to the core.

"The wind is really going to push me out to sea," I thought. "They're going to find my body washed up on shore, and wonder why this dumb California tourist went swimming. This is how I die."

But instead of blowing out to sea, I clawed my way back on my feet. A few minutes later, the wind blew me over again. Hours passed. All of the fretting was driving me mad, so my primitive mind again took control of the wheel. The sun sank behind the sea wall, and the sky turned a deep shade of orange. The trail dipped into a gully that trapped wind-driven snow, forcing me to wade through knee-deep drifts.

Along the coast, golden sunlight streamed through holes in derelict log cabins. This was "Old Shaktoolik," a village that stood since 1839 but was abandoned in 1967 when a destructive storm forced residents to move to a more sheltered location. New Shaktoolik was three miles downstream on the Shaktoolik River, which parallels the coast just a few hundred meters from tidewater. "Sheltered" was a relative term out on this wind-swept peninsula that probably held more water than land. After five decades, the abandoned village was little more than rubble. I gazed longingly at the disintegrating buildings, imagining the prospect of shelter.

"Three miles, only ninety more minutes to town!" I said out loud, startled by the hoarseness in my voice. This sounded ridiculous when spoken out loud, but ninety minutes is what it took.

Shaktoolik is derived from a Unaliq word meaning "the place of scattered things." Native peoples have occupied the region for at least six thousand years, and Russians moved in during the 1840s. For nearly that long, white people have been perplexed by Shaktoolik. "The place of scattered things" is still an apt description. The wind blows incessantly here. During the fall, southerly storms slam into the coast, eroding the thin strip of sand on which the village sits. Winter brings the North Wind, and a wooden snow fence on the northern side of the river does little to prevent homes from being buried to their roofs in drifts. Spring arrives late and summer is a deluge of rain and mosquitoes. In 1900, a Nome-bound Gold Rush cyclist called Shaktoolik "the lousiest place you ever saw." More recently, a Fairbanks-based scientist asked a local elder why Shaktoolik had been located where it was, when just eight miles away there were foothills and forest to provide shelter from the wind, firewood, and better access to building materials.

"We like the wind," the elder replied. "It brings us fish, and the animals like to be in the wind. The wind is the Eskimo's friend."

Beneath violet dusk, I finally pulled onto the ice road that cut through New Shaktoolik. I was shivering because my labored but slow pace was no longer producing enough heat to keep me warm. Survival mode prevented me from becoming traumatized so far, but as I neared safety, a quiet panic intensified. I was deeply exhausted after fighting eight miles of crosswind. The next section brought fifty miles of intense headwind, and just the tiny Little Mountain shelter for respite. I still hadn't figured out how to eat or drink properly in this weather. What would happen when my body was too depleted to produce heat, but too far from shelter to stop?

A group of children inundated me outside the village school. Many seemed remarkably under-dressed for the weather. They peppered me with questions about where I was from, and became fixated on the GPS unit mounted to my handlebars, asking if they could touch the screen. They continued to swarm as I pushed my bike inside the building. Stepping through the door was like diving from a hurricane into a warm lagoon. Suddenly everything was bright and different, but still chaotic. The gym was filled with people watching a Friday night basketball game, and more children rushed into the entryway to see this visitor and her strange bike. The crowds were nearly as overwhelming as the wind, so I mumbled something about finding the teacher's lounge and ducked out the door.

Spending a day in a sub-Arctic hurricane is one thing, but re-emerging from shelter — no matter how brief — is violently breathtaking. Ice shards slammed into my face as I stumbled down the alleyway, gasping for air. Just venturing a hundred feet around the school felt as treacherous as winter mountaineering. A group of teenagers passed, wearing only thin hoodies and walking calmly toward the gym. This amazed me. The people of Shaktoolik must be some of the toughest people on Earth.

I found another side door to the teacher's lounge. This was the room where I set up my refugee camp while I waited out the storm that never went away in 2015. I intended to do the same this year. First I removed all of my outer layers — all thickly coated in rime — and draped them across overturned chairs to dry. While heating water in the microwave, I scrolled through weather reports on the public computer. The forecasts had become even more discouraging. This storm was as good as eternal.

I was sitting at a tiny desk, eating still-crunchy noodles out of a bag when a woman entered the room and sat down next to me. She introduced herself as Gloria, the Shaktoolik School custodian. Gloria was a petite Native woman who looked to be in her mid-thirties. Her demeanor was strange — she spoke in terse sentences and her eyes darted back and forth, as though she expected to be ambushed at any moment. We struck up a conversation, and I learned that she'd only recently taken this job after an incident, which she didn't disclose, left her with post-traumatic stress disorder. Before the traumatic incident, she was a health worker. She loved that job, but couldn't do it now. Her husband was the school's maintenance technician, and helped her get work cleaning the building, which she was grateful to have. She had a teenage daughter who wanted to go to California and was "very into makeup and stuff." Gloria herself had never traveled outside Alaska, and had no interest. I asked her how long she'd lived in Shaktoolik.

"Thirty-five years," she said, which I assumed was her age. She spoke of autumn storms that were becoming increasingly more powerful, carrying away chunks of the beach and a few structures in their wake. Like many in rural Alaska, Gloria worried about the future of her village as climate change ravaged their way of life.

"What is Shaktoolik like in the fall?" I asked, imagining dark skies and salt-water hurricanes battering the driftwood sheds that lined the beach.

"Oh it is beautiful," Gloria said. "Very beautiful."

It was clear Gloria genuinely loved her life in this village, even with her traumas and hardships. I admired her simple passions and strong work ethic. In turn, I felt ashamed of my own frivolous pursuits, and for the fear and loathing that I harbored for Shaktoolik.

"It is beautiful here," I agreed.

Hello, North Wind.
We Meet Again.

Somehow the open floor of the Shaktoolik school library felt too exposed, so I set up my nest in cramped space underneath the librarian's desk. As sheltered from the wind as I could possibly be, I tossed fitfully and shivered on top of my sleeping bag. An hour of fretting finally conceded to sleep, and it was right about then that I sensed another presence and startled awake. Mike was standing over me, still wearing his fur-lined hood and sunglasses. It was after midnight.

"Windy out there," he said.

"How was the ride in?" I asked.

"That was tough," he said. "Really tough. I got blown over a few times."

"Just a few?"

"It's nice here," Mike said. "I had a nice chat with Moses, the maintenance guy."

"I didn't meet him," I said. "I met his wife. Talked with her for a while. I've been here since seven. When did you leave Unalakleet?"

Mike shrugged. "Maybe noon. So when are you planning to leave tomorrow?"

"I guess whenever you get up," I answered with a not-subtle groan. "I'll wait for you." I wasn't sure I was ready to leave this indoor sanctuary at all, but I certainly didn't want to leave before sunrise, alone.

"How long until Koyuk do you think?"

"Conservatively, twenty to twenty-five hours nonstop," I said. "The trail is not going to be better than this last section, and the weather will be worse. I don't even want to consider going for it in one day. My plan is to push for Little Mountain tomorrow and assess from there."

Mike look dazed. He'd left Unalakleet twelve hours ago, still believing he'd roll into Koyuk by midnight. Now, he didn't balk at my assessment that the next fifty miles was going to take two full days.

"That sounds like a plan," he said.

I was up by seven in the morning, and stomped around the library loudly enough that Mike stirred as well. The online weather report showed a temperature of eight below zero and north winds steady at thirty-eight miles per hour. The headwind was just as dire as the previous year, and it was even colder. My lower lip quivered. Could I really face this once more? I didn't ride my bike seven hundred and fifty miles across Alaska only to be shut down in Shaktoolik, again. But I didn't want to die.

After checking the race tracker, I discovered Beat was in Ruby. I presumed he'd be at the same bed and breakfast where I stayed, so I looked up the number online, pulled a calling card out of my wallet, and picked up the library phone.

On the other line, Beat sounded sleepy and slightly annoyed. "I was just about to leave," he said. "Peter is going to drop out of the race. He's okay, just done. Eric shouldn't be far behind me."

I pressed Beat for more information about Peter quitting, since it's rare for an Iditarod racer to make it so far and then drop out unless something goes drastically wrong. Beat speculated that Peter struggled after falling in the Tatina River, and finally lost his resolve when he realized that after everything he'd been through, he was still only halfway through the race, five hundred miles from anything else. I considered this for a moment and then launched into my concerns, which boiled down to conviction that the North Wind would certainly kill me. I hinted for Beat's approval to drop out of the race myself.

"Just go to the cabin," Beat said. "Rest up and then decide. You've come a long way. I know the conditions are very dangerous, and you have to be careful. But this is what it comes down to."

"I know," I said. "This is the crux."

Beat gave me tips for facing the North Wind: Put on a down coat every time you stop. Don't expose your skin for more than a few seconds. Your bivy is probably capable of saving your life, but avoid it at all costs.

I'd been naive to believe the Iditarod Trail would let me off so easily. The hand numbness, the battering crashes, the endlessly bumpy trail and fatigue — these were challenges. But I could breathe and I was alive, so it had been all too doable so far. The sea ice was the real test. If I passed, I still might not finish the race. But if I triumphed against my fear of the North Wind, that might be the largest victory of my life — even greater than reaching Nome.

The sky was clear and the wind as fierce as ever by the time Mike and I finally ventured outside. It was ten in the morning, and Shaktoolik's single street was empty of traffic and covered in drifted snow. We took a minute to readjust all of the layers we'd carefully applied — for me, every single piece of clothing I brought with me besides my down pants, down coat, rain shell, and extra under-wear and socks. My goggles were firmly tightened beneath a balaclava and two hoods, but I panicked when a patch of fog appeared inside the lens and loosened them slightly. A piece of windproof fleece draped over my nose and mouth, with a strip of silnylon to capture the moisture from my breath and drain it into an ice goatee below my chin. Mike wore his puffy jacket with the fur-lined hood cinched as tight as possible. Ice clung to strands of fur beneath his chin, which made him look like Bumble the Abominable Snow Monster, with a human nose. I asked him if the hood obstructed his vision.

"It's like this Chewbacca tunnel," he replied.

On our way out of town we encountered Iditarod volunteers who directed us to the trail intersection, which I'd already forgotten after one year. Pedaling over relatively clear glare ice, we paralleled a mostly demolished snow wall until it ended. A wooden tripod marked the passage beyond. It was here that we left the last vestiges of wind blocks and turned due north. The wind's low howls be-came deafening, and air pushed so forcefully against my face mask that I felt like I was being smothered with a wet towel. All around us was an unbroken white expanse, encircled by distant mountains.

Mike offered to lead, and I tucked in behind him. Drafting off another cy-clist in this wind was like hiding behind a telephone pole in a hurricane. In short, why bother? Following a target provided a helpful psychological boost, however. With my head lowered, I admired Mike's big boots as they churned methodically into an invisible wall.

After forty-five minutes my breathing had become shallow, so I announced that I needed to pee. With not even a blade of grass to duck behind, this task was as incommodious as it sounds. I stepped a few feet off the trail into a knee-deep drift, pulled down four layers of pants and underwear as the flash-freezing windchill slammed into my exposed backside, turned to squat with my face to the wind, emptied my bladder as quickly as possible, then turned around again, admiring the impressively long yellow fan in the snow as I yanked up my pants so hastily that I missed a layer or two. I yanked at my tights wedgie as I sprinted back to the trail.

"How far do you think we've gone?" Mike asked as I grunted to lift the enormous bike off the ground. "Four, five miles?"

"Do you really want to know?" I said, and before he could refuse, answered. "Two miles. Not quite."

"Two?" he said, shaking his Chewbacca tunnel in disbelief. While standing still we faced south, where Shaktoolik's single row of buildings lined the horizon. They still looked close enough to hit with a stone.

"It's going to be a long day," I said.

Over soft, ever-shifting trail, Mike and I churned into the wind. Occasionally closing my eyes to "rest" them, I imagined the world's steepest sand dune. We were both laboring at that strenuous limit where most cyclists choose to step off their bikes and start pushing. Still, every time we declared a "walking break," the effort became no easier, and our paces slowed from the two-mile-per-hour range to less than one. My GPS wouldn't even register these speeds. It declared us stopped, and we might as well have been.

Each walking break ended in a snack break. Mike and I would turn our backs to the wind, pull apart face masks and hoods, yank the drinking hoses from nooks deep beneath our coats, and ingest as many calories as we could before the North Wind tore all the heat from our bodies. Full stops were tolerable for three or four minutes at most, so I had to choose which bodily function was most pressing — hunger, thirst, or elimination. After my third pee break, I announced that the task was simply too awful, so I would give up drinking for the remainder of the day. Calorie intake was something I needed to continue, because a bonk could lower my body temperature to dangerous levels. This is what it had come down to. Eating was an excruciating but necessary chore, dehydration was preferable to skin exposure, and stopping was more exhausting than pedaling, which itself was the most exhausting physical effort I'd ever experienced.

"How far have we gone now?" Mike asked after three hours. Behind us, Shaktoolik was still visible on the horizon.

"Six now."

Mike lowered his ruff and looked back toward town. "I hate that GPS."

Still, I felt more relieved with each passing mile. The North Wind was blowing thirty-five miles per hour and the windchill was below minus thirty, but we were managing well. As long as we were moving I felt reasonably well, although tired. My breathing was raspy but controlled. I was thirsty and hungry, but I no longer believed I was going to die. Traveling with Mike helped quiet my doom-fueled imagination and kept me anchored in reality, which was pretty bad, but could be so much worse.

After four hours and eight miles, I caught my first glimpse of the shelter cabin. It was still little more than an abstraction — an orange square straddling a blurry line between white and blue expanses. I knew the shelter was still six miles away, so I said nothing as we descended from a shallow hill at slower than walking speed, then pedaled toward the shore of Reindeer Cove. Wanting to document the momentous occasion of wheels hitting sea ice, I reached into my vest to grab my camera. The pocket was empty. My stomach sank. I hadn't used my camera since my first pee break, when Mike and I also took a few moments to document our ridiculous costumes. When I put the camera away, I must have missed the vest pocket and slipped it down my coat instead. There was no way of knowing where it fell out. It might be three hours back.

"I dropped my camera," I lamented to Mike. "And I have to go back for it. I promise I'll only backtrack two miles at the most. If I don't see it by that point, I'll just have to be sad."

Logging bonus miles out here was an unpleasant idea, but I couldn't give up on my camera without a fight. The device itself wasn't important, but the card containing hundreds of images meant more to me than a finish in this race. Without documentation, all of the beauty would be left to memory, and all of my feelings and observations would have to be pieced together from scratch. Documentation is not just important to me, it's vital. Otherwise life simply slips away, and then what's left? I create narratives to make sense out of the chaos of life. It's a selfish endeavor in a world bombarded with so many photos and recorded words that they're losing all meaning. But this doesn't matter all that much to me, because stories still give my life meaning. I won't apologize, but I admit that this passion becomes problematic when survival depends on forward motion, but I opt to move backward just to preserve stories.

Pedaling south, the North Wind shoved me violently. A thick layer of abrasive snow kept my speed down, and the wind was so powerful that I could scarcely steer straight. But even through shallow, slightly panicked breathing, I could pedal eight or nine miles an hour with ease. At least this confirmed that our extremely slow progress was a direct result of the wind, and not inexplicable inertia. Of course I couldn't enjoy the tailwind, knowing every lost meter would have to be gruelingly regained. But for a few stolen moments, I was free.

After a half mile, I spotted a black speck amid the white expanse. My heart leapt. Not only did I recover my camera, but it was much closer than I expected. I celebrated the small victory and turned to rejoin Mike, who was stumbling drunkenly while pushing his bike through ankle-deep drifts. When I caught up to him, he asked how much farther it was to the cabin.

"About three miles," I said, gesturing toward the orange structure that now appeared prominently on the peninsula.

"Where is it?" he asked.

"Right there, next to the cliff. It's bright orange. See?" I'd been staring at that cabin for more than two hours, becoming increasingly more agitated when it never seemed any closer.

Mike lifted his Chewbacca tunnel and squinted.

"Wow, you really can't see anything, can you?"

"Is it that black thing over there?" Mike pointed at the relatively large landmass to the left of the cabin.

"I think you're looking at Little Mountain."

We reached the shelter just before five in the afternoon — seven hours and fourteen miles after leaving Shaktoolik. Fourteen miles was an unconscionably short day of travel, but neither of us was in the mood for race heroics. Even Mike was showing signs of deep exhaustion, with glazed eyes and slumped shoulders. Both of us staggered slightly as we entered the plywood structure and removed our headgear. This crossing had been easier than the previous year, but not by much. I still couldn't conceptualize thirty-five more miles into this wind. We both agreed we needed to rest and replenish first.

"If the wind dies during the night, we get up and go," I suggested. "Otherwise, first light is our best chance to not get lost and wander out to sea on some random caribou hunter's track."

"Out to sea" was a relative term. The next thirty-some miles stretched over salt water, but this far edge of the Norton Sound was slightly more protected from warm currents and volatile weather than the rest of the Bering Sea. This allowed a comfortably solid layer of ice to freeze and hold tight to the shoreline. Open water was just a few miles west, and it wouldn't take much confusion to veer onto thin ice and disappear forever. The thought of navigating a featureless expanse of ice covered in just enough snow to mask fatal weaknesses, in the dark, was frightening beyond words. I was grateful to avoid the task, for now.

The interior of Little Mountain cabin was significantly cleaner than the previous year, and the stove had been fixed. I put on my down coat and pants, then returned to the gale to gather snow for water. All of the surface snow had solidified, and my aluminum pot couldn't even make a dent in the crust. Instead, I stomped a hole with my boot and hurried to scoop up shards of snow before the wind blew them away. Back inside, Mike and I fired up our stoves and settled in for a much-anticipated meal. As we shoveled hot mush in our mouths, we heard the high-pitched whine of a snowmobile approaching the cabin.

The door swung open but the visitor remained on the porch as frigid wind rushed into the room. He wore a bright red snowmobile suit and a coyote fur headdress that draped down to his butt. He stepped into the cabin but left the door wide open, and removed his goggles and hat to reveal a shock of gray hair wrapped in a bandanna. He introduced himself as Lance, a snowmobile tourist from Minnesota. He started his trip in Fairbanks, and planned to drive north until he reached the Arctic coast. Mike offered Lance some Fireball-infused hot chocolate.

"Wow, you two know how to travel in style!" Lance exclaimed. He told us about his wooden trailer that he built himself. It was heavy, his snowmobile was old, and the bumpy trails were murder on his back. He carried a tent but preferred to curl up in the animal-skin cover on top of his trailer, and loved sleeping outside. He asked how far it was to Koyuk.

"About thirty-five miles," I said. "Is that where you're headed tonight?"

"I'll see how far I get," Lance said. "I may just camp out a few miles from here."

"It's open sea ice like this the whole way," I said. "Are you sure you don't want to stay here?"

"Na," Lance said. "Cabins are too crowded and hot."

Mike explained what he and I were doing and the fun parts of the trail, but admitted that this section was just brutal. I joked about the wind blowing us back to Shaktoolik.

"You want a ride?" Lance asked. "You could throw your bikes in the sled."

I pondered this for a moment — not because I was seriously considering his offer to help us cheat, but because my initial reaction to this suggestion was surprisingly strong repulsion. Even though I still believed that the North Wind could kill me, and even though my heart was filled with dread, the idea of skipping the sea ice felt like a fate worse than failure. I would rather turn around and admit defeat than take a ride with Lance. We all like to believe we'll do the right thing, but when our ethics are tested during times of weakness, it's interesting to gauge how we really feel. I may fail and fail again, but I will never cheat.

"We can't take rides," Mike said. "But thanks for the offer."

Mike and I ventured outside to inspect Lance's artisan trailer and decades-old machine, and waved as he puttered away. Twenty minutes later, I glanced out the doorway, and could still see Lance's speck crawling over the white expanse.

Mike decided to split two large logs that had been discarded outside, then built a small fire in the stove that was still too dilapidated to emit much heat. We hovered next to the open hatch, holding our rime-coated clothing over the flames. I expected these hours of waiting to pass slowly, but in a seeming instant the sun began to set. I watched pink light spread across Little Mountain from the tiny cabin window, then ventured outside once more to collect snow. A gust ripped the hood off my head, and I gasped amid a bombardment of ice pellets. It never stops being shocking, the North Wind. It never stops.

The North Wind knocked loudly against the walls all night long. I tossed and turned, anticipating a lull that never arrived. By first light I had again worked myself up in a lather of doom, and packed up my bike as though I were getting my final affairs in order. Mike's rear tire had gone flat overnight, and he handed me the old tube so I could patch the hole while he installed a new one. There was so much draft inside the cabin that I couldn't detect airflow, and tried spitting on the rubber to look for air bubbles. Instead, every wad of spit froze within seconds. When I handed the tube back to Mike, it was still leaking and coated in a thick layer of frozen saliva.

"Sorry," I apologized sheepishly.

As we applied our final layers of clothing, Mike observed me struggling to pull my goggles on.

"How bad is your hand?" he asked, assuming this was the problem because I'd complained about it frequently.

"It doesn't take much for it to get cold, and once that happens my fingers go rigid and it's more like a stump than a hand. When it's warm, it's painful and tingly. I've never had hand numbness like this. It's scary."

Mike suggested that it was better to have a numb hand than painful knees — his main complaint.

I shrugged. "Maybe. But a bad hand makes me pretty helpless. It wouldn't take much to become stranded. Even a flat tire would be an ordeal … I'm not sure I could even change a tube."

The temperature inside the cabin was three below zero. As we pushed our bikes outside, Mike suggested the wind was blowing fifty miles an hour.

"It's probably more like thirty," I said. Still, this was the light morning breeze. Pulling down my mask to take a drink of water felt like sticking my face into the blades of an industrial air conditioner.

We dropped off the peninsula and surveyed the ice. The Iron Dog stakes had become sparse — most likely blown away by the wind — and I was fearful that we wouldn't locate the trail. Barring this, we'd have to take a compass bearing and cross this volatile body of salt water on an untested line, which was terrifying. Mike was the first to spy an orange stake, and as we approached it, I noticed a blue flag attached to the end. Blue flags were the markers of the Iditarod Sled Dog Race. Ahead, we could see a line of these blue-flagged stakes. It was clear they had just been placed.

"The Iditarod trail breakers," I surmised. "They must have come through last night."

In the sled dog race, trail breakers travel a few hours ahead of the leading mushers, marking the trail as they go. They place extra stakes to warn of hazards, or in areas prone to whiteouts. It's quite luxurious when you think about it, and Mike and I had become lucky benefactors of this service at exactly the right time. Indeed, there were stakes every fifty meters now, lined up along the wind-sculpted snow in a way that reminded me of birthday candles on a frosted sheet cake.

"Geez, why do they need so many stakes?" Mike said. "Do you think they do this for a thousand miles?"

"Probably," I said. "Those mushers sure are spoiled." But I certainly wasn't complaining.

The sea ice was an ocean frozen in motion. Snow dunes were considerably larger on the north side of the peninsula, and the surface crust frequently collapsed under our wheels. The trail broken by Iditarod volunteers a few hours earlier was churned-up sugar snow, and even less rideable than the virgin crust. Negotiating the unpredictable surface in gale-force headwinds required every molecule of mental energy I had left in my reserves. Our steering was too squirrelly to continue the illusion of drafting, and Mike and I sometimes split apart by hundreds of meters as we hunted for the best line through petrified waves.

Similar to the previous day, I feared the chore of peeing more than the dangers of dehydration, and avoided drinking and eating until my vision began to blur. Mike and I regrouped to declare walking breaks, which continued to be slower and more strenuous than pedaling — but they were less mentally taxing. The best comparison I can make to this effort is small-craft seafaring — riding was like paddling a canoe into breaking waves as a strong current pulled us backward. In such volatile conditions it feels more difficult to pilot a craft than just swim, but when we stepped off our bikes, we were even weaker and more vulnerable to being buffeted by the wind.

After several hours of staggering, we stopped for a real break. I ate a few nuts out of my top-tube bag, and then walked a few feet away to pee. Upon returning, I hoisted my bike and discovered the bag was empty — a quart-sized bag of trail mix, several candy bars, a cigarette lighter, and a chapstick were gone. As I scanned the surrounding snow, there was no evidence of any of it — not even a scattering of nuts. It was nearly two pounds of supplies, whisked into oblivion in a matter of seconds. I made a mental note to keep a firm grasp on everything.

Throughout the day, traffic along the sea ice increased. First there were a few small planes, then a helicopter, and then another Cessna circling overhead. A snowmobile with two passengers passed, and the duo stopped to anchor a tripod and camera next to the trail.

"What is all this?" Mike wondered as we took a snack break several hundred yards past the photographers.

"The sled dog race," I said. "They caught us."

Sure enough, the first dog team approached a minute later. We took the excuse to extend our break by waiting to cheer the first musher, although his approach took a lot longer than we expected. We'd become so accustomed to being passed by snowmobiles that we didn't conceptualize the five-mile-per-hour pace of the huskies that were leading the Iditarod Sled Dog Race. I was shivering profusely by the time the dogs passed, heads lowered and tongues lolling out despite the fierce windchill. Their faces were coated in rime and their legs moved in long but protracted strides, as though we were watching a filmstrip in slow motion. The musher was hunched behind his sled but stood as he passed to yell something at the dogs.

"Dogs are incredible athletes," I said to Mike as the huskies trotted away at a quarter of the speed they were capable of running in better conditions. "I would kill to be able to run that fast."

The photographers passed behind the team and told us there were about fourteen more miles to Koyuk. I was convinced the remaining mileage was closer to seventeen. "How long do you think it will take?" Mike asked me.

"Six hours," I said. I believed it would be closer to eight.

"Oh good," Mike said. "So we'll get there by nine."

A couple of hours went by before we saw the next dog teams — the father-son rivalry of Mitch and Danny Seavey, traveling together. The gap between first and second place surprised me, as I expected to be inundated with traffic once the sled dog race caught up to us. We hadn't seen a single snowmobile since the photographers passed. The race leader was clearly executing a breakneck pace, and apparently few tourists or media were willing to venture out on the sea ice in this wind. Mitch and Danny were both sitting on platforms on the back of their sleds, with hooded heads lowered so we couldn't see their faces. When they passed us at waist level, they didn't even nod. I couldn't say I blamed them. My own mood was turning sour as survival became more of a sure thing, which highlighted the tedium of pedaling against an invisible wall at two miles per hour.

"Mushing seems like a pretty good gig," Mike said. "Just sit on your butt."

"I don't envy those guys either," I said. "They probably haven't slept since Monday. Cooking up dog food, doling out snacks, laying out beds of straw, having to take care of sixty-four feet. I have a hard time taking care of my own feet."

I respected mushers, but the huskies were more relatable to me. I watched them race toward the horizon with warm admiration. These were new emotions, as I've never been a dog person. A couple of biting incidents as a youth and chasing incidents as a cyclist fueled a prevailing fear of dogs, and I'd prefer that even the friendliest mutts left me alone. But these huskies were impressively driven — racing through this windy hell for nothing more than salmon mush, kibble, and the praise of their musher. Before I came to Alaska, I was one of those animal-rights supporters who assumed that sled dogs were manipulated and tortured into this task. But after walking their trails, witnessing their body language and sharing real interactions with them, I have no doubt that huskies simply love to run. They love running with an innocent passion that I can't quite fathom, but aspire to achieve, all the same.

At that point, my own passion was severely diminished, dragged through the trenches by fatigue, nutrient depletion, and the ever-roaring North Wind. Mike and I continued to weave drunken paths that were vaguely side-by-side, but could only speak to each other when we stopped. Despite the terrifying chills that set in every time, our breaks became more frequent.

"It is beautiful out here," Mike said.

I nodded. "I keep reminding myself about the incredible vistas, and how much I love wide-open spaces, because otherwise I might just go insane with frustration."

"Did you ever think you'd find yourself in a place like this?" Mike asked.

"I used to think I wanted to ride a bike across Antarctica," I said. "But not anymore. I don't think there's anything I want less."

At sunset we caught our first glimpse of the lights of Koyuk, sparkling from the slope of a rounded hill. "We're almost there!" Mike exclaimed.

"We're six miles away still," I said.

"Well, we can see it, so we know we're going to make it," Mike retorted.

Evening brought dusky skies that quieted the gales. Even as the wind settled to an almost-calm fifteen miles per hour, we still labored for two more hours to cover this "almost there" distance. As we pedaled into the village, happiness and gratitude were muted by fatigue. I didn't quite register the momentous occasion of successfully crossing the sea ice. Still, my memory recorded yellow street lights over a cozy row of cabins, so I'd always have an image to recall when I reflected on my greatest accomplishment.

"Koyuk," I croaked. "We survived!"

I was so tired that I had little concept of where we were or what exactly came next, but Mike deftly located the school and a maintenance man to unlock the door. The building was crowded with volunteers and journalists who flew into Koyuk, as well as a large group of Norwegian tourists who passed us on snowmobiles an hour earlier. The maintenance man took pity on Mike and me because we arrived under our own power, and gave us the empty kindergarten classroom for the night. We hung our rime-coated gear on children's coat hooks and spread out damp sleeping bags on desks. I washed my face in a tiny sink and finally relieved myself in a tiny toilet. It felt amazing to pee without gasping into the wind, and the skin on my buttocks didn't even freeze.

My chest and throat warmed, prompting a coughing fit that dislodged a considerable amount of mucous. Later, I could hear a pronounced wheezing in my breaths. Fourteen hours of heavy breathing into the wind, with its minus-thirty windchill, had taken its toll. This congestion was undoubtedly more than just the residue of a hard day. As I coughed and coughed again, I feared the early stages of bronchitis.

The weather forecast indicated strong northwesterly winds would persist for at least two more days. The Iditarod Trail headed southwest for a short distance, and after that the wind would largely be a strong crosswind or headwind for the remainder of the route into Nome. I feared I didn't have the strength for such a battle. More than that, as I held my hand to my chest and choked up gobs of phlegm, I feared I didn't have the lungs for such a battle.

Gratitude

A couple of hours before sunrise, I managed to drag myself up from the Koyuk classroom floor. I collected my thawed clothing — now stiff with dried sweat — and waddled to the teacher's lounge to sort through my post office box, groaning at the contents. The supplies were exactly the same as they had been since Ruby — two freeze-dried meals, sour gummy bears that scraped the top of my already-raw mouth, disgusting fruit and nut mix, Snickers bars, chocolate, oatmeal, and peanut butter. I regretted the skepticism that prompted me to pack these boxes with a bunch of throw-away garbage, because now I had to suffer the consequences.

I kept the freeze-dried meals — I never threw these away even though my hoard had grown to seven or eight — and reluctantly included a fresh supply of trail mix and chocolate. The rest I left in the box with a note for students to help themselves. For breakfast I forced down four packets of oatmeal, then waddled down the hall.

The classroom door was locked, and I had to pound on it for almost a minute before Mike woke up.

"What time is it?" he asked, slurring all of the words.

"Not early. Just after eight," I answered. "I'm about to take off."

"Oh," he said, blinking rapidly as though he fell asleep wearing his contacts. "I feel worked. That was a hard day yesterday."

"It was," I agreed. Mike and I covered thirty-three miles over the sea ice in fourteen and a half hours with minimal stops. Those fourteen hours comprised the most mentally and physically strenuous day of my life so far. At the time, I was so focused on survival that I didn't notice the searing burn in my legs, the soreness in my lower back, or the lung congestion. All of that had returned this morning, and my fatigue was magnified by knowledge of all of the harsh miles still ahead. It was gratifying, though, to learn that even Mike felt sore after two days on the sea ice.

"GPS says we averaged two and a half miles per hour yesterday," I said. I'd checked the statistics earlier that morning, and was excited to share the numbers with Mike. "It's thirty-three miles with fifty-two feet of elevation gain. That track is going to look so pathetic on Strava!" This was my way of making a joke. Mike didn't even crack a grimace.

"So what's the plan for today?" Mike asked.

"Elim, I think," referring to a village that was about fifty miles away. "Maybe I'll go for one of the shelter cabins beyond if things are going well. But I really don't want to push it. I'm worried I might be coming down with bronchitis."

Mike nodded. "Elim sounds good." I watched him plop back down on his sleeping bag. Quietly, I closed the classroom door and rolled my bike toward a sunlit foyer. Local school children were on spring break this week, and Koyuk's school halls remained quiet. Still, they looked like any school halls in Kansas or New York, making it easy to temporarily forget I was in Alaska. Although I'd been on the Iditarod Trail for fifteen days, it was still a shock to step out of a building to a view of a white, frozen sea. Snow-covered streets and metal roofs were saturated in pink light, so vibrant that I had to squint as I pedaled out of town. The air was eerily calm, and the North Wind's absence intensified the morning silence. My breath was raspy and every body part hurt, but I was alive. This realization sparked a smile. I was still alive.

Beyond Koyuk the trail was heavily drifted, and the soft layer of snow had been stirred up by dog feet and sled runners. A couple of mushers passed, and one spoke to me in a woman's voice. I assumed it was Aliy Zirkle, the musher who gave Beat a bag of bacon several days earlier. She was farther back in the field than I would have expected, since she was leading the race when she passed Beat in the Interior. Later, I learned that she and her team were attacked by a drunken man on a snowmobile outside the village of Nulato. Several of Aliy's dogs were injured as he looped back several times, intentionally buzzing her sled. This man also attacked another popular musher, Jeff King. One of his dogs was killed. Despite the tragic setback, both mushers decided to continue toward Nome.

"You must be tired," she said in a muffled sing-song voice that sounded as though she'd just woken up as well.

"I'm okay," I replied. "You must be tired yourself."

Aliy nodded, although I couldn't see her face beneath her hood and mask. I was similarly bundled up in my balaclava and goggles, as the temperature was still in the negative single digits, and I expected the wind to return. Other mushers seemed taken aback when we exchanged greetings, and I presumed they weren't expecting to hear a woman's voice. When Jeff King's team approached, I moved over early and shot a half dozen photos before belting out a cheerful hello. Jeff's face was uncovered and I could clearly see a scowl as he passed without saying a word. At the time I didn't know about the Nulato attack, and assumed he was one of those Iditarod mushers who didn't support sharing the trail with kooky human-powered folks. The snub left me feeling surprisingly wounded. It was clear my emotions were still on edge.

Several miles later, I stopped to have a longer conversation with a charismatic young musher who was resting his dogs. His encouragement bolstered my self esteem, and boosted a short but steep climb over a low-lying ridge. The views from five hundred feet above the sea were breathtaking, with an expansive white valley and mountains sparkling in the sunlight. The North Wind picked up strength during the descent, blurring the trail with fast-moving ground blizzards.

Crosswind pummeled me across the Kwik River Valley, and I teetered and swayed in a constant battle to stay upright. A shelter cabin stood at the center of this exposed flood plain. The flat, treeless location made for an unappealing campsite, but that wasn't the purpose of the Kwik River cabin. Along Alaska's western coast, these weathered plywood structures have been built specifically to protect travelers during storms, which rage incessantly, year-round. Funded and maintained by Native organizations rather than the federal government, the cabins' amenities are limited to bunk beds and a stove — bring your own wood — and are scrawled with the graffiti of past travelers. A large message on the wall begged users to clean up after themselves. "This cabin may save your life someday."

I considered what it would be like to arrive at this cabin in a pitch-dark blizzard rather than in this bright — albeit cold and windy — afternoon. Even a palace could not be more luxurious than life-saving shelter when it's truly needed. I ducked inside and fired up my stove for hot chocolate and freeze-dried noodles: the only foods I looked forward to eating anymore. Hot lunch was another high luxury, and I felt guilty for wasting the time. Still, my breathing became worse the longer I stayed out in the wind, and seemed to improve with rest. I was convinced these breaks were vital if I wanted to avoid sputtering out before Nome.

I was back on the trail after an hour, hot on the heels of the young musher who passed me again, and feeling more revitalized than ever. After skirting an abandoned airport at Moses Point, the trail joined a road — unmaintained, but distinctly improved with guardrails and gentle grading over a succession of hills. As I grunted and wheezed up a steady ascent, a sound similar to jingling bells startled me off my bike. I turned just as a dog team passed within a foot of my left leg. The lead dog, a beautiful white husky, gave a polite "woof" and a nod as it trotted past. I nodded back at my canine superior, sensing that we were just two lead dogs acknowledging each other on this difficult climb. The musher was kneeling on the sled platform with his chin buried in his coat. He didn't return my hello. As I watched the team continue up the hill, the musher's body swayed back and forth like an unsecured bag.

"He's asleep!" I exclaimed, and shook my head. Good thing that lead dog had everything under control and knew where the team needed to go. My respect for sled dogs increased every day.

At the crest of the hill, my throat erupted in a horrible coughing fit that lasted several minutes. Unfazed, I used my left hand to wrap the useless fingers of my right hand around the brake lever — now a necessity for every long descent — and launched down the steep ramp. The road had climbed five hundred feet above the sea, and the forested slope revealed a layered vista of white ice, blue water, and distant mountains. Even with the rear brake locked in place, I barely maintained control. Within seconds I was approaching the sleeping musher's team at high speed. Not wanting to startle my husky friend, I grabbed the front brake too forcefully, causing the wheel to lock and the bike to spin sideways on glare ice. Over I went, unfortunately landing on my bruised right side with a hard skid. Quickly I bounced back up, hoping only that the huskies hadn't noticed my crash. I genuinely wanted their approval.

I rolled into Elim just as the sleeping musher's dog team trotted happily toward the checkpoint tent. My right shoulder was throbbing and my throat was raw. Coughing fits had become more frequent throughout the day, and I was convinced I'd lapsed into an early stage of bronchitis. Even though it was still light outside, I intended to get a full night of sleep indoors before continuing any farther.

A group of children directed me to the school, where the athletic director let me set up my sleeping bag nest in a cozy side room next to the library. A post office box waited for me there as well, though it contained the exact same supplies I'd schlepped from Koyuk. For dinner I mixed instant mashed potatoes with freeze-dried chicken and noodles, which did little to quell a gnawing appetite for protein. I was already asleep when Mike knocked on the door just before ten.

"How was your day?" he asked.

"Pretty uneventful," I said. "I've developed this horrible cough, but at least the wind was better today."

Mike told me he'd spoken with his wife on the phone, and she asked whether I was trying for the women's record.

"If you want to get up in a few hours and go for it, I will go with you," he said. It was a genuine offer.

"Oh no," I said. "It's a hundred and thirty more miles. I'm not exactly sure what the record is, but I'm pretty sure I have to get to Nome by tomorrow afternoon to break it. Even if we left right now, it's unobtainable."

"Oh okay," Mike said, sounding both relieved and disappointed.

"But thanks for offering," I said. "Really."

✳ ✳ ✳ ✳ ✳

During the night, I woke up choking on phlegm. This was unnerving, and evoked memories of struggling to breathe during the Tour Divide, after my illness became so bad that I needed to lie down on the side of the road to catch my breath. Out on the Bering Sea coast, with the frigid North Wind slicing across exposed valleys, where I needed to move to survive, there was no such luxury. Again I fell asleep with cold panic burbling through my veins, soothing myself with a quiet chant: "Breathe, just breathe."

I woke up feeling strangely refreshed and left Elim in pre-dawn darkness, when the wind was still a whisper but the cold was cavernous. Finding the way out of town proved confusing, and I ventured down a few side streets before locating a streak of dog feces that led to a trail marker. The route dropped onto the sea ice, skirting the base of marble cliffs that the star-lit sky rendered in stunning contrast. Similar to most mornings on the Iditarod Trail, I floated through disorienting sleepiness, one moment laughing at scattered dog booties, and the next fuming at the incomprehensible maze of jumbled ice. To spark alertness I fired up my iPod, and soon found myself standing out of the saddle, sprinting over blue ice, and singing out loud to Imagine Dragons:

"I've got this place that I filled with empty space, so I'm trying not to face what I've done … I'm in this race and I'm hoping just to place, so I'm trying not to face what's become of me …"

Singing sputtered into coughing, and I ripped my face mask down as a large glob of mucous dislodged from my throat. This brought a brief taste of unobstructed air, and I took big, greedy gulps as the tip of my nose and lips went numb. The sudden injection of oxygen propelled me up a steep sea wall and onto the slopes of the second longest climb on the Iditarod Trail, a mountain that mushers call Little McKinley. Little McKinley gains a thousand feet in fewer than two miles, which this late in the race feels like climbing the Big McKinley that Alaskans call Denali. A rose-colored sun glistened through the trees behind me, casting striped pink reflections on the snow. When I glanced over my shoulder I could see a dog team approaching, and pedaled as hard as I could to stay in front of them. I managed to hold them off for a few hundred feet of elevation, but hard breathing in the cold air tightened my airways. I started coughing again, and slumped off my bike to let them pass.

It was dumb to push myself so hard, but for those few minutes my lungs were clear and my legs were strong, and everything about that felt incredible. Still, indulging in my temporary strength extracted a high price, because when I sputtered out, I wasn't anywhere near the top of Little McKinley. Suddenly the full weight of gravity threatened to pull me back to the ocean. The bike pressed into my already tight chest as I leaned into the handlebars, feeling as though I were pushing a stone up a sand dune.

By the time I crawled to the high point, the peach light of dawn had given way to a glaringly bright day. The trail contoured a broad ridge above tree line. I imagined these bald, rolling hills as a white sand desert, with wind-sculpted dunes sparkling beneath a hot sun. As I continued to battle for oxygen, a haze settled between perception and reality, and the desert imagery became more intense. Memories flickered of hiking in the Grand Canyon with my dad, of camping beneath sandstone buttes in the San Rafael Swell, of riding a mountain bike across South Africa.

Amid this collision of past and present, I arrived at a saddle. Here the trail dipped into a steep gully, plummeting a thousand feet to Golovin Bay. This side of Little McKinley was much more bare, with a patchwork of sugary snow and brown tussocks. I stopped to take a few photos, manually locked my numb hand around the brake lever, and launched into the abyss.

My heart raced as I screamed down the bumpy trail, holding my breath amid a rush of adrenaline and fear. Time twisted entirely, and I slipped into a memory from two years earlier, when I was descending a steep canyon in South Africa's Stormberg Mountains. As I dodged lumpy tussocks, I saw only rocks. Snow-swept hillsides became sandstone buttes. Ice-covered Golovin Bay became the Karoo, a vast South African desert. Every piece of my consciousness was back in

South Africa, and for long minutes, I believed this unquestioningly. The delusion was so complete that as I approached a lone building, I thought, "There's a shepherd's hut." There was a strong breeze gusting off the bay, which caused me to think, "Maybe the shepherd will let me come inside to get out of the wind."

After rolling up beside what was in fact the McKinley Creek shelter cabin, I spent several seconds looking around for the shepherd. But there were no people, no sheep — something wasn't quite right. I began blinking rapidly as though waking from a deep sleep.

"Where am I?"

As pieces of reality began to snap back together, my confusion only deepened. "Snow, but how? What year is this?" The McKinley Creek shelter cabin stood stoically, buried to its windows in hardened snowdrifts. The sight of these drifts finally revealed the answers. Alaska. 2016. The Iditarod Trail. Did I really ride my bike all the way to Golovin Bay? As perception rose to the surface from an ocean of memories, I looked back at the mottled gold-and-white hillside. This landscape was completely displaced from the one I just witnessed, and I marveled at the intensity of my hallucination.

I pedaled onto the smooth ice of Golovin Bay and continued to ruminate on the strangeness of the experience. It couldn't have been more real to me if I had physically traveled back in time to relive a few minutes of the Race Across South Africa. If I were more inclined toward superstition and hadn't experienced endurance-related hallucinations in the past, I might insist that this is actually what happened. That I'm a time traveler. I'd be convinced of it. It's unnerving to ponder an imagined experience compared to known experiences and conclude that perhaps none of them were real. Maybe everything is a hallucination. Individual perception is our only window into whatever's actually out there, and it's jarring to realize you can't trust perception. Why, then, should we believe anything we see or feel?

This is how I entered the village of Golovin six miles later — coughing, exhausted, and fearing for my mental health. I wasn't in the mood to interact with normal humans, so I quickened my pace through the village street, which stretched across a thin peninsula that divided Golovin Bay from Golovin Lagoon. I'd nearly reached the other side when two girls darted out of a youth center building. They looked to be about seven or eight years old and were wearing cute pastel outfits that I considered inadequate for the zero-degree temperature.

"Will you sign our coats?" the taller girl asked. There was a hand-painted sign in front of the youth center welcoming mushers to Golovin, and I got the sense the girls were watching out the window for dog teams.

"But I'm not a musher," I said, "I'm a bicyclist, see?" I patted my handlebars.

"Here," the girl shoved a cheap marker in my hand, then pointed to a spot on the chest of her puffy coat.

"Are you sure? That looks like a nice coat. I don't know if your Mom will like me writing on it."

"No, it's okay," she insisted, and pointed to another scribble that a real musher had left on her back.

The marker was frozen and my hand was similarly stiff, but I managed to scrawl a faint and sloppy autograph on the coats of two little girls in Golovin, and I have to say, it made my day.

Just beyond town, two men on a snowmobile pulled up next to me. The younger man introduced his father and then asked if I would pose for a photo. The old man stood stiffly next to me as I gave an awkward thumbs up. I felt embarrassed but bemused about my apparent celebrity status in the tiny village of Golovin. There was a bulky canvas sack in the back of their sled, so I asked if they'd been hunting.

"Yes," the younger man said, adding no details. This was typical of my interaction with Native Alaskans. Questions brought honest and succinct answers. There was never a hint of bloviation, even when it seemed warranted.

As I pedaled beyond the meager protection of the peninsula, the North Wind raged across Golovin Lagoon. After four long days on the coast with many hours of pedaling directly into the wind, I'd become resigned to the Sisyphean grind. My thoughts flickered, again searching for memories of anywhere else, when suddenly the bike stopped cold. My body lurched forward, hitting a wall of wind that bucked everything sideways before tossing me awkwardly on the ice.

Still lying on my side, I spun around to see what I'd hit. The ice was clear. When I brushed my arm over the rear wheel, it wouldn't budge. For long minutes I examined everything from the brake pads to the crank to the derailleur. Just when I was utterly stymied, I realized that the obstacle was a strap from the rear rack, tangled in the cassette.

As I tugged at the tight knots, the windchill sucked all the heat from my arms, forcing me to rewarm my hands by stuffing them in big mittens and swinging my arms wildly. My right hand had so little strength that I couldn't make a fist. Untying knots was out of the question, even before my hands became cold.

It was hardly an emergency, but my mental health was fragile and every emotion was exaggerated. I panicked. "I can't untangle this. I'm stuck!"

Tears streamed into my face mask as I tugged and slammed the wheel against the ice, only tightening the strap and making things worse. Since McGrath, I'd feared the minor mechanical that was going to end my race. This had to be it. I removed my left hand from the mitten and pulled a tiny pocket knife out of my vest, then tried slicing at the strap. The blade was dull, not even as wide as the strap, and seemed just as useless against the knots as my dead right hand. My fingers froze to the point I couldn't move them at all.

With two numb hands and mounting frustration, I plopped down on the ice, filled with irrational but paralyzing fear. I was only eight miles beyond Golovin, with perhaps eight more miles to the village of White Mountain. Neither were too far to walk, but the distance seemed insurmountable if a seized wheel reduced me to dragging my bike on its side. I scanned the white expanse for movement — anyone who could pluck me away from being stranded on sea ice. All was still, except for the North Wind.

As I sat, shivering and becoming colder, a whisper of rationality crept in — if only one end of the strap is tangled around the cassette, the other end must still be free. Of course. The other end of the strap was still hooked to the rack. All I needed to do was release the buckle, and the strap would be loose enough to loop it backward around the cogs until it was untangled. The knife, knot wrangling, hyperventilating and panic — especially the panic — were never necessary. How embarrassing.

This sheepish embarrassment about my own ineptitude lingered as I reached the edge of Golovin Lagoon and pedaled into low-lying hills surrounding the Fish River. Physically I was having a good day after the early coughing fits, but between the hallucination and overreaction to the strap incident, I feared my mental state was not nearly so solid. It was still early in the day, the weather was relatively decent, and I'd considered blazing through White Mountain in favor of seeking out a shelter cabin or even making a big push to Nome. But the comfort of the village beckoned. I rationalized a vital need for sleep before venturing into what can be the most dangerous stretch of the Iditarod Trail, a mere fifty miles from Nome: The Solomon blowhole.

I also knew White Mountain was the home of a beloved trail angel, Joanna Wassillie. Joanna lived with her husband and two young children in a small cabin off a bank of the Fish River. She first became associated with the race ten years earlier, when she spotted a light moving slowly up the river. Fearing this was an injured hunter who had lost his snowmobile, she fired up her machine and raced out to meet him. She found a man alone, dragging a sled, and shuffling with a pronounced limp. When she urged him to hop on her snowmobile, he said in a thick Italian accent: "No, no. I race."

Joanna looked around, confused. Race? It was late at night, at least twenty below, and she hadn't seen another runner come through the village in, well, ever. The man was Marco Berni, an Italian runner competing in the 2006 Iditarod Trail Invitational. Through miming and interpreting his broken English, Joanna gave Marco directions and invited him to rest at her house.

Marco ended up staying with Joanna for two days. He'd fallen on ice and hurt his hip, and the long rest allowed him to recuperate enough to finish the final eighty miles to Nome. Joanna joked that Marco ate only Parmesan on the trail and smelled strongly of sweat and old cheese, but he refused to take a shower. He spoke almost no English, but they carried on boisterous conversations all the same. This was her introduction to the "ITI crazies," and she's opened her home to human-powered travelers ever since. Beat had spoken fondly of his time with Joanna and her family, who clear out their own bedrooms to make space for visitors, and prepare coffee and homemade meals at any time of the day or night.

I rolled into town on a bright Tuesday afternoon, and scanned the hillside for the official screen-printed sign that Joanna pinned in front of her cabin. She ran toward the river wearing a colorful kuspuk with a fur trim, and waved for all of the three minutes it took to ride toward her house. With a strong embrace, she welcomed me to White Mountain and ushered me inside.

"I've been watching for you," she said. "I made French press coffee. Do you like coffee?"

Even though I'd never visited White Mountain nor met Joanna, it felt like coming home. Any weak ambitions I harbored for a big push to Nome melted with this question. I nodded vigorously.

After I'd finished my coffee, Joanna asked if I wanted to take a bath.

"A bath?"

"I bought these Epsom salts," she said, holding up a fancy-looking package. "I thought it might feel nice for you guys after a long day on the trail."

"I'd very much like that," I said.

Twenty minutes later, I lowered myself into Joanna's tub and dunked my head beneath the water, relishing the comfort of complete sensory deprivation. I examined my body for the first time in sixteen days — skin speckled with purple and black bruises, a patch of windburn across my lower back, slightly swollen calves and feet, missing a few pounds around my torso and thighs. All in all, nothing looked too bad, and now I was a mere eighty miles from Nome, reclining in a warm bath. A bath! What forces in the universe were responsible for this kid-gloves treatment on the famously ferocious Iditarod Trail?

"Beat is going to tease me about this," I thought.

Of course, submerged in warm water, it was easy to forget about the North Wind and the dangerous task that still lay ahead. The race was far from over. For the final leg, I would need to climb over the notoriously steep and exposed Topkok Hills, then drop back onto the coast. There the beach butts up against mountains, and for the next twenty miles I'd pass narrow canyons that serve as straws, siphoning the frigid air of the Interior toward the ocean. Wind speeds in this area can top a hundred miles per hour, and gusts of at least fifty miles an hour happen nearly every day of the winter. For every nice story I'd heard about the final stretch to Nome, there were ten stories about the horror of the "blowhole."

After the bath, I sat down to spaghetti dinner with Joanna and two other women who were ski-joring — skiing while harnessed to two huskies — from Unalakleet to Nome. Laura and Robin, both Alaskans, swapped trail stories with me as we speculated about the upcoming weather and route. I found this conversation empowering. Here we were, three intrepid travelers and a life-long resident of this harsh land — all women — sitting at one table.

Laura knew of a weather station that recorded wind speeds in the Solomon blowhole, with graphs posted online. She'd checked it earlier in the day, when the North Wind was cranking at fifty-five miles per hour. By dinner time, it had fallen to thirty-five. She figured they'd hit that stretch two days later, when the forecast called for a reduction in wind speeds. My plan of going through late the next morning was more risky.

"I'd get up really early," Laura cautioned. "Avoid going through there after noon."

"I can always wait it out at the Topkok cabin," I said. Previous ventures into winds near sixty miles an hour had knocked me off my feet, even when I didn't have a seventy-five-pound bike and only one good hand. There was a real chance I wouldn't be able to move amid such powerful gusts, and the land was so exposed that hunkering down was impossible. It would sure be a pity, so close to the end, to blow out to sea and never be seen again.

The Saga of Jason Mackey's Ski Pole

Although the cabin had just one and a half bedrooms, Joanna set me up in the bed where she and her husband, Jack, usually slept. Mike showed up around sunset, just as I was rifling through leftover supply boxes to discover a treasure trove of peanut butter cups, jerky, and trail mix that was not my trail mix. I hoarded it all — just in case I was pinned down in the Topkok shelter cabin for two days — and went to the entrance to greet my elusive trail companion.

"I'm going to try to leave by five at the latest," I informed Mike, who laughed at me.

"That's the coldest part of the morning," he said.

"But it could be really windy by afternoon," I countered.

Just before dark I connected with Beat via Joanna's home phone. He was making his way over the Kaltag Portage and planning to rest at the Old Woman cabin. The weather in those hills had become much colder — thirty-six below — and he felt worn down by his own solitude. Tim Hewitt was three days ahead, and Eric Johnson was two days behind. As he spoke, I imagined clouds of frozen breath swirling around Beat's face as he marched through that lonesome, haunted valley. Beat said he was proud that I'd made it so far, but gave me some light-hearted grief for taking a bath at Joanna's house.

"It was so amazing. If Joanna lived somewhere farther down the trail, like Kaltag, I'd probably never leave," I said. "But since it's only eighty miles from Nome, I guess I have to go."

Just before 5 a.m., I crept into the kitchen to heat water for instant coffee. Despite trying my best not to make noise, Jack rose from a nearby couch and offered to cook pancakes. Joanna made a bleary-eyed appearance as well, apologizing for "not being a morning person."

"Neither am I," I said. "But Nome is still a long way from here."

I was surprised Joanna and Jack made an effort to see me off, and thanked them profusely. Here on the harsh Bering Sea coast, kindness and hospitality are worth more than any material reward. Soaking in the warmth of White Mountain felt just as fulfilling as finishing the race. As I indulged in the most peaceful sleep of my trip, I almost convinced myself that the journey was complete. Of course there was still that frayed end of the Iditarod Trail, a lonely and dangerous stretch that just won't let it be over until it's over.

Outside Joanna's cabin, the morning was eerily still. Surprised by the absence of motion, I held my breath, as though the North Wind was a predator that would swoop in if I made my presence known. Instead, a sharp chill latched onto my skin. The thermometer at the house registered minus thirteen, which isn't terrible. But it was likely to keep dropping, especially on the river, until the sun came up.

I made it about two miles up the Fish River before I was already hungry again, and pulled out a particularly special treasure that I excavated from another racer's drop bag — miniature white chocolate peanut butter cups. Looking back toward the village, I saw a glittering speck in a vast indigo void. Wisps of ice fog hung over the village lights, accentuating their glow. White Mountain was so inviting that I instinctively moved toward it, taking several steps before I realized what I was doing. Turning to face west again, I saw only yawning darkness. It was very cold.

The snack break proved costly. By the time I was back in the saddle, my whole body was quaking with shivers. This sparked a quiet panic, which prompted me to sprint up the river. I pedaled with all of the strength my cold muscles could muster to pump warm blood back to my limbs. The furious effort quelled my shivering, but it wasn't enough. I wanted to be warmer. I rode harder.

Breath poured into a swirl of fog so thick that I could scarcely see through it. I wasn't wearing goggles, so frost collected on my eyelashes and eyebrows, freezing into large white clumps. Steam rose from the collar of my jacket, because I was beginning to sweat heavily. I knew I shouldn't invite this, but it felt so wonderful to be warm, to breathe cold air, and to ride fast. I was doing it! I was riding to Nome!

The biosphere within my clothing continued to produce heat and moisture as dawn broke. Violet light appeared above the black profile of distant hills, accentuating the expansiveness of the valley. The sky brightened to a deep shade of blue, and all of the snow-blanketed land was the same color, just a few degrees lighter.

There was a cluster of anemic spruce trees at the mouth of a canyon. This was the gully that would take me into the infamous Topkok Hills — thirteen miles of steep, rolling terrain at the head of a narrow peninsula. These trees would be the last I'd see on the Iditarod Trail. Beyond here, the trail was wind-swept, exposed, and shelter-less, save for a few cabins in varying states of dilapidation that were specifically built to save lives.

I made a quick stop to pee, and within seconds I was again wracked with shivering. Racing toward the climb, I reached for a heat-generating peanut butter cup, only to find the bag's zipper had frozen shut. The entire top tube and left side of my frame bag were coated in clear ice —droplets of respiration formed from hard breathing, which then funneled down my face mask and rained onto the bike, where the water instantly froze. The front of my jacket was an ice bib as well. My base layers were as soaked as they could possibly be. Being this wet wasn't a good thing. One might argue it was the worst mistake I'd made on the Iditarod Trail.

Feeling desperate for calories, I forced myself to stop and yank at the frozen zipper with my one good hand. When it was freed and I had a few peanut butter cups in my stomach, I felt brave enough to check my thermometer. "Oh geez, it's minus twenty-four!" I yelled. Minus twenty-four isn't unusual or extreme for this part of the world. Minus twenty-four would be fine, really, if I'd worn all the correct layers to begin with, and I wasn't soaked in my own sweat. But because I was wet, a chill clamped down the moment I stopped, and every second compounded the danger. If warmth becomes violent shivering in five minutes, one can only surmise the proximity of deadly hypothermia.

Riding so hard from the outset was a critically poor choice, but now there was little I could do about it. I could put on my down coat, but I still considered that coat for true emergencies. Wearing it while riding remained my "only if you think you're going to die" game plan. The moisture clinging to my body would seep into the coat's insulation, so its life-saving properties would be nullified. Since I wasn't quite so desperate, my best option was to keep riding and wait for the sun. It would come up eventually. It always did.

The Topkok Hills provided an undulating wave of varied but consistent pain. The first climb out of the meager forest brought a whisper of heat, just before the grade steepened enough to force me off my bike. My throat gurgled as I coughed, spewing a fountain of snot and breath fog that turned quickly to ice. As I pushed up the hill, heat drained from my core. I'd reach the top shivering again, knowing I had to descend a hundred feet into the bowels of Hell frozen over.

Then the next climb repeated the pattern. My body's power meter plummeted, and I had to gasp and gurgle my way through a ploddingly slow push. Warmth was an elusive phantom, emanating from my hard-pumping heart, only to escape through porous weaknesses in my arms and legs. All the while, a strip of pale pink light stretched across the snow a half mile to the north. As I climbed and descended, the light never stretched any closer.

"This is a life of quiet desperation," I thought. "Not sitting at home. This."

I wanted to cry, only because I was so desperately uncomfortable, in this mess of my own making, and there was no relief. The battle against hypothermia had consumed all of my energy, and stopping to cram a few peanut butter cups into my mouth just made things worse. Soon heavy fatigue and low blood sugar added to my woes. Climbs became impossibly steep, descents unbearably cold. My good hand tingled and my bad hand went numb. If I tried to pedal or push any harder, I became dizzy and lapsed into coughing fits. I did start to cry, but only briefly. Tears froze to my cheeks, a shocking sensation that cut the faucet immediately.

"Quiet desperation," I repeated, if only to remind myself of the relief that awaited if I managed to survive the ride to Nome — the wonders of boredom and lying barefoot on carpet and never putting myself through another adventure, ever again.

Fear trickled into my gut like cold water, and I berated myself for continuing to put unearned faith in my body's ability to keep moving through any difficulty. A year of failures already debunked this delusion. When was I going to accept that I was no longer strong enough for such extreme adventures? Entrusting my survival to these legs and lungs was sheer foolishness.

Was it ever not foolish? There is nothing special about me — I have no remarkable athletic gifts, no unique powers of endurance or ability to withstand the cold. There's only one quality that separates me from other humans who don't ride bicycles across Alaska in the winter: desire. When I lie in bed on a hot summer night, I dream of wind-swept tundra. When I push a cart around a grocery store, I imagine crossing frozen swamps beneath a sparkling night sky. The desire to return to Alaska is so strong that my daydreams occasionally take over, leaving me blinking in confusion at a row of cereal boxes, wondering how I arrived at this bland existence so distant from the intensities I've known.

Then there is reality — the frail and fearful human that can't withstand these intensities, at least not to the satisfaction of my desire. This desire will never be satisfied. Ten years of cowering in the cold, crawling up and down mountains, fearing for my life — it will never go away. Desire is a raving maniac, cackling as I struggle through insidious situations, pushing me blindly toward peril. If I fail, desire grows louder, and if I succeed, it becomes deafening.

So I suppose I'm mad. This is just another reason why I'm not special. We're all mad, driven to our own idiosyncrasies by the absurdity of life. It's probably just a fluke of fate that I think amassing wealth is a waste of time, and riding across frozen tundra is desirable. This is my way of living large, and living large always comes with a higher price.

Many hours but only twenty miles beyond White Mountain, sunlight finally connected with the trail. The temperature had risen to minus eighteen. At that point I was shivering lightly, but consistently. Climbs no longer provided a shot of warmth. My body was too depleted to produce extra heat. The Topkok Hills continued rippling toward a sharp blue horizon. Those too would never end. The fingers on my right hand were entirely rigid; I didn't even bother wrapping them around the brake lever anymore. With the front wheel locked and the rear wheel unhindered, the bike fishtailed wildly. I didn't care. I almost hoped for a swift end to my misery.

But I didn't crash, and I didn't succumb to hypothermia. Eventually the sun rose above the ridge, eliminating shadows. Solar reflection from the snow melted the ice sheet from my jacket and bike bags. I could afford to stop long enough to eat more peanut butter cups, returning some semblance of energy to my muscles. Fatigue still gnawed at my limbs, casting a heavy curtain over my thoughts. This wasn't sleepiness, though. It went deeper than that, into places hidden from me, where my desire resides. I no longer cared whether I made it to Nome or quit somewhere just shy of the end. This too is the absurdity of life — wanting something so badly that we smother all desire in pursuit of it. Desire would rebound, of course, but for those moments I would have given anything to return to a dull life. I fantasized about sitting in traffic, doing dishes, or pushing a cart around a grocery store.

Arriving at the crest at what I was certain would be the last climb, my jaw dropped at the sight of another wall in front of me. It truly was a wall, launching out of a stream bed and straight up a near-vertical slope, gaining five hundred feet in what had to be less than a quarter mile of trail. I could see hollows where snowmobiles spun their tracks at full throttle, tearing up what little snow remained on the trail.

Just as I entertained an urge to start crying again, I heard a jingle and looked back. A dog team was approaching, with faces coated in frost and tongues flapping wildly. The musher dug a ski pole into the snow, meekly pulling his sled along.

"These hills are crazy," he said with a guttural growl.

"They sure are," I answered, and watched as he passed. His blue coat was emblazoned with the word "Mackey," which led me to surmise he was Jason Mackey, brother of the legendary four-time Iditarod winner Lance Mackey. As a hopeless Iditarod fan, I knew about their family and back story, and Jason was a person I admired. I watched as his team floated down the hill before hitting the wall, where they ascended a short distance and stopped moving. Jason walked to the front, grabbed the harness of his lead dog and guided them up the headwall. After three minutes, he remounted his sled and commenced poling up the slope while his dogs clawed and wove all over the wide trail. I stood and watched until they were over the crest and out of sight, seething with envy at their strength.

My own ascent was a slobbering, coughing, backsliding mess. There wasn't enough energy left to be upset, nor was there enough oxygen left to cry. The surface crust was solid and slick, forcing me to kick steps into the snow to leverage the weight of the bike. Every hoist of the handlebars felt like bench-pressing a hundred-pound barbell. I'd take a few gasping breaths, kick another step, and shove the bike forward. One step at a time, for five-hundred vertical feet. By the top I was choking on phlegm, exhausted, and dizzy. My throat was ragged from the cold air, and my legs were quivering. I threw my bike down and sat on the trail, burying my ice-crusted face between my knees. When I regained enough composure to sit up straight, I noticed a black pole lying across the trail a few feet in front of me. Picking it up, I recognized the crooked profile and medical tape holding two broken pieces in place. It was Jason's ski pole.

For several seconds, I clutched the pole in a mittened hand while scanning the landscape ahead. From that altitude, I could see more than fifty miles in all directions. The fathomless blue water of the Bering Sea filled the horizon, rimmed with a sandy shoreline and miles of glare ice. Bald, white mountains came within a few miles of the coast, but I could tell the route along the shoreline was flat. If the legendary blowholes were cranking, I saw no evidence — the air was clear all the way to Cape Nome, a snow-covered bluff some forty miles away.

"This is my window," I thought. "I need to get through there before the wind picks up."

Then I looked down at Jason's pole. His team had beaten me to the top of this hill by at least forty-five minutes. There were still fifty more miles to Nome. My leg muscles felt like refrigerated gelatin and my lungs were filled with shards of ice. "It's mostly flat," the thought process continued. "I wonder if I can catch Jason and return this pole?"

That thought was like a shot of adrenaline, spurring me to frenzied action. I stuffed the pole underneath a bungee cord on my front rack and launched into the steep descent. It was another fishtailing mess, but exhilarating all the same. In a blur of blue sky and frozen tears, I unraveled seven hours of energy-bankrupting hardship. Without changing anything but my attitude, I arrived at the driftwood-strewn shoreline feeling as though I'd just woken up in White Mountain all over again — renewed.

Sunlight reflected off frozen tide pools, baking the air to a balmy five degrees above zero. As I stripped off layers that were still crusted in frost, a red fox darted across the trail. The fox stopped briefly and sniffed at the air, then moved a few steps toward me. As I waved my hand, it made a small leap and swiveled mid-air before nonchalantly trotting away.

"I'm going to catch Jason!" I said out loud to the fox that did not care.

Iditarod dog teams typically travel between seven and ten miles per hour. My moving average over the entire route was closer to five and a half. Jason Mackey's dogs were meticulously trained athletes possessing the bloodlines of Idiatrod champions dating back to the 1970s, while I was a fading shadow of a human athlete who was not much of a competitor to begin with, and who now had Jell-O legs and scarred lungs. But never mind all that. I was going to catch Jason!

Beyond the Topkok shelter cabin, the first two miles of flat trail traversed a frozen lagoon. I was too timid to open up my effort on the slippery ice, and continued to lose ground on Jason. But once the trail rose onto a wind-scoured, bumpy jeep track, I laid into the pedals. I wasn't sure I had much left to give; I only knew I'd be spending it all. It wasn't about returning a broken ski pole to a musher who couldn't possibly care, or about showing up a random team of canine superiors at the very end of a long race, or even about reaching Nome more quickly. I'd told myself "no" too many times during the past year. There were so many "you can't" and "you're too weak," and a number of "you're not talented enough" and "you're too old." I was tired of all the doubt. I was tired of holding myself back. I was just tired.

Instead, I defied "you can't" by pedaling as hard as I possibly could. Mounds of frozen dirt undulated beneath my wheels as the North Wind brushed my side — a whisper at ten miles per hour. I kept glancing to the right for evidence of the Solomon blowhole — snow blowing from the hillsides or the blurred horizon of a ground blizzard. The air was clear, but I'd heard stories of gusts erupting out of seemingly nowhere, and didn't let my guard down.

My breathing was shallow and swift, in an oxygen-starved environment I knew all too well — the cusp of my lungs' limit. It was a place I feared and avoided, but for this day — with the North Wind whispering quiet threats and my imagined competition outpacing me somewhere beyond — I was ready to embrace the literal suck. In and out, in and out, breathe, breathe, breathe. In this focused meditation, life became refreshingly simple, swiftly retreating from the scariest place on the Iditarod Trail. The North Wind had me cornered in its most fearsome territory, and yet it held back, as though conceding this battle out of sympathy for an already broken opponent. Quietly, my confidence returned. I was going to catch Jason.

I pulled into Safety Roadhouse, the final sled dog race checkpoint, a few minutes before four in the afternoon. Just twenty-two miles from Nome, the roadhouse has origins dating back to the Gold Rush, when twenty-two miles was considered a good day's travel. Safety earned its name because it's just beyond reach of the Solomon blowhole, so travelers knew they were safe. These days the roadhouse is only open for summer tourism and one week in March. Iditarod fans take helicopter rides from Nome to have a drink at the bar, volunteers sit next to the fire, and mushers rush in and out for one final push to the finish line.

A handful of spectators who were standing on the porch clapped politely and asked if I needed anything. I pulled Jason's bent ski pole off the front of my bike.

"I found this on the trail; I think it belongs to Jason Mackey," I said. "Is he here?"

"Sorry, he just left," one man said. "He was in and out in under five minutes."

"Oh," I said, feeling deflated. I'd been averaging more than ten miles an hour since shortly after Topkok. In twenty-five miles, I'd nearly caught up to Jason after losing an hour to his team on the last Topkok hill. But the trail had become increasingly soft as it crossed into an area more protected from the wind, and the final twenty-two miles featured a rolling climb over Cape Nome. I'd already calculated that if I didn't catch Jason by Safety, I wasn't going to catch him.

"In that case, is the bar open?" I asked. "I'm really thirsty."

I removed my outer layers and wrapped them around a bar stool, where I sat down and ordered a can of Pepsi. The bartender was an older Native man, probably in his seventies, engaged in an animated conversation with two veterinarians. As I guzzled the soda he turned his questioning to me, asking about my day so far, and how long I thought it would take to ride to Nome.

"Probably four more hours," I said. "There's that big climb over Cape Nome, and my brakes basically don't work anymore, so I might have to walk downhill." (Not only was my right hand too weak to press the rear brake lever, my front brake pads were also nearly worn out.)

"Those guys who came through a few days ago took the road, went around the cape," the bartender said.

"Really?" I didn't mask my surprise. Between Nome and Safety was a gravel road that wasn't maintained or regularly traveled during the winter, so the wind-blown snow covered it in deep drifts. I attempted to ride this road two years earlier, while I was waiting for Beat to arrive in Nome. It was a mess, and at one point I was buried to my waist in the sugary snow.

"No, I think the road is a bad idea," I said. "It's always drifted in."

"The Iron Dog went that way, and it's still clear," the bartender insisted. "I think those bikers got through fast."

I finished my Pepsi and considered the bartender's suggestion, but didn't hurry out the door. Instead I struck up a conversation with a veterinarian, who interpreted my praise for the dogs' athleticism as disapproval of their treatment. It took several minutes of circular arguing to set him straight. I guessed that he'd fielded a number of complaints about animals spending long days running nonstop through cold and difficult terrain — but I was a human doing exactly that, and it's what I admired about them.

As the minutes passed, the bartender watched with a disapproving look on his face. It was strange, but I was reluctant to leave. The Safety Roadhouse was cold and musty, and not really a place I wanted to linger. But the prospect of ending this adventure suddenly held me back.

I left Jason's ski pole propped against the door — perhaps it would help another musher over Cape Nome — and ventured into the breezy afternoon. The temperature was ten degrees, so I stood outside with only a thin hat and jacket, and no gloves. Three tourists who had just arrived by helicopter watched me pack up my bike.

"Aren't you cold?" one asked.

"Not anymore," I answered.

I rode a quarter mile up the trail while glancing toward the coast. A row of shuttered fishing shacks lined what I assumed was the road. At the last minute I changed my mind and pedaled overland across punchy crust to connect with it. It isn't like me to trust trail information from bystanders. Although I still believed the bartender was wrong about the road being the faster way to go, a part of me just had to find out.

The first few miles were covered in a thick layer of snow, but it was well-packed and smooth. I enjoyed watching green mile markers count down the remaining distance to Nome. The road wrapped around the base of Cape Nome, where it was blown clear of snow. My tires crackled loudly on the icy gravel. On the other side of the broad hill, the road intersected the Iditarod Trail once more. Familiar orange stakes indicated the Iron Dog snowmobilers took the trail. The road continued on a parallel route one mile to the north, and its condition was unknown. After twelve hours of strained breathing and striving, my thoughts were as scattered as drifting snow. Without ruminating, I followed the road.

There was a mile of glare ice interspersed with soft snowdrifts, which were more frequent as I became more committed to my choice. The now-hidden road dropped into a shallow drainage, which trapped a winter's worth of wind-driven snow in drifts that were more than six feet high — true snow dunes that could swallow me whole. Even as my logical mind lamented my mistake and visualized turning around, my primitive self blindly went forward. The front wheel pressed into a fan of powder and — to my logical mind's astonishment — effortlessly rolled onto the surface of a snow dune. A hard crust had formed over the drift, with a texture and shape not unlike the slickrock formations of southern Utah. The combined weight of my bike and body barely made an imprint as I rolled up and over steep mounds of petrified snow, giggling like a child.

White slickrock gave way to a sheen of glare ice, then a patchwork of ice and gravel. The road took a sharp turn back to the coast, where I could see a cluster of modern buildings and people standing next to parked cars and trucks. This was the "end" of the Nome-Council Road during the winter months, and people had driven out from town to watch mushers cross the road at a trail intersection. As I pedaled past on my behemoth bike with head gear coated in rime, they ignored me. It wasn't unusual to see a random person on a fat bike out here. We were only six miles from Nome.

I pedaled onto clear gravel, mind fluttering and heart in a state of disbelief. The final six miles to Nome were a plowed road. There were no longer any obstacles between me and the finish, short of being hit by a truck. A thousand miles across Alaska. Was it even real? I glanced to the north, where the wind still blew at a steady ten miles an hour. Directly beside me, on the trail that now paralleled the road a hundred meters away, there was a dog team driven by a musher wearing a blue coat. I recognized that coat. Could it be? Was that Jason?

Without further thought, I lowered my shoulders, tucked my chin over the handlebars, and launched into a full sprint. I had a thousand hard miles on my legs, a numb hand, glycogen-depleted muscles and oxygen-deprived brain, so it probably wasn't much. But that sprint was truly everything I had left to give. I crossed a bridge over the Nome River, and then there were three miles to go. My heart was racing so fast that it vibrated. Trucks and cars streamed past. A few drivers honked their horns. Distant buildings grew in size until I could make out windows and doors. The gravel road gave way to pavement, and then there was one mile to go.

It's become a tradition of mine to press the forward button on my iPod Shuffle when there's one mile left in a race. It's a memory-generating ritual, letting fate determine the song that will remind me of this moment for years to come. Although my iPod had been turned off since early-morning anxiety about the cold prompted me to shut the thing up, it was still clipped inside my coat and there were still buds stuffed inside my ears. I turned it on. Immediately I heard the rasping voice of the pop star Sia, singing "Dressed in Black."

"I had given up. I didn't know who to trust. So I designed a shell. Kept me from heaven and hell."

Ten years of striving carved a path that was littered with failures, and it was true. I had given up. When the way ahead looked impossible, I continued to sabotage myself. I emotionally withdrew from this race before it started, sent myself supply boxes full of garbage, lingered at every possible quitting point as long as possible … and yet, here I was.

"And I took to the night. I'd given in to the fight. And I slipped further down. I felt like I had drowned."

Fog continued to cloak my thoughts, even as I strained to focus and absorb every detail of this final mile. The towering hospital building with glass windows gleaming in the afternoon sunlight. The dirty piles of snow lining the street. The jumbled ice of the Bering Sea. The bitter taste that lingered on my tongue after weeks of poor nutrition. The rawness of my throat as I gasped the cold air, which was infused with exhaust — a taste so familiar and yet so foreign. The tingling in my fingers. The trembling in my chest.

"Life had broken my heart, my spirit. And then you crossed my path. You quelled my fears, you made me laugh. Then you covered my heart in kisses."

A grin spread across my face. Of course. The Iditarod Trail. Ever since I put a wheel to this trail ten years earlier, I'd anthropomorphized its existence and exalted its influence on my life. It was beautiful and benevolent, it was cruel and calculating, it was cold and indifferent. It was the ghost trail that disappeared in the summer only to be reborn every winter, cutting an ever-changing path through a seemingly timeless land. It was not unlike the God of my youth, doling out a barrage of brutality with a promise of redemption at the end.

"I was hopeless and broken. You opened the door for me. Yeah I was hiding and you let the light in, and now I see — that you do for the wounded, what they couldn't seem to. You set them free.

The burled arch came into view, with its whimsical black lettering burned into wood: "End of Iditarod Sled Dog Race, 1,049 Miles." A small crowd was assembled around the finish line, awaiting mushers. Some clapped, but others seemed confused as I pedaled up the snow ramp and came to a stop just a few feet shy of the arch. An announcer with a microphone figured out I was "one of those Iditabikers" and peppered me with questions. How did it go? How was the trail?

"Oh, it was beautiful," I said hoarsely to a live recording that was being broadcast all over the world.

Others approached as they realized that I had pedaled this bike all the way from Knik, and blasted me with more questions. I felt overwhelmed. Sia was still playing quietly in my ears, and I couldn't find the iPod to turn it off. A woman took a few photos and then a big man with a green coat and a Santa Claus beard approached. I recognized him vaguely, and he introduced himself as a long-ago acquaintance of mine, Hunter from Ketchikan. Although I had a few friends in Nome, I saw no other familiar faces. My mind was still foggy, my breathing labored. Hunter placed a hand on my shoulder and guided me to a narrow opening through the plastic fence surrounding the ramp.

As we stood together on the pavement, the town siren went off, announcing the approach of the next finishing musher.

"Is that Mackey?" a nearby woman remarked, and despite another crowd growing around my bike, I sidled up to the fence to watch. A musher wearing a blue coat pulled up the ramp. The announcer introduced him as Jason Mackey. Crowds assembled around his team, doting on the clearly elated dogs. I would have given just about anything in that moment to walk up to Jason, congratulate him on a good race, and return his ski pole, but I had left it back in Safety. Instead, I lingered shyly at the fence, quietly relishing my ten-minute victory.

I switched on my satellite phone to check for a message from Beat, and saw a text from my father, congratulating me on setting the record. The record? I scoured my foggy mind for any evidence of the record. It was past two in the afternoon, which meant it was past day seventeen. I'd forgotten to check my watch at the finish, but it was six in the evening, and with the daylight savings time adjustment, it was less than seventeen days and four hours. Seventeen days was a decent finish — it had been the best overall time in the Iditarod Trail Invitational up until 2014. Of course, trail conditions determine speed more than anything else, and I wasn't about to indulge in smugness about nearly beating one of Mike Curiak's best times while I rode the icy trails of 2016. But the record?

Later, after I located my friend Phil and sat down to leftover pizza at his home, I looked up the statistics on his computer. Ausilia's record was seventeen days, six hours, and twenty-five minutes. I finished in seventeen days, three hours, and forty-six minutes. It occurred to me that if I hadn't engaged in my impromptu race with Jason Mackey, I probably would have spent much more time dawdling during the final section — especially after all of the difficulties I experienced in the Topkok Hills.

Before I found Jason's pole, I'd planned to stop at the Topkok shelter cabin, eat a hot lunch, and try to shore up strength for the final push to Nome. I was so certain that my body was spent, but all it took was a ski pole lost on the trail to shift this perspective. Instead of resting and conserving energy, I sprinted with a zeal I hadn't felt in at least a year, before all of these breathing difficulties arose. If it wasn't for that unhindered burst of energy, I likely would have been slower than that two-hour margin, and the record wouldn't have fallen.

"The Iditarod Trail provides," I thought, imagining Jason's ski pole propped against the door at Safety. I bit into a piece of pizza, which tasted like the bitterness that lingered on my tongue. I was so tired, and my brain was so muddled, that my only emotion was disappointment that I didn't feel something more. It always takes time for the weight of an accomplishment to settle in, but I sensed that soon this would mean much more than a simple fairy tale about a benevolent trail that took me in wounded and set me free.

"The Iditarod Trail provides."

Epilogue

One week later, snow as fine as dust streamed around my boots while I trudged up the western face of Cape Nome. The spring equinox had come and gone, the midday sun was directly overhead, and white slopes glistened with such intensity that I had to squint into my sunglasses. It was another brilliant Wednesday afternoon. The sun made the eighteen-degree temperature feel almost hot, even as a headwind froze beads of sweat on my forehead. My heart fluttered with anticipation, because I expected to see Beat on the other side.

After finishing the Iditarod Trail Invitational on Wednesday, March 16, I spent one night convalescing at the home of Phil and Sarah Hoefstetter. Phil was an administrator at the Norton Sound Regional Hospital, and had ridden a bike from Knik to his doorstep in Nome four times since his first Iditarod Trail Invitational in 2008. In 2016, he won the race in eleven days, five hours, and fifteen minutes — only one day behind Jeff Oatley's record.

Phil had a genuine shot at this record, but he was beset with mechanicals throughout his ride. The final straw snapped when his chain broke during the Norton Sound crossing. He replaced the broken link, but it broke again. After three frantic repairs on the exposed surface of the sea ice, Phil ran out of spares and had to hike the rest of the way into Koyuk. There he waited nineteen hours for a replacement chain to arrive from Nome while constructing a makeshift tool to install it.

One day after Phil finished, the Alaskan trio of Bill Fleming, Kyle Amstadter, and Jay Cable arrived in twelve days, eight hours, and forty minutes. The three traveled together for most of the race, forging a camaraderie that became unbreakable. Three miles from Nome, the cassette popped off of Jay's rear wheel. He urged his companions to go on without him, but they insisted on setting up a tow system so they could pull Jay the rest of the way to Nome.

Three days later, the next finisher was Robert Ostrom — the man who took a ride on Mike's back across the Happy River. This was Bob's third and fastest finish in fifteen days, eight hours, and thirty minutes. He arrived like a phantom in the night, quietly leaving town before the handful of fans in Nome even knew he was there. Bob truly rode solo, sometimes more than a hundred miles separated from any other person. He managed to cross the sea ice before the windstorm that pinned Mike and me down, but later fought sixty-mile-per-hour gusts that knocked him off his bike.

I came in just under two days later, the sixth finisher overall. That night I microwaved my own finisher's banquet of leftover pizza and hot chocolate, then sat at Phil's computer to refresh the race tracking site and gauge Mike's finishing time. Despite my best efforts to keep my eyes open, I dozed off after sunset. Mike rolled under the burled arch just before eleven that evening, finishing in seventeen days, seven hours, and forty-seven minutes. All of Nome's hotels were booked for the Iditarod, so he found a church, crashed under a pew, and then caught a flight back to Anchorage early the next morning. By the time I woke up, he was gone. My one regret in the race is failing to congratulate my trail companion at the finish. We didn't ride together often, but Mike was always on the periphery. Knowing he was usually just a few hours behind me helped boost my confidence in tackling the more remote segments of the trail. I would have been exponentially more alone without him.

I felt guilty about missing Mike as well as disappointed that my own finish line experience had been so anonymous and strange. So the following evening, I made an effort to greet the next cyclist to arrive in Nome, Troy Szurkowski. Troy was Australian, and the first person from the Southern Hemisphere to finish the Iditarod Trail Invitational. Other Australian ultra-endurance athletes I know never seem to take anything seriously, so I was surprised by Troy's steely demeanor when he rolled under the burled arch just after sunset. His finishing time was eighteen days, six hours, and fifty-nine minutes. Without acknowledging anyone else, Troy propped his bike under the burled arch and began fumbling around with a lightweight tripod and camera. A chorus of spectators offered to take his photo, but he just shook his head and acted as though no one else was really there.

After he took a self portrait, a famous musher named Martin Buser — who just happened to be waiting under the arch for somebody else — teased Troy about all of the gear piled on his bike. Troy was adamant that everything was important, and meticulously detailed the individual pieces. Martin started laughing, which caused Troy to become more flustered and confused until I guided him off the ramp. A local woman, Nora, invited us both to dinner and gave us directions to her house. It was two miles away, and Troy raced as though a wolf was chasing him. I was one day into my own deep recovery, and no longer had any steam left in my lungs or legs. I bonked badly after one mile, and felt dizzy and disoriented by the end of the second mile. By that point Troy was more coherent and ready to be around other humans, while I slurred my words and battled sleepiness throughout the meal.

That night I moved out of Phil's house and went to stay with a physician named Roxy, who offered me a spare bedroom in her apartment. She whisked me to numerous social events around town, ensuring I never went hungry. She also offered medicine for my bronchitis — which was already improving — and advice for my numb hand. After several tests, Roxy determined my issue was almost certainly carpal tunnel syndrome. Subsequent nerve tests would confirm a grade five case, and surgery three months later revealed a significant buildup of scar tissue around the ligament. The best theory available is that a wrist injury — either old or recent — caused scar tissue to form, compressing the nerve. My crash on the ice during the first day of the race was likely the final kink that resulted in a sudden and severe neuropathy.

Two more finishers arrived on Friday — Bill Dent of England and Donald Kane of Scotland, in nineteen days, four hours, and thirty-seven minutes. The United Kingdom contingent teamed up for most of the race, even though Donald rode a pre-2005 steel fat bike with first-generation, non-studded tires. How he stayed upright on top of glare ice remains a mystery.

The Northern Lights were rippling overhead on Friday night when Roxy and I, along with another doctor named Eric, set out to watch Tim Hewitt march the final miles into Nome. The North Wind howled as we ducked behind Roxy's car and propped cameras on the hood, trying and failing to capture a focused shot of the aurora. A bright headlamp appeared in the distance and we waited ten minutes for it to finally reach us. Each one of us was shivering profusely and cheering weakly when Tim passed. Suddenly Eric shouted loudly, "You can do it!"

"What?" Tim called out from the trail fifty meters away.

"You can do it!" Eric yelled more forcefully. Tim lingered for several more seconds, likely confused, before Roxy and I yelled, "Go! Go."

We teased Eric — not just for quoting a bad Adam Sandler movie, but because Tim was nine hundred and ninety-seven miles into a thousand-mile journey. Obviously he knew he could do it.

Tim also added somewhat of an epilogue to my Jason Mackey ski pole saga. The broken pole was still propped outside the door when Tim arrived in Safety two days after I left. Tim lost one of his trekking poles while crossing the Happy River above Puntilla — some eight hundred miles back — and decided to grab it so he'd have two for the final stretch to Nome. He carried the pole most of the way over Cape Nome before deciding he was better off with one, and tossed it into the night. I was disappointed that Jason's pole made it so far without reaching the finish, so on my way to see Beat the following week, I scoured the slopes in search of a bent ski pole. I never found it, because I'd misunderstood Tim's story all along. He briefly considered taking it from Safety, but changed his mind. The pole likely still sits on the porch of the roadhouse, waiting for another Iditarod to arrive.

A crowd of inebriated revelers trickled out of the Front Street bars and gathered under the burled arch for Tim's midnight finish. The group cheered wildly as he arrived under threads of colorful lights after nineteen days, nine hours, and thirty-eight minutes.

"Where did all of these people come from?" Tim exclaimed. His smile was as bright as the aurora still dancing in the sky. His ninth finish of the thousand-mile hike shattered the previous foot record, which also belonged to him. To set it, Tim had to walk more than fifty miles a day, dragging a thirty-five-pound sled, sleeping an hour here and there, and traveling most of the distance alone. Most who understand the race agree that while Jeff Oatley's ten-day ride is stout, another racer — such as Phil — could best it in near-perfect conditions. Tim's record, however, is more likely to stand forever. He was sixty-one years old.

Beat was the next in line to finish the race, and I didn't expect him for four or five more days. Most people depart quickly after finishing the Iditarod, but I lingered in Nome for more than a week, waking up with night sweats, staying up late with Roxy, and pedaling my bike slowly along the icy streets of Nome. Iditarod Sled Dog Race festivities continued into the weekend, and I enjoyed spectating the final mushers, sharing overpriced restaurant meals with new acquaintances, and attending the Iditarod finisher's banquet. Nearly a thousand people were crammed into a gymnasium that could barely hold six hundred. For fifty dollars we dined on overcooked salmon and strawberries while sponsors rambled on for more than six hours. Roxy and I only made it through three hours before we squeezed our way outside, laughing at what a spectacle this was for a town of three-thousand people in the middle of nowhere. The sled dog race is a big deal. Not many people care about the cyclists and walkers, which is just fine with us.

Even though my legs were toast and my hand hurt more each day, my lungs recovered quickly. Whatever crud I picked up in Koyuk vanished after two days. My embarrassing bonk with Troy kept me more vigilant about eating regular meals— even though it would take another week to pick up an appetite. Two days after my finish, I was itching to get back on the trail, and quelled these desires with long rides out the unmaintained roads beyond Nome. These roads were coated in glare ice and concrete snow, and climbed into the foothills en route to the isolated interior of the Seward Peninsula. I would pedal until my legs began to hurt once more, then look at my GPS and realize I was twenty miles from anywhere. This realization would always cause a brief moment of panic about whether I'd find the energy to propel myself back to Nome. After I calmed down and resigned myself to the return, I'd gaze wistfully toward the Kigluaik Mountains — craggy, snow-capped, pummeled by the North Wind, and more wild than the wildest segments of the Iditarod Trail.

"Next time," I assured myself quietly.

Sam and Katie arrived the day after Tim, and had their own sights set on possibly extending their ride farther north. We spent more than five hours at a tiny coffee shop, entertaining ourselves with trail stories and cleaning the place out of coffee and pastries. They spent the rest of the day at the library, looking at maps and scheming a route to Kotzebue, but ultimately decided to return to Anchorage. Comfort is difficult to leave, no matter how much the unknown beckons.

After Beat, there were two more finishers: Eric Johnson, and an Austrian man, Klaus Schweinberger. After six McGrath finishes and at least three failed thousand-mile attempts, Eric finally made it to Nome in twenty-five days, eighteen hours and twenty-four minutes. Less than three miles from town, he became lost in a snowstorm and wandered several miles out of the way. Beat and I watched his progress online from Nome, yelling at my phone as Eric drifted farther north. Eventually he drifted back, but threw his trekking poles in a huff when he finally found the burled arch. Two minutes later, all was forgotten, and he jovially consumed two breakfasts at the last restaurant in town still open after the Iditarod.

Klaus had walked to Nome once before, in 2013. The journey took him thirty-two days, which was past the race's designated thirty-day cutoff. He achieved his first official finish in twenty-nine days, twenty-three hours, and seven minutes — with just fifty-three minutes to spare. Klaus joked that he was the slowest of the slow, but I disagreed. Anyone who can walk a thousand miles across frozen wilderness, let alone in fewer than thirty days, is incredibly strong.

Beat finished during the evening of March 23, after twenty-four days, three hours, and fifty-nine minutes. It was officially spring, and on this far western edge of the Alaska time zone, daylight lingered after 10 p.m. I tracked Beat's progress and started pedaling east in the late morning. After several days of long sightseeing rides, fatigue gnawed at my legs. The Nome-Council Road was still coated in ice and concrete-hard snowdrifts, but wind gusts had deposited enough new snow to slow progress considerably. The North Wind had shifted during the week — now the breeze came directly from the east, into my face. There were a host of discomforts and protests from my body to remind me that the race was over, I had survived, and I really shouldn't have to do this anymore. My primitive mind begged me to turn around, but eagerness about seeing Beat drove me forward.

At the edge of Cape Nome, I stood five hundred feet above the coast, scanning a thoroughly white landscape for a single dark speck. When I failed to locate Beat, I descended off the steep eastern face — still throttling a barely working front brake for speed control — and continued pedaling toward Safety. The Iditarod Trail was in terrible shape — covered in soft mounds of power that had been tossed around by irregular snowmobile traffic — but I was still able to pedal. It occurred to me that during my seventeen-day journey to Nome, trail conditions were rarely unrideable. My own legs and lungs were usually the limiter, as the bike stayed afloat even in this inconsistent fluff. Eriksen truly was an incredible bike, and this had been an incredible year.

I caught my first glimpse of Beat from at least two miles away, judging by how long it took us to meet. At first he was a barely discernible dot, and then a squat silhouette, and then I could make out the rhythmic motion of trekking poles slicing through the snow. His smile was apparent from a half mile away — that same dominating grin that I found so captivating at the finish of the Swan Crest 100 in Montana, five and a half years earlier. The rest of his face was hidden behind dark sunglasses, beige tape and a four-week beard. When we finally stood side-by-side, I could see his eyes were drooping and dull. We shared a long kiss and then I asked, "How are you?"

"I'm tired," he said. "I can barely stay awake. I almost took a nap back at Safety, but I'm too close now."

My GPS registered sixteen miles since I left Nome. For Beat, the distance would take least five more hours. I couldn't tell whether he knew or cared, but I didn't share this information.

It was clear Beat didn't want to linger long, so I turned my bike around and pushed it beside him, sharing updates that we never covered during our brief satellite phone conversations. I told him about Troy's finish and Roxy's hospitality, Phil's new house and the horrible condition of Tim's feet. Beat had little to add.

"I'm glad to see you," he said. "But I'm just so tired."

Beat had been walking for twenty-four days, stopping only a few hours a day to sleep, make water, and cook. With the thirty-day clock running and spring approaching, time was a precious commodity. He didn't waste any minutes that he could control. In Beat's race, there were no baths, no nine-hour recovery sleeps, no Fireball hot chocolate or twenty-mile sprints to pizza. Although it's obvious that walking a thousand miles on the Iditarod Trail is more challenging than cycling, even I had a hard time conceptualizing the magnitude of difficulty. Beat's sallow expression revealed a harsh truth.

We walked for a few more minutes in silence, and then I said, "I should go. Let you finish your own race."

"Sorry," Beat said. "This is all I can focus on right now." His chin was lowered and his eyes were fixed on the trail, although he was still walking with his signature broad stride that made it look as though he never became tired and never slowed down. This was how he covered more than forty miles per day in all conditions — by pressing forward at the same pace regardless of how shattered he felt. I'd learned a lot from Beat during the past five years.

"I understand," I said. "I'd feel the same way in your place."

We both looked up toward Cape Nome. From this vantage point, the headland appeared as steep as a fortress wall.

"I'm going to ride around the cape on the road," I said. "I will see you on Front Street in a few hours."

Beat cracked another broad smile. "Looking forward to it," he said.

I veered off the trail onto a fragile crust, which collapsed into airy layers of older crusts. Despite the pastry-like snow conditions, I managed to keep pedaling. The effort was taxing and I stopped often to look back. Beat's silhouette moved stoically across the horizon until he was again just a black speck in an expanse of white and blue.

Although the fishing shacks that lined the coast appeared to be less than a mile from the trail, I battled breakable crust for more than three miles before I finally found my way to the road. There had been considerable drifting during the past week, and the road surface had become soft and punchy.

"A lot can change in a week," I thought.

I pedaled around the cape in slow motion, observing a number of details I'd missed the previous week — wooden crosses marking a century-old grave site, jumbled ice blocks strewn across the beach, and an old cabin. My leg muscles quivered and I again wondered if I'd drained too much energy to propel myself back to civilization. But there always seemed to be enough left. Even if it was barely enough, it was always enough.

At the trail intersection, I stopped to watch for Beat. I'd traveled seven miles versus the four he needed to walk to reach this point. Although nearly an hour and a half had passed since we parted, I saw no sign of him.

"Well, it was a steep climb," I thought. "Maybe he decided to stop and take a nap after all." This last thought brought me comfort.

I didn't dawdle long. As slow as I'd been riding, I knew I needed to keep a steady pace to reach Nome with enough time to ensure a proper greeting for Beat. After the sled dog race ended, the burled arch was moved to an alleyway next to a liquor store. I intended to clean myself up, purchase some beer and perhaps Fireball from the liquor store, chips and ice cream from the grocery store, and gather up the friends I'd made in Nome to cheer Beat into the finish.

I could see the hospital building with windows glistening in the sunlight, even though it was twelve miles away. It seemed such a daunting distance, and I pondered how I ever found the wherewithal to travel a thousand miles, even when there was no finish in sight and danger lurking around every bend. I hadn't forgotten how fearful I'd been, or how I'd longed for warmth and comfort. Still, I managed to thrive in that savage world. I was fierce, yes, and I was strong — even though my human insecurities never left. As long as I kept moving, I could ignore their whispers in the shadows. But the insecurities grew exponentially louder whenever I stood still. I'd stayed in one place for an entire week, and now I was deeply intimidated by a measly twelve miles.

"It's funny how easily we slip into a feral mindset," I thought. "And how quickly we lose it in the so-called real world."

The easterly wind had shifted to the south. The breeze blew hard at my side, so I turned to face north. There the sky was an electric shade of blue over a sharp profile of white mountains. I was stunned at the clarity of the northern horizon, because a hazy darkness was hovering over the sea.

"South wind," I thought. "A storm is coming."

Danger approaches from all directions. Maybe this storm would close in before I reached Nome, during a simple day ride when I was lacking most of my survival gear. Maybe I would have to hunker down somewhere along the trail, wondering why I didn't just remain where it was warm and dry, why I rode out to see Beat, why I even started this silly adventure at all. It didn't turn out this way, but for a few more hours I was again locked in a race against time, against my own fears, pedaling as though my survival depended on it.

I suppose that's life. For all of our effort and toil, our joy and grief and fierce love — surviving to see another day may be our only reward. But it is a great reward.

Acknowledgments

This book would not have been possible without the support of family and friends. Thank you to Bill and Kathi Merchant, for their exhaustive efforts with the Iditarod Trail Invitational and good will in the Iditarod community, which helps both racers and independent human-powered travelers.

Thank you to Dan Bailey and Amy Sebby in Anchorage, Corrine Leistikow and Eric Troyer in Fairbanks, Libby Bakalar and Geoff

Kirsch in Juneau, Carey Restino in Homer, Phil and Sarah Hoefstetter, Roxanne Richards and Shana Theobald in Nome for providing their homes as Alaska base camps over the past five years.

Thank you to Mike Beiergrohslein for being an ever-upbeat companion on a brutally difficult trail.

I'm grateful to the Petruska family in Nikoali, Peter and Tracy Schneiderheinze in McGrath, River's Edge Bed and Breakfast in Ruby, Larry Hausmann in Galena, and Joanna Wassillie in White Mountain for your wonderful hospitality.

Thank you to Liehann Loots, Leah Plack and Jan Berka for being wonderful training companions in California.

I'm grateful to Ed Plumb, who started the White Mountains 100 in Fairbanks, which inspired my continued dedication to Alaska after I moved away in 2010.

Also thank you to Danielle Coffman for your part in coaxing me back into winter racing madness in 2011.

I'm grateful to Tonya Simpson for her editing work.

Thank you to blog and book readers who have supported my writing, emotionally and financially, since I launched my blog in 2005.

Thank you to my father, Jed Homer, for inspiring my love of the outdoors and continuing to share this passion, and my mother, Sheri, for her support despite my questionable life choices.

I'm grateful for my sisters, Lisa and Sara, who also think I'm crazy and love me anyway.

Most of all, thank you to Beat Jegerlehner, my number one supporter and partner in the adventure of life.

About the Author

Jill Homer is an outdoor adventure enthusiast, freelance journalist and designer living in the forested foothills above Boulder, Colorado.

She was a community news journalist — pale-faced and risk-adverse, with a body better suited to shelving library books than scaling mountains — when her then-boyfriend convinced her to move to Homer, Alaska, in 2005. There she discovered the unique sport of snow biking, which launched her into a whirlwind lifestyle of endurance racing, travel, and adventure sports.

Her athletic accomplishments include a women's bicycle record for the 1,000-mile Iditarod Trail in Alaska, a former women's record for the 2,740-mile Great Divide Mountain Bike Route, and nearly fifty ultramarathon finishes. Deep down, she's still the awkward, timid girl she was while growing up in the suburbs of Sandy, Utah.

She has authored three memoirs, a compilation of personal essays, and co-authored a biography about a man who has walked across Alaska eight (now nine) times.

Follow Jill Homer's adventures on her blog,
jilloutside.com

Books by Jill Homer

Jill Homer has an outlandish ambition: a 2,740-mile mountain bike race from Canada to Mexico along the rugged Continental Divide. *Be Brave, Be Strong: A Journey Across the Great Divide* is the story of an adventure driven relentlessly forward as foundations crumble. During her record-breaking ride in the 2009 Tour Divide, Jill battles a torrent of self-doubt, anger, fatigue, bicycle failures, crashes, violent storms, and hopelessness. Each night, she collapses under the effort of this savage way of life. And every morning, she picks up the pieces and strikes out anew in an ongoing journey to discover what lies on the other side of the Divide: astonishing beauty, unconditional kindness, and boundless strength.

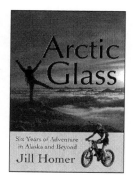

Arctic Glass: Six Years of Adventure in Alaska and Beyond compiles the best essays of "Jill Outside" from the thousands of posts that have appeared on the Web site. The essays chronicle the adventures of an unlikely athlete who takes on harsh challenges in the frozen wilderness of Alaska, the Utah desert, and the Himalayas of Nepal. Endurance racing, overcoming challenges, and self-actualization amid stunning outdoor landscapes are common themes in these vignettes about "The Adventure of Life."

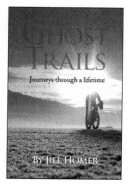

Ghost Trails: Journeys Through a Lifetime is the inspirational journey of an unlikely endurance athlete locked in one of the most difficult wilderness races in the world, the Iditarod Trail Invitational. Through her struggles and discoveries in Alaska's beautiful, forbidding landscape, Jill begins to understand the ultimate destination of her life's trails.

What compels a man to run, walk, and trudge a thousand miles across Alaska? "Because it's there" isn't an adequate explanation. "As a challenge" or "for the adventure of it" are closer, but still too vague. The thousand-mile dog sled race on the Iditarod Trail is often called "The Last Great Race" — but there's another, more obscure race, where participants don't even have the help of dogs. The Iditarod Trail Invitational challenges cyclists, skiers, and runners to complete the distance under their own power and without much outside support. By 2014, Tim Hewitt had completed the race an astonishing eight. Six of those, he won or tied.

"8,000 Miles Across Alaska: A Runner's Journeys on the Iditarod Trail" chronicles Tim Hewitt's adventures across Alaska — the harrowing weather conditions, breathtaking scenery, kindness of strangers, humorous misadventures, humbling setbacks and heroic victories. From fierce competition with his fellow racers, to traveling backward on the trail to ensure the safety of his wife, to battling for his own survival, Tim Hewitt has amassed a lifetime of experiences. This is his story.

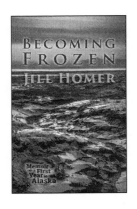

In *Becoming Frozen: Memoir of a First Year in Alaska,* Jill Homer takes a job at a weekly newspaper in Homer, Alaska, and forges a new life in a town where artists and fishermen drive the local economy, grizzly bears roam through back yards, social outings feature death-defying ski trips or kayaking rough seas in freezing rain, and business attire means wearing three sweaters to an unheated office. As Jill adapts to Homer's idiosyncrasies, she finds her own quirky hobby — riding a bike on snow. Despite having little in the way of an athletic background or talent, Jill signs up for a hundred-mile race across frozen wilderness. As the harsh Alaskan winter sets in, she launches a tenacious training routine that takes her far out of her comfort zone. Here, under the Northern Lights, battling exhaustion and extreme cold, Jill discovers the heart of Alaska.

Available from Amazon, Barnes & Noble, iTunes and other online retailers.

Printed in Great Britain
by Amazon